THE TOTAL DOG MANUAL

Adopt a Pet .com

THE TOTAL DOG MANUAL

David Meyer, Abbie Moore, and Dr. Pia Salk

weldonowen

CONTENTS

Introduction from *Adopt-a-Pet.com*

About *Adopt-a-Pet.com*

BASICS

001 Find Your New Best Friend

002 Make a Friend for Life

003 Check the Rules

004 Create a Safe Environment

005 Choose the Right Dog for Your Lifestyle

006 Find a Match for Your Child

007 Look for the Perfect Roomie

008 Size Up Your New Pal

Do Bigger Dogs Always Need More Space?

009 Address Allergies

010 Find the Perfect Running Buddy

011 Make Time to Settle In

012 Give Them Some Exercise

013 Invest in the Essentials

014 Consider Costs

015 Tag and Chip Your Dog

016 Choose an Adult Dog

017 Adopt a Mutt

018 Rescue a Purebred Dog

019 Introduce a Feline Friend

020 Adopt a Pet and Save a Life!

021 Look in the Right Places

022 Check Out an Animal Shelter

023 Catch One Today

024 Visit Your Local Humane Society

025 Research a Rescue

026 Avoid Puppy Mills

027 Pick a Name

028 Bring Your Dog Home

Double the Pets, Double the Trouble?

029 Adopt a Bonded Pair

030 Get Your Furry Fix by Fostering

🐕 BEHAVIOR

031 Know Your Dog: Senses

032 Let 'Em Sniff!

033 Meet and Greet

034 Recognize the Play Bow

035 Encourage "Roll" Play

The "Alpha Roll"

036 Learn to Speak Dog

037 Teach Your Kids How to Behave Around Dogs

038 Understand Ear Signals

My Dog Keeps Scratching His Ears. What Might Be Wrong?

Cropped-Ears Controversy

039 Look Into Their Eyes

040 Resist Their Gaze

Oxytocin Release—The Look of Love?

041 Exploit Your Looks

042 Bat Those Eyelids

043 Clock His Tail Position

044 Spot Telltale Tail Shapes

Is Tail Docking a Necessary Evil?

045 Watch Those Wags

046 Spot a Dominant Dog

047 Read Her Lips

Why Is My Dog Constantly Chasing His Tail?

048 Interpret Growls

049 Play Tug-of-War (Maybe!)

050 Never Intervene

051 Lead the Pack

052 Spay or Neuter Your Dog

Does Fixing Dogs Change Their Personalities?

053 See the Signs of Submission

054 Recognize Fear

To Breed or Not to Breed?

Arthur's Tale

055 Deal with Submissive Urination

056 Give a Shy Dog Some Space

057 Pet, Don't Pat

How Can I Help My Dog Learn to Play with a Toy?

058 Calm Separation Anxiety

059 Adopt a Friend

060 Help Your Dog Stop Crying

061 Understand Jumping Behavior

062 Keep Paws on the Floor

063 Plan Official Jump Time

Keep Your Feet on the Floor

064 Lick That Licking Habit

065 Minimize Mouthing

066 Meet the Relatives

067 Understand Your Dog's Prey Drive

068 Stop Your Dog Chasing Runners

069 Pet a Pit

How Healthy Are Purebreds?

070 Get to Know Breeds

071 Identify Types of Dogs

072 Track Down a Hound

Does It Matter If My Dog's Nose Is Wet or Dry?

073 Meet Ten Typical Hounds

074   Recognize a Retriever

075   Play Ball to Release Energy

076   Meet Ten Typical Sporting Dogs

077   Stand By a Working Dog

        Beware of Dog?

078   Get Past Resource Guarding

        Why Won't My Dog Stop Barking?

079   Beat Boredom Barking

080   Meet Ten Typical Working Dogs

081   Round Up a Herding Dog

082   Discourage Ankle Biting

083   Whistle While You Work

084   Enjoy Agility

085   Meet Ten Typical Herding Dogs

086   Dig a Terrier

087   Understand Why Dogs Dig

088   Deal with Digging

089   Designate a Digging Area

090   Meet Ten Typical Terriers

091   Play with a "Toy"

        Bag a Dog?

092   Pamper a Pooch

093   Meet a Mixed Breed

🦴 TRAINING

094   Allow a Little Breathing Room

095   Take an Obedience Class

096   Stock Up on Treats

097   Learn the Ten Training Commandments

098   Never Hurt or Frighten Your Dog

099   Be Consistent

100   Be Patient

101   Use Positive Reinforcement

102   Teach the "Lifesavers" First

103   Start Slowly and Safely

104   Keep Sessions Short

105   Know Your Dog's Learning Style

106   Keep It Going

107   Have Fun

108   Pay Attention to What You Want

109   Teach Your Dog His Name

110   Use a Team Name

111   Train Your Puppy

112   Know When to Say "No"

113   Invest in Training Equipment

114   Introduce Your Dog to Other Pets

115   Socialize Your Pup

116 Introduce Your Puppy to Children

117 Choose the Right Time for Crate Training

118 Consider How Long to Crate

119 Select the Right Crate

120 Decide Where to Put the Crate

121 Get Your Puppy Used to His Crate

122 Close the Crate Door

123 Train Your Children

124 Cope with a Puppy and a Young Child

125 Create a Child-Puppy Bond

126 Nip Nipping in the Bud

127 Survive Teething

128 Teach Table Manners

129 Keep Your Dog Off the Furniture

130 Practice "On" and "Off" the Sofa

131 Housetrain Your Dog

132 Pad Train Your Pooch

133 Get Your Puppy to Go on Command

134 Teach Your Dog to Sit

135 Train Your Dog to Lie Down

Basic Training Hand Signals

136 Use Hand Signals

137 Stay!

138 Stay a Little Longer

139 Teach Your Dog to Come on Command

140 Play "Here Boy!"

141 Try a Whistle Call

142 Roll Over, Rover

143 Say Please!

144 Teach Fetch and Drop!

145 Play Fetch from Water

146 Swim Safely

147 Equip Your Sea Dog

148 Understand Clicking

149 Start Clicker Training

150 Add a Verbal Command

151 Get a Bark on Command

152 Stop Your Dog from Barking at Home

153 Keep the Peace at the Fence

154 Fit a Collar

155 Try a Martingale Collar

156 Choose a Leash

157 Leash-Train Your Dog

158 Know When to Use a Harness

159 Avoid Retractable Leashes for Training

Choke Chains: Correction or Cruelty?

160 Prevent Pulling on the Leash

161 Consider Using a Head Halter

162 Create a Greeting Ritual

163 Plan Some Time Out

164 Have a Safe Trip!

165 Never Leave Your Dog Alone in the Car

166 Head for the Great Outdoors

Sam and Bertie

167 Run with Your Dog

168 Bike Together Safely

169 Acclimate Your Dog to Riding

170 Consider Other Cycling Options

171 Play Hide-and-Seek at Home

172 Freeze Like a Statue

173 Park Your Pooch

✂ CARE

174 Prepare for a Puppy's Arrival

175 Vaccinate Your Puppy

176 Vet a Vet

177 Plan for Veterinary Expenses

178 Buy Pet Health Insurance

179 Get Help with Vet Bills

180 Establish a Routine

181 Make Your Home Safe

182 Create a Dog-Friendly Backyard

183 Beware of Water Hazards

184 Build a Doghouse

185 Understand Canine Nutrition

186 Keep Water Accessible

My Dog has Diarrhea. What Should I Do?

187 Learn the Ten Commandments of Feeding

188 Provide Separate Food Bowls

189 Choose the Right Prepared Foods

190 Count Calories

Dogs Eat Meat, Right?

191 Understand the Importance of Play

192 Stock Up the Toy Chest

193 Check Out the Ultrasonic Option

194 Learn the Advantages of Ball Throwers

195 Let Leaping Dogs Fly

196 Avoid Dangerous Toys

197 Know When Enough Is Enough

198 Pick Up Your Dog Properly

199 Learn Some Bath Time Dos and Don'ts

200 Prep Your Dog for Bath Time

201 Gear Up for Bath Time

202 Associate Bathing with Good Things

203 Bathe Your Dog

My Dog Has a Lump on His Skin. What Does This Mean?

204 Prepare for Post-Bath Pandemonium

205 Make Bath Time the Best Time

206 Visit the Dog Wash

207 Call In the Professionals

208 Turn Scary into Fun

209 Recognize Canine Coat Types

210 Choose the Ideal Grooming Kit

211 Prep Your Dog for Grooming

212 Clean Fido's Face

213 Prep for Dental Cleaning

214 Take It Slow

My Dog Keeps Shaking His Head—What's Up?

215 Clean Your Dog's Teeth

My Dog's Breath Smells Awful. What Should I Do?

216 Clean Your Dog's Ears

Are Bones Good for My Dog?

217 Deep Clean Those Ears

218 Prep for Nail Trimming

219 Trim Your Dog's Nails

220 Groom a Smooth Coat

My Dog Has Dry Skin. How Can I Help?

221 Groom a Short Coat

222 Groom a Long Coat

223 Groom a Silky Coat

224 Clip a Coat

225 Handstrip a Wirehaired Dog

226 Dress to Impress

227 Consider Canine Couture

Dog Hair to Dye For?

228 Dress Up for Halloween

229 Take Pics of Your Pooch

230 Get the Facts on Fleas

231 Check Your Dog for Fleas

232 Free Your Home from Fleas

233 Recognize Common External Parasites

234 Terminate That Tick

235 Use a Tick Lasso

My Dog Rubs His Rear Along the Ground. What's Up?

236 Deal with Internal Parasites

237 Give Year-Round Care

238 Watch Out for Winter Hazards

239 Explore the Snow

240 Give an Adoption Option for the Holidays

241 Dress for Winter

My Dog Has Hypothermia! What Can I Do?

242 Keep Your Dog Safe in Summer

243 Beat the BBQ Blues

Callie

244 Cope with Fear of Thunder

245 Plan Your Vacation Carefully

246 Travel Safely with Your Dog

247 Hire a Dog Walker or Sitter

248 Check Out Kennels in Advance

249 Calm Your Pet on the Fourth of July

250 Find Your Lost Dog

251 Deal With a Dog Bite

252 Treat an Insect Sting

253 Handle a Toad Encounter

254 Keep a Canine First-Aid Kit

255 Manage a Snake Sighting

256 Avoid Rattlesnakes

257 Recognize Rattlesnake-Bite Symptoms

258 Spot the Signs of Ill Health

My Dog Eats Grass. Is This Okay?

259 Nurse Your Pooch

260 Give Your Dog a Pill

261 See the Signs of Old Age

262 Change Your Elderly Dog's Routine

Jasper

263 Just Say No to Joint Pain

264 Give Your Dog a Hand to Stand

265 Talk about Your Dog's Last Days

266 Remember Your Dog

267 Share Your Grief

268 Find a New Friend

Index

Credits

INTRODUCTION

Welcome to the world of having a dog in your home. If you have never shared your life with a dog, you are about to learn why dogs really are "man's best friend."

We at Adopt-a-Pet.com have written this book to help you find a dog to share your life and home with, and to help you have the best possible relationship with your dog throughout his or her life. Understanding more about your dog will help you have a great relationship that will hopefully last for many years.

Animals enhance our lives and we can enhance theirs. They remind us of our connection to nature, and they give us the unconditional love we often forget to give ourselves. As humans, we have a special responsibility to animals— to treat them with love, respect, and compassion. And as anyone who has lived with a dog or cat (or other companion animal) will tell you, they give us back so much more than we give them. A dog can help a shy child gain confidence, add joy to families, give comfort and assistance to the sick or disabled, and provide needed companionship for the elderly. And all they need from us is love and the basic care needed to keep them safe and healthy.

So sit, stay, and enjoy this book and learn from it. Whether you are planning to get a dog, or have one (or many) already, on these pages you will find things that help you understand your dog and enhance your relationship. Like any relationship, you will get out what you put in. And even if you can't adopt a pet, do visit Adopt-a-Pet.com, find a pet you want to help, and share that pet with your friends. That small act can save the life of a pet in need.

Wishing you nothing but wags,

David Meyer,
Abbie Moore, and
Dr. Pia Salk

ABOUT ADOPT-A-PET.COM

Adopt-a-Pet.com is the world's largest non-profit homeless pet adoption website. Thousands of animal shelters, humane societies, SPCAs, and animal rescue groups post hundreds of thousands of pets for adoption, and millions of potential adopters use Adopt-a-Pet.com each month to search for pets. Our service is entirely free, and is made possible by the passionate pet lovers at Nestlé Purina Pet Care, Bayer HealthCare Animal Health, and the Petco Foundation.

Our mission is to ensure that every companion animal has a safe and loving home. This means that

1. every pet that is born has a loving home,
2. the human/animal bond is strong and people have all the knowledge and resources they need to have a happy life with their pets, and
3. when a situation arises where a pet really does need a new home, a new and loving home is found.

Our primary tool to help animals is technology. We use the internet to get homeless pets seen and adopted, and to deliver information that allows people to have happy and successful relationships with their pets. We also support animal shelters and companion animal protection organizations of all types by providing technology to help them work faster and smarter.

Technology, however, is not the only
tool we use to help companion animals.
We also conduct real-world events
and publicity campaigns, such as
our annual "Pooch Smooch" around
Valentine's Day, an event to raise awareness
of companion animal issues. Additionally, we
conduct campaigns in various cities, featuring
local sports stars championing our cause.
Those campaigns involve media events, printed
billboards, and local radio and TV.

Our team is made up of a small, dedicated
group of animal lovers, who themselves are
often volunteers for local animal shelters and
pet-rescue organizations, fostering pets in their
homes and helping with weekend adoption
events. Our staff played a key role in rescuing
many thousands of animals who were stranded in
New Orleans in the aftermath of Hurricane Katrina,
and are often involved in important issues when we
see a way to help animals.

Please visit
Adopt-a-Pet.com
to learn more and
find a pet to adopt
near you today.

BASICS

66 No matter how little money and how few possessions you own, having a dog makes you rich. 99

LOUIS SABIN

You know the saying, "A dog is a man's (or woman's) best friend"? To make it come true, remember that friendship is a two-way street. As with any friend, you need to understand your dog without a word being spoken. You need to care about his or her needs, and find the activities that you both enjoy doing together. In short, a great relationship with your dog begins with a basic understanding of who your friend is and what it is he or she needs to be happy.

A dog's breed is not at all as important as you might think. It is important to realize that while specific breeds do have tendencies that most dogs in that group will exhibit (perhaps high energy or enjoyment of swimming), all dogs—no matter what breed or mix—are individuals. Their behaviors and needs will be as diverse as those of any two people, even if both people are from the same ethnic group or household. Are you exactly like your brother or sister? Just like people, dogs have different personalities—even siblings who were raised together. And a dog's personality, just like a person's, is influenced by his environment, his age, and his unique nature. So when you look at a dog, try not to see a poodle or a Chihuahua, but instead try to see the individual. Is this dog friendly? Is this dog high energy? Is this dog large, and will she need a lot of space?

Bringing a dog into your life will mean years of joy for you and your family, but it comes with responsibility. You need to be able to pay for the things your dog needs—most notably food and occasional medical care. You need to make the time to take your dog on walks and give him love and attention. You will need to be able to arrange for your dog's care if you choose to travel. All of these responsibilities last not just for this month or this year, but for the life of your dog—and dogs can live for 15 years or more.

001 FIND YOUR NEW BEST FRIEND

If you think making new friends is hard, then it's time you met a dog. When you bring a dog into your family, you get a lot more than a loyal pet. Quite apart from the unconditional love that dogs offer their human families, research has repeatedly shown that dog owners are generally fitter, less stressed, and live longer than their dogless counterparts. Regular exercise with your dog helps you maintain a healthy weight, reduces blood pressure, and improves cardiovascular fitness. Psychological benefits include higher self-esteem and a lower risk of mental health illnesses such as depression. Such therapeutic benefits are evidenced by the increasingly common employment of canine companions in hospitals, prisons, and nursing homes.

Studies show that senior dog owners experience less stress and loneliness, better nutrition, and a stronger focus on the present. Dog walking boosts parasympathetic nervous system activity, which promotes calm and rest in the body. It can also help a dog owner to make friends, since dogs are so keen to meet and greet other dogs, bringing their human companions together in the process. Taking care of a dog gives you a sense of responsibility that contributes to your overall well-being.

Children, especially, tend to instinctively adore dogs. Here are some of the positive benefits of bringing a pet home for your kids.

TOP 10 BENEFITS

- Children who grow up in homes with pets have less risk of developing common allergies and asthma.
- Recent scientific research suggests that playing with dogs may help lower blood pressure.
- Kids with pets get outside more—to go for walks, run, and play—and enjoy all the associated health benefits.
- Pet owners require fewer doctor's visits.
- Emerging readers often feel more comfortable reading aloud to a pet.

- Nurturing a pet is a good way for children to "parent play," to practice being caregivers.
- Feeding and caring for a pet encourages childhood responsibility.
- Children with pets display improved impulse control, social skills, and self-esteem.
- Sharing the love and care of a family pet forges an additional common bond among siblings.
- Cuddling a pet reduces stress, loneliness, and anxiety.

002 MAKE A FRIEND FOR LIFE

Remember, a dog is for life. In return for the devotion that a dog gives freely and unconditionally, you need to make a real commitment to caring for your pet for its entire life, no matter what that entails. Be prepared for the dog to affect other parts of your life for up to 15 years if you opt for a puppy. And if you know you can't commit to a dog for more than a few years, then consider adopting an older dog. Your pet's well-being will have to be considered in all kinds of decisions, including travel, social life, relocating to a new home, adopting other pets, and having children. Never acquire a pet on a whim or because you feel it's love at first sight. Do your research and carefully consider all the implications of adopting before you make a decision (the fact that you're reading this book is a good sign!). And never, ever, give a dog as a surprise gift!

003 CHECK THE RULES

Verify in advance that you're allowed to keep a pet where you live, especially if you rent or belong to a homeowners' association. As obvious as this sounds, in a recent survey of more than 180 pet shelters and rescue groups, this simple advice was listed in the top ten most important points to consider before committing to dog ownership. This simple oversight still leads to far too many dogs (and other pets) ending up homeless.

004 CREATE A SAFE ENVIRONMENT

Lock away any poisons or harmful substances your dog could possibly get to, and hide away wires that can be chewed (if your dog is a puppy). If you have an outdoor space that your dog can enjoy, it's crucial to make sure there is plenty of shade, access to clean water, and no way your dog can get under or over your fence. Every year, countless pets are lost, injured, or killed because their owners didn't take sufficient precautions to secure their safety at home.

005 CHOOSE THE RIGHT DOG FOR YOUR LIFESTYLE

Finding the best pet for yourself or your family should start with an understanding of your ideal pet personality. Consider this: Do you need a dog that is low-key and good with kids, or are you looking for an energetic pal who is into trail running? Perhaps you need a dog that will get along well with your existing pets—another dog, a cat, a house rabbit, or all three! The dog rescue centers that host hundreds of local pets near you are experts at matching you with a dog who will love the life you can provide. But first you need to think carefully to figure out the size, age, and energy level that would fit best with your particular situation and lifestyle.

006 FIND A MATCH FOR YOUR CHILD

Introducing a pet when you have children can seem daunting, but rest assured that the friendly experts at your local rescue center will guide you every step of the way. Meanwhile, here's some basic, tried-and-true advice to help you to ensure that the dog you bring home will blend.

TRAIN YOUR CHILDREN Yes, we all know the importance of training your dog (it's one of the most vital things you can do to make your relationship a success), but it's equally important to teach your children how to interact with dogs in a safe manner. Before you bring any dog home, make sure your kids know how to approach a new dog: extend a hand, palm down, and allow the dog to approach and sniff. If the dog gives your child the "okay" signal (wagging tail, kissing, no signs of aggression, fear, or nervousness), your child should pet the dog on his side rather than reaching over his head. There's plenty more on this subject later in the book, but the golden rule is quite simply to teach your kids to treat their dog with the respect and gentleness she deserves.

CHOOSE AN ADULT DOG Puppies are great, but they're not ideal for very young children. They mouth tiny hands with pin-sharp teeth, they jump, and they're also easily injured. Also, contrary to popular belief, you can't always tell what personality traits your puppy will develop. When you adopt an adult dog, what you see is what you get. It's much easier to tell if an adult dog is already great with kids than it is to guess if a puppy will grow up to be.

ADOPT FROM A RESCUE CENTER Many rescue organizations keep their pets with foster families who have a chance to observe their dogs around children and other animals, so rescuers have a pretty clear picture of their pets' personalities.

BE RESPONSIBLE If you're adopting a pet for your kids, understand that the responsibility is yours. Kids, by their nature, often tire of things that were once new and exciting, including pets. You will most likely end up being the one who provides most of the pet's care.

007 LOOK FOR THE PERFECT ROOMIE

Live in an apartment, but longing for some canine companionship? Not to worry. Many, many apartment-dwellers have successfully adopted dogs. In fact, though most people in New York live in apartments, the city is very dog-friendly. If they can do it, so can you! You just need to take a few things into consideration.

PERMISSION Remember item 3: Make sure your current apartment allows dogs, and understand that if you move to a new apartment, you'll need to find another one that allows dogs. Again, too many dogs end up abandoned because their owners move into new homes without checking this critical detail.

NOISE You may need to provide training to make sure your dog doesn't bark incessantly and disturb the neighbors while you're away. This is a situation in which adopting from a rescue group, where dogs have been in foster homes, can really make a difference. They'll know already if a dog is prone to excessive barking.

EXERCISE You will need to make sure your dog has adequate access to the outdoors for some exercise and potty breaks. A dog-walker and doggie daycare are great resources to use if you work long days.

SIZE Size matters, but keep an open mind when you begin searching for a canine roomie. Many large breeds do surprisingly well in apartment life. For instance, Great Danes and Greyhounds make great apartment companions. Though they are very large, both breeds are generally quite happy to be couch potatoes when indoors as long as they can enjoy some outdoor activity each day. Conversely, some small dogs, such as Jack Russell Terriers, have very high energy levels and need lots of exercise.

008 SIZE UP YOUR NEW PAL

Although size might not be the only deciding factor when choosing a dog, you will definitely need to consider the pros and cons of owning a massive mastiff or a pint-sized pooch. Big dogs take up more space (on the couch and in the car, at least), they require bigger crates, have bigger appetites (resulting in bigger food bills), and you will be required to clean up correspondingly bigger poops. Also, really big dogs have shorter lifespans than smaller dogs. Despite their many conveniences, small dogs often have big personalities and may like to vocally remind you (and your neighbors) of their presence. Really tiny dogs, often referred to as "toys," are more prone to injury in busy households where they find themselves under people's feet.

SHOULDER THE BURDEN If your dog was ever ill or injured and needed to be carried to the car or taxi to get to the vet, could you pick him up, or get him onto a sheet and enlist a neighbor to help you carry him?

KNOW YOUR STRENGTH Even very well-trained dogs can get excited and yank on their leash if a squirrel darts across their path. You should be strong enough to be able to hold on to the leash, for the safety of your dog, for the safety of drivers, and for the safety of the squirrel.

LEARN THE RULES Just as some landlords forbid multiple pets or ban specific breeds from their property, landlords and homeowners' associations may impose weight restrictions on permitted pets, so bigger dogs can limit your rental possibilities.

SPEND WISELY Bigger dogs do eat more food! It's not surprising that a Great Dane consumes ten times as much food as a Yorkshire Terrier (and the costs rise accordingly). But bear in mind that more active dogs, even when relatively small, also require more energy input—which means more food. Supplies for a bigger dog (collars, leashes, harnesses, beds, and coats) are more expensive, too.

DO BIGGER DOGS ALWAYS NEED MORE SPACE?

Although bigger dogs inevitably take up more space on the carpet or couch, energy level is a much more accurate indicator of how much space a dog needs in a yard or home for running and playing. A Great Dane with his mellow energy level can live happily in a small apartment with just two or three short daily walks. A Jack Russell might require hours at the dog park every day to be happy in the same size home without feeling the need to bounce off the walls every evening! Energy is not only determined by size and breed, of course—age is also a very important factor. Older dogs tend to enjoy longer rest periods and prefer shorter walks.

009 ADDRESS ALLERGIES

Can certain breeds of dog really be suitable for people who are allergic to dogs? The answer is yes... and no. "Allergic to dogs" is actually a very general term. Before you consider adopting a dog, find out if your allergy is to pet dander, saliva, or urine. If you're allergic to saliva and your doctor approves of you adding a canine family member, you can ask your local rescue groups to keep an eye out for an adult dog that doesn't lick people. There are also many "low-dander" dogs out there.

OLDER DOGS If your allergy is to pet saliva, you need a mature dog whose licking behavior is established and manageable—unlike that of a puppy, whose instinct is to lick anything and everything and whose behavior has yet to become permanent. Make sure you wash your hands after playing with or petting your dog, especially if your hands come in contact with toys that have been in your dog's mouth.

LOW-DANDER DOGS While no dog is 100 percent non-allergenic, if you're allergic to dander, you may be able to tolerate a so-called "low-dander" dog. Several breeds, including Bedlington Terriers, poodles, and schnauzers, are known as low-dander dogs. These dogs have coats that are more like hair than fur, and they tend not to shed much. They also usually require a lot of grooming, due to their constantly growing hair.

MIXED-BREED DOGS Many mixed breeds involving one of these low-dander breeds will also be appropriate for dander-allergic people. For instance, most poodle mixes are low-dander. The current craze for "designer dogs" has generated a plethora of poodle mixes, hence the names Cockapoo, Jackapoo, Poogle, Labradoodle, and Cockadoodledoo (we may have made up the last one).

HAIRLESS DOGS Many people with allergies also do well with hairless breeds like the American Hairless Terrier or the Chinese Crested Hairless. Not surprisingly, such dogs don't tend to do so well in colder climes. If you want a low-dander dog, you can find lots of options in shelters and from rescue groups.

010 FIND THE PERFECT RUNNING BUDDY

Though all dogs require some level of exercise to remain happy and healthy, not all breeds have the physique or energy level to make good running partners. Some dogs make great short-distance or sprinting companions, and others can run marathons. Your dog will let you know when he has had enough. Just make sure you carry extra water and a collapsible dish, and pay close attention to your dog for any signs of fatigue. Never push your dog beyond his comfort level. Please keep in mind that dogs should not be run long distances or at great speeds until they are fully grown. Running a dog too fast or too hard at a young age can result in serious joint problems that will plague him for life.

ALL-ROUNDERS Some of the best running partners are mixed-breed dogs. Almost any healthy dog can be a running companion, with the exception of short-nosed breeds like Boston Terriers and bulldogs.

JOGGING PARTNERS*

Australian Shepherd
Beagle
Vizla
Golden Retriever
Pit Bull
Labrador Retriever
Rough Collie
Rhodesian Ridgeback

LONG-DISTANCE PARTNERS*

Weimaraner
Poodle
Dalmatian
Border Collie
Jack Russell Terrier
Australian Cattle Dog
Siberian Husky
Belgian Shepherd

*Mixed-breed dogs similar to these breeds are just as suitable.

011 MAKE TIME TO SETTLE IN

Whenever you introduce a new dog into your home, allow for a several-week adjustment period when you can expect some challenges. This applies even if you are adopting a housetrained dog, but is especially true if you are getting a puppy. Although he will quickly adapt to his new family, a puppy will initially miss his mom and littermates. It's important to be at home as much as you can for the first few weeks to keep a constant watch on your new family member, to start the housetraining process, and begin to forge a friendship that will last a lifetime.

012 GIVE THEM SOME EXERCISE

Walk dogs according to their individual needs, and bear in mind that all dogs, no matter what breed or type, require some level of exercise to remain happy, healthy, and well behaved. An under-exercised or bored dog can become quite destructive in any home. So if you know you are going to have to work long days, be sure to factor in the cost of hiring a dog-walker or daycare. For mental stimulation, provide playtime and toys for both indoor and outdoor use, and most importantly, spend time each day just petting and talking to your dog. Having multiple dogs can help keep them stimulated, as they play and interact with each other.

013 INVEST IN THE ESSENTIALS

Head down to your local pet store or look online to stock up on some essential equipment before introducing your dog into his new home. Provide your dog with a comfortable bed and a selection of his own feeding bowls. Select a couple of basic grooming tools, such as a bristle brush and a fine- or wide-toothed comb depending on the length of your dog's coat. All dogs should be allowed a few toys for that all-important playtime. Last, but most important, your dog should have his own leash, collar, and identity tag.

COLLAR AND LEASH Your dog should wear a properly fitted collar at all times, indoors and out. A leash is vital for exercise and training. Collars and leads are available in a wide variety of styles and materials.

IDENTITY TAG An identity tag engraved with your cell number should be secured to your dog's collar at all times to help ensure your dog's safe return should she get lost.

BED Wicker baskets and fabric beds can make attractive pieces of furniture, but bear in mind that they won't look so great after your dog has chewed them for a couple of days. Go for a plastic basket if you think your dog is likely to chew his bed, which is almost guaranteed if he is still a puppy.

BEANBAG Beanbags are great because they are comfy, light, and retain body heat. They often have convenient removable covers that can be easily washed. A beanbag makes an excellent second bed if your dog likes to join you as you work in your home office or kitchen.

BOWLS Food and water bowls come in a wide variety of materials and sizes. Stainless steel bowls with a rubber rim to prevent sliding are practical, but a heavy ceramic bowl might be the best choice for a larger, energetic dog. Select an appropriate bowl for your dog's size.

GROOMING KIT Metal combs and brushes are important for removing tangles from longer coats, while a bristle brush is needed for a short-haired dog. Make sure that you use brushes that are correct for your dog's coat type.

CHEW TOYS Dogs can amuse themselves for hours with a decent chewy toy. Make sure, however, that the chew toys you choose are an appropriate size for your dog and don't present a choking hazard. Dogs love squeaky toys, but if your dog is an especially enthusiastic fan, you may—for the sake of your sanity—want to limit such play to the yard, or to a short period of time each day.

CRATE While not an absolute necessity, a dog crate can provide comfort and security for your dog. It should have a comfortable, chew-proof mat and a water bowl or dispenser. It must be big enough for your dog to stand up and turn around comfortably.

014 CONSIDER COSTS

When you are getting ready to acquire a pet, it's vital to figure out what you can afford—and to prepare for the unexpected. Being a good, caring pet owner involves many things that don't affect your wallet, like your time and love, but there are definitely some costs involved. Consider the likely costs that come with caring for different dog types. Apart from the setup costs for essential equipment, which can mount up to a few hundred dollars, you also need to consider the running costs—the annual cost of food and vet care. Finally, put something aside for unexpected costs, such as emergency vet care, behavior training, or boarding or petsitting if you travel.

016 CHOOSE AN ADULT DOG

Some people think that getting a new dog means getting a puppy. Puppies are cute, but they quickly grow out of that cuteness and for about three years are full-sized dogs that act like puppies (jumping and chewing). Raising a puppy is a lot of work, and just as with raising a child, there's no guarantee what your dog's personality will be like when she grows up. When you adopt full-grown dogs, you get to see and know the dogs you are adopting. Their size will not change, and their personality is fully developed. What you see is what you get. You can see if they are playful and friendly, if they like kids or other animals, and if they are dominant or submissive. Contrary to common belief, it's the puppy who is the mystery, and the adult dog who is the known quantity.

015 TAG AND CHIP YOUR DOG

Your yard might not prove to be as secure as you had hoped, or someone might leave a gate open, and it only takes that one moment for a pet to be out on the street and in danger. Your neighbors might find your dog, but they can only contact you if they know who you are. So it is essential that you purchase a good-quality identification tag engraved with your cell phone number, and perhaps the number of your veterinarian. Tags can fall off, though, so it is also essential that your dog be "chipped" to allow a vet or shelter to scan her for your contact details. Your dog may already have a microchip, in which case make sure that the associated registry has your correct contact information.

017 ADOPT A MUTT

People tend to think of dogs based upon breed, and certainly that can make sense given the hundreds of breeds that exist today. But more people now appreciate the great benefits of having a mixed-breed dog. Mixed-breed dogs, or "mutts," actually tend to be more genetically healthy than purebred dogs, which of course means a better quality of life for the dog, and lower veterinary costs for you over the dog's lifetime. Mutts are often more rounded characters without the sometimes obsessive behavior you may see in dogs bred over decades to perform specific tasks. Mutts are often unique individuals, with coloration and physical features not seen in other dogs. They're truly one of a kind.

018 RESCUE A PUREBRED DOG

It's much smarter to choose a dog based upon his observed personality rather than making assumptions about a dog's behavior based on breed. However, some people really love the look or general traits of a particular breed, and prefer a purebred dog. The good news is you can get the satisfaction of adopting a dog in need, and still get that purebred you might seek. Anybody (including someone with a purebred dog) can face a situation that obliges them to find a new home for their pet, so there are often plenty of purebred dogs of all types in shelters. The easiest way to find a specific dog near you is to go to Adopt-a-Pet.com or Petfinder.com and search for that breed.

019 INTRODUCE A FELINE FRIEND

Many dogs can get along perfectly well with cats, but there are a few things to be sure to do when bringing a cat-friendly dog into your home. First off, you will need to feed your cats on a countertop or behind a closed door so your dog cannot eat your cat's food. Cat food is not good for dogs, and can give your dog stomach trouble. Second, you should be sure to orient or cover your cat's litter box in a way that prevents your dog from getting in and possibly eating kitty poop, which some dogs like to do (go figure!). Finally, trim your cat's nails so that if she takes a swipe at your dog, she cannot easily scratch his eye or nose.

020 ADOPT A PET AND SAVE A LIFE!

Any dog can end up in a shelter, and it usually has nothing to do with any issue with the dog. It's often simply a matter of someone needing to move, losing a job, becoming ill, or some other circumstance that causes a dog to end up homeless. It's a great feeling to find a wonderful companion, and also to know you have given a home to an animal in need. In fact, people who have adopted frequently say such dogs are more loyal and somehow seem to know they were given a home when they needed help. Adopting a pet has never been easier: Just follow these four simple steps to save a life and find yourself a loyal pet.

STEP 1 Use Adopt-a-Pet.com or Petfinder.com to search for pets at all your local animal shelters, humane societies, and pet rescue groups without leaving the comfort of your own home. You can see a pet's distance from your zip code and select a desired breed, gender, size, color, age, and much more.

STEP 2 Call or email the shelter, and arrange to visit the pet in person. You might go to an animal shelter or to a different location where the pets are being shown (like a pet-food store). It may be best not to bring your children at this stage to avoid disappointing them if things don't work out with a particular dog.

STEP 3 For some organizations, you will be asked to fill out an application. In the case of some smaller pet rescues, you may need to be approved, which could include someone coming by to check out your home and make sure it seems safe for a new pet.

STEP 4 If the dog you want is available for you to adopt, bring your kids to assess compatibility. If all is well, there will be an adoption fee to help pay for the cost of caring for pets at the shelter, which often includes vaccines, spaying or neutering, and microchipping. Then it's the really exciting part—time to take your furry friend home and start your new life together.

021 LOOK IN THE RIGHT PLACES

Start your pet search by going online and using Adopt-a-Pet.com, or by going in person to a local animal shelter, humane society, or rescue group. Here you will find wonderful, healthy pets of all ages, shapes, and sizes in need of caring homes. You will meet trained and professional people to help answer all of your questions. Pets from these organizations have almost always had all their vaccines, and often already have an ID microchip. However, it's worth looking into the organizations near you, as they may operate differently.

022 CHECK OUT AN ANIMAL SHELTER

Your local city shelter could be called Animal Services, Animal Control, or even "the pound"—but get that depressing and dated *Lady & The Tramp* image out of your mind. It is true that many large city shelters are overwhelmed with the numbers of pets coming in. If they have an "open door" policy, that means they do not turn away any animals, but it also means that as more pets come in than get adopted or found, they humanely kill animals to make room. This is a hard and depressing reality, but many modern shelter facilities are nevertheless bright, clean, and inviting, and the pets are ready and waiting to be adopted by someone like you!

TAKE YOUR TIME While some dogs at a public shelter have information available about their history, some do not, so it is good to put some extra effort in to get to know the pet you are considering. Once you find a dog you like, bring your entire family along to say hello, and spend plenty of time outside of her kennel in an adoption office play yard, or even in a hallway or lobby. Watch how she responds to each family member.

ASK FOR ADVICE Many shelters have volunteers who help the adopting public, but most don't have much of a formal screening process—it is up to you to select a pet that will be a good match for your home.

BE PATIENT Be prepared to spend the first few months learning about your pet after you bring her home. You may even need to call in the assistance of a professional trainer or pet-savvy friend to help you through the normal adjustments of a new pet in a new home, especially if you have other pets or children. A little extra effort and patience now will pay huge dividends in the long term.

VISIT YOUR VET Also, even if your new pet seems completely fit and healthy, take her to your local vet for a full and thorough checkup, and understand that you may have to help her get through a common shelter cold in the first few weeks.

023 CATCH ONE TODAY

For centuries, sighthounds have been bred for speed, and the Greyhound, which is the world's fastest dog, can accelerate to over 45 mph! Tragically, tens of thousands of these majestic animals are abandoned each year when they reach the end of their racing careers at around five years old—although they can live for 14 years or longer. These canine "couch potatoes" are actually incredibly calm creatures that require only a short period outdoors each day, and love nothing more than lazing around the home looking elegant. However, they are not the ideal pet for inexperienced dog owners since they have a very strong prey drive and need careful handling around small animals. There are many rescue organizations dedicated specifically to abandoned racing dogs.

024 VISIT YOUR LOCAL HUMANE SOCIETY

Did you know that Humane Societies and SPCAs are all independent organizations, not connected to each other? The differences may be confusing. Some humane societies and SPCAs are "limited admission"—they only take in pets when they have space. Limited admission organizations may have their animals for many months, and use foster homes. Consequently, they usually know a lot about their dogs' characters and habits. Other humane societies are "open door," just like a city shelter, so they may euthanize to make room for more pets. These shelters may have some dogs for weeks and know their behavior traits, but may also have known some of their dogs for only a few days.

025 RESEARCH A RESCUE

A rescue "group" can be a private citizen or a nonprofit organization. Rescues are typically "limited admission" and use foster homes or boarding kennels. Because they pour so much time, effort, love, and money into their pets, their adoption fees generally range from $150 to $400. They will usually ask you to fill out an adoption application, conduct a phone or in-person interview, and will generally ask to visit your home to evaluate it for the safety and suitability of the particular pet you're interested in adopting. The price and process may sound like a lot, but in return you typically get a lot—a pet whose behavior and medical history are well known, after-adoption support with training, and a solid return policy should the pet surprise everyone and not be a match for your home. But since each rescue is so different, make sure to ask about their policies.

026

AVOID PUPPY MILLS

Canine behavior specialists, trainers, humane organizations, rescue groups, and kennel clubs all agree that people should never buy a puppy from a pet shop, or from a kennel that has puppies shipped in from commercial breeders. These are known as "puppy mills," where the animals are usually housed in less-than-humane conditions and the mother dogs endure miserable existences. Many unscrupulous pet stores perpetuate this exploitative treatment and only exacerbate the problem of canine overpopulation—unfortunately, as long as there is any demand, puppy mills will continue to provide a supply. Also be sure to avoid irresponsible individuals, often called "backyard breeders," who typically breed just for profit and do not provide an adequate standard of care. Again, buying from such people only perpetuates the problem.

027 PICK A NAME

As pet parents, you can have just as much fun coming up with names as human parents do. Plus, the process allows for more creativity; you don't have to worry about mean playground rhymes or making relatives happy. If you're leaning toward getting creative with your pet's name, wait and get to know his furry little personality first. The Rottie mix that you were going to call Bonesaw might turn out to be more of a Muffin. Just remember that the name you choose has to be something that your partner and kids are comfortable calling out in the local park—"Cleopatra" or "Cupcake" might be too much for your teenage son.

AVOID CONFUSION If you are going to practice verbal recall training with your dog, choose a short name that is easy to call out at a distance. Don't choose a name that sounds like a command, such as Beau or Noah.

BE HAPPY Smile when you call your pet; if she sees you are happy, she'll be more likely to respond to you.

THINK AHEAD Select a name that will grow with your pet. "Fluffy" might seem right when your little ball of fluff is a puppy, but if he hits 80 pounds (36 kg) it might not seem like such a good fit anymore.

CHANGE A NAME You don't have to change your dog's name if you like the one she was given by the shelter or foster home, but if you do want to change it, then positive reinforcement is a great way to train her to respond to her new name.

SEEK INSPIRATION If you feel you need a little inspiration choosing a name, browse through 100+ possibilities here, or look online for hundreds more.

TRADITIONAL	CUTE	POP CULTURE	BUTCH	NOSH	LITERARY
Bella	Acorn	Bono	Apache	Bagel	Ahab
Bonnie	Bianca	Bowie	Bear	Burger	Argos
Buddy	Birdie	Blondie	Butch	Chowder	Auden
Buster	Booboo	Britney	Boxer	Couscous	Bilbo
Chum	Bootsie	Clooney	Caesar	Doughnut	Beaudelaire
Coco	Bubbles	Dylan	Chief	Dumpling	Blake
Cody	Candy	Elton	Coyote	Flapjack	Chandler
Charlie	Coco	Elvis	Cruncher	Fudge	Chaucer
Jake	Cupcake	Kiefer	Diesel	Meatloaf	Dante
Jasper	Daisy	Gaga	Fang	Noodle	Gandalf
Lady	Honey	Madonna	Goliath	Nutmeg	Gatsby
Lucky	Keiko	Marilyn	Growler	Pickles	Ghost
Maggie	Lil'bit	Marley	King	Pudding	Homer
Milo	Lilypie	Oprah	Shadow	Roly-Poly	Milton
Missy	Lulu	Prince	Spike	Ravioli	Romeo
Monty	Suki	Rihanna	Terminator	Sausage	Rosebud
Max	Tutzi	Ringo	Thor	Sesame	Sancho
Sheba	Zizi	Zappa	Wolf	Waffle	Sherlock

028 BRING YOUR DOG HOME

The way you introduce your new dog to your home is a crucial step in making her comfortable and well adjusted. If you have other dogs, it is good to let them meet your new dog in a neutral and safe location, like a fenced park. That way, everyone can be relaxed and not feel territorial or protective over toys or food. Even in this setting, it is best not to let your new pet off-leash outdoors unless you are 100 percent positive that the area you are in is completely secure and your new dog already has a collar and ID tag. In this case, it might make sense to let your new dog off-leash so that she can have the full freedom to approach your current dog at her own pace, circle around, and greet and sniff as they see fit.

Once inside your home, your new dog may be very curious and want to explore. Or, she may feel a little scared at first in the strange new environment. If your dog appears nervous, pick one room that feels safe and spend some time alone with her in that room. Also, show your dog where the water and food will be and be sure to give her plenty of chances to go outside so she knows where to go when nature calls.

BONE OF CONTENTION
DOUBLE THE PETS, DOUBLE THE TROUBLE?

If you think that having two pets is always double the work, think again. Adopting a pair of pals can actually end up being less work! Many destructive behaviors are due to boredom or separation anxiety, and a built-in playmate naturally provides the stimulation and security needed to reduce the potential for such neurotic behavior. It can also alleviate concerns about leaving a companion animal alone while you're at work. And the emotional and physical benefits of having a best bud are not reserved for humans alone. Studies actually show that animals bonded to one another live longer and healthier lives.

029 ADOPT A BONDED PAIR

Shelters and rescue groups often receive animals that have lived together for years and formed a strong bond. It is not always just two pals coming in together, but sometimes three, four, or more. No one should ever have to lose their BFF, but that is what often happens when one of the animals is adopted without the other.

Remember, a bonded pair (or threesome, or foursome) can be made up of a variety of critters—a dog and cat, a mama and her pup, a dog and a goat—yup, you'd be amazed at the buddies that come into shelters together. Also, many animals actually meet and become bonded at the shelter, so giving them a chance to stay with a new friend is important, too.

Adopting bonded pals means the animals are spared the trauma of a second painful separation (having already lost their original human family), and will be less inclined to feel lonely in their new home.

030 GET YOUR FURRY FIX BY FOSTERING

If you can't adopt a pet, but want to get a temporary furry cuddle fix, support the work of your local rescue groups, and save lives, then fostering is for you. Fostering is one of the most compassionate and rewarding actions an animal lover can take. A foster home can make a lifesaving difference for a homeless dog. Many people envision rescue groups as having large facilities and a full staff—the reality is more informal than that.

GIVE TIME Many rescue groups are only able to take in as many needy animals as they have fosters for. They work tirelessly to find homes for the animals in their care and to network the ones in municipal shelters, but all too often the time needed to find a home exceeds the time an animal has left. Foster homes provide the critical time needed to connect the dots between an animal in need and an adoptive home.

GIVE PROTECTION Foster homes help in ways that extend beyond simply saving lives. By getting to know a pet's personality, a foster helps the rescue group to properly place that pet into a suitable home. A brief stint in a safe environment can also help provide the socialization needed to facilitate a smooth transition into a new home.

GIVE LOVE And let's not forget the fun part! A foster parent gets to have a furry fix for a short stint without a lifelong commitment that may not suit her lifestyle. It's like getting to spoil a favorite niece or nephew when they come to visit.

BEHAVIOR

66 In times of joy, all of us wished we possessed a tail we could wag. 99

W. H. AUDEN

Understanding your dog's innate behaviors and tendencies is an important part of having a great relationship with her. While dogs can't speak, they absolutely do communicate in many ways, and it is up to you to learn to speak their language.

It can be helpful to understand that many of the behaviors dogs exhibit relate to pack behaviors and issues of dominance and submissiveness, with you as the pack leader. But it is also important to remember that dogs are far away from their wild ancestry, and in many ways, they are simply like little children—testing boundaries, looking to feed their cravings, and seeking your love and attention.

Dogs almost always just want to please you. Whatever a dog does, even if it upsets you (chewing your favorite shoe, tearing through your kitchen trash bag, or urinating in the wrong place), you must always remember that this was not intended to upset you. Don't take it personally. Again, a dog is like a small child and just needs to learn the rules.

Remember, too, that dogs are not their breeds—they're individuals. We can't emphasize this enough. The various breeds were originally bred for specific tasks, but these days, breed mostly just relates to how a dog looks (size, body shape, hair, etc.). Do you judge others only by their looks? When it comes to the true nature and behavior of a dog, they, like people, are individuals, and mixed-breed dogs are as valuable and worthy of "best in show" as any other dog. Just ask someone with a mixed-breed dog, and see what they say.

031
KNOW YOUR DOG: SENSES

To begin to understand why your dog does what she does, you first have to learn about how she sees the world—or rather how she *smells* the world, since smell is by far a dog's most important sense. Dogs obtain information about other dogs (and humans), including their emotional states, from scents. Hearing is dogs' second most important sense and they can locate the source of a sound far more quickly than we humans can. Sight is a clear third and, again, dogs' visual sensitivity to movement and night vision is far superior to ours. Your dog's heightened senses explain many of the mysterious canine "superpowers": How does my dog know it's me pulling into the driveway? How does she seem to sense when I'm feeling unwell?

SMELL

It's hard for us mere humans to comprehend the power of a dog's sense of smell, which can be many thousands of times more sensitive than ours, depending on the type of dog. The area in a dog's brain dedicated to smell is 40 times larger than the equivalent area in our brain. Dogs use their sense of smell to find food and investigate strange objects. By sniffing each other's fur, mouths, and especially genitals (see item 33), dogs glean information such as where another dog has been, what he's eaten, and what mood he's in. Recent research suggests that dogs are even able to smell human illnesses, including some cancers.

HEARING

A dog's hearing is extremely acute and far superior to ours. Humans can detect sounds within a range from 20–20,000 hertz (depending on age), whereas dogs can detect sounds in a range from 40–60,000 hertz. This is why dog whistles, which are higher than 20,000 hertz, are inaudible to us. Plus, dogs can hear sounds over greater distances than humans and are far more discerning when it comes to sound quality—your dog would still recognize the sound of *your* car's engine even if all of your neighbors owned the same make and model! A dog's ears are independently mobile and are able to pinpoint the source of a sound almost instantaneously.

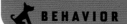

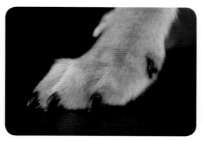

SIGHT

Dogs' eyes evolved to see best at dusk or dawn, which is when wild dogs hunt, and they are particularly adept at spotting the slightest movement. A dog's eye's are placed in such a way that they have a wide field of vision with good binocular sight in a relatively narrow central area (binocular vision in dogs is approximately half of that in humans). Also, dogs do not see colors in the same way as we do. Studies indicate that dogs see colors in various shades of blue, gray, and yellow. Orange, yellow, or green toys will appear the same shade of yellow as grass to your dog. A blue toy will be easier for your dog to spot.

TOUCH

Dogs are born blind and deaf, and even their astonishing sense of smell doesn't develop for a week or two. Touch is the first sense dogs develop as they are licked and nuzzled by their mothers. A dog's entire body is covered with touch-sensitive nerve endings, and touch-sensitive hairs called vibrissae grow above the dog's eyes and on its muzzle (which is why you should never trim a dog's whiskers). In a natural pack, dogs constantly send signals through physical contact to other pack members. And affectionate physical contact with human pack members is vitally important for a dog's health and happiness.

TASTE

Because the sensation of taste is closely linked with smell, you might expect dogs to be the true gourmets of the animal kingdom. However, dogs have far fewer taste buds than do humans, and their sense of taste is unsophisticated to say the least. As pack animals, dogs are far more concerned about getting as much food as they can into their stomachs as quickly as possible, before someone beats them to it. This behavior is more common with certain breeds, such as Beagles, which have a tendency toward obesity. A dog's Jacobson's organ, located in the mouth, allows her to quite literally taste the air when hunting prey or searching for a mate.

032 LET 'EM SNIFF!

As intelligent social animals, dogs have developed a complex and highly sophisticated range of communication skills. This includes a certain amount of verbal communication in the form of whines, woofs, and warning growls, but far more important and subtle are the messages communicated by a dog's body language and the invisible alphabet of odors. Urine markers left in strategic locations send complex signals to other dogs. As frustrating as it can be for human pack members who don't want to stop every 30 seconds so Fido can sniff at every lamppost en route, it is important to indulge your dog and give him time to catch up with the local canine news in the doggie *Daily Post*.

033 MEET AND GREET

When we humans meet each other, we perform brief rituals of greeting that vary from one culture to another. People may give an almost imperceptible nod of the head by way of greeting or we may bow deeply to each other; we may kiss each other on the cheek one, two, three, or more times; we may shake hands and smile. Psychologists can go much deeper than this, and can identify subtler signals passed by, for example, the firmness of a handshake and the warmth of the accompanying smile or the duration of eye contact. When two dogs meet, they perform their own distinctive (and universal) greeting ritual. Their body language may suggest a meeting of equals or there may be unmistakable signs of dominance and submission. Most uncomfortably for many of us, the ritual involves urine scenting where the dogs sniff each other's genitals—more submissive dogs may raise a rear leg or even roll over to accommodate the more dominant dog. Whatever embarrassment you may experience during these encounters, resist the urge to pull your dog away. Remember that it's as natural as shaking hands and just good doggie manners.

034 RECOGNIZE THE PLAY BOW

One of the most distinctive and endearing of all doggie signals is the classic play bow, or "puppy play position." Here, the dog faces his human or canine playmate and crouches with his front paws extended in front. His rear end is raised comically and his tail is up and wagging at a rate roughly corresponding to the enthusiasm with which his invitation is greeted. The body language may well be accompanied by an equally characteristic "Let's play!" bark. The type of game he's proposing will inevitably involve some form of chase interspersed with regular bouts of rough-and-tumble mock fighting.

035 ENCOURAGE "ROLL" PLAY

Dogs play-fight with each other all their lives, and even though it can sound and look alarming to us humans, it's actually an important part of their development. Puppies play-fight with each other to learn how to assert authority and signal submission. The dominant dog will usually roll his playmate onto his back and pin him down. As pups get older, they play-fight with adult dogs they share their home with, as well as with each other. This way, they learn to understand how much pressure it is acceptable to apply with their jaws. If they hurt the adult dog or each other, the adult may reprimand them with a swift nip. In the wild, such play helps individuals to find their rank in the pack; with domestic dogs, it's a vital part of socialization and a great source of fun.

BONE OF CONTENTION
THE "ALPHA ROLL"

Because dogs naturally submit to more dominant dogs by rolling onto their backs and exposing their vulnerable underbellies, some trainers advocate a "rank reduction" technique to correct aggressive or dominant behavior by forcibly rolling a dog onto his back and pinning him down to show who's boss. It is unsurprising that a lot of people get bitten when performing the "Alpha Roll"; by forcing an animal to submit in this way, you make her think that you intend to harm or even kill her, and she may well feel obliged to defend herself. As ever, a more patient, positive-reinforcement approach gets far better results.

036 LEARN TO SPEAK DOG

Given that a well-trained dog can learn to differentiate between, and respond appropriately to, hundreds of verbal commands from her human family, it is only right that we should make an effort to understand what our canine companions are trying to say to us. We all know that a growl is a warning, and a yelp is a sound of distress, but there are so many verbal signals in between those two sounds, and they all communicate different messages. Below are a few of the most common bark signals, to help you to understand what your dog is trying to say.

SIGNAL	Groups of three or four barks at a mid-range pitch.	Continuous barking at a mid-range pitch.	A series of barks with a significant pause between each bark; can be at a mid-range pitch, but may become higher-pitched after a period of time.
MEANING	A call to action. Something, whether friend or foe, is entering our territory. We need to investigate this.	A call to arms. At this point the potential threat is much nearer, and the pack should be ready to defend itself.	"I'm lonely and bored. Is there anyone there?"
TYPICAL SCENARIO	 Your dog is near the window as someone walks past or approaches your home.	 Your dog moves to the front door, as the "intruder" is now very close.	 The dog is alone in the house and is experiencing separation anxiety. He pauses to listen for a return call or, better still, a key turning in the door.
SIGNAL	One or two short, sharp barks at a mid-range or high pitch.	A single short sharp bark at a high pitch.	A "stutter-bark" at a mid-range pitch.
MEANING	"Hello!"	"What the . . .?"	"Let's play!"
TYPICAL SCENARIO	 A potential intruder has been recognized as a friend and is being welcomed by your dog's standard greeting.	 Something unexpected has occurred and your dog is expressing surprise (but not fear or annoyance).	 This distinctive "arrr-Ruff!" is often accompanied by the dog's delightful play-bow (see item 34).

037 TEACH YOUR KIDS HOW TO BEHAVE AROUND DOGS

Many children instinctively love dogs and want to pet every dog they meet, but not every dog likes to be petted by strangers. Here are some basic rules to teach your kids about doggie etiquette.

ASK FIRST Always ask for permission to pet a dog. If the dog's owner says it's okay to pet the dog, approach slowly and present the back of your hand to the dog so that he can sniff you, which is his way of saying hello. Never approach a dog when his owner isn't around, especially if the dog is tied up on a lead or chain and feels vulnerable.

BE QUIET AND CALM Dogs can be scared by loud noises and fast movements. Do not jump around with a strange dog, even in play. Such actions may stimulate the dog's instinctive desire to chase. Remember that dogs play rough and use their mouths to hold on to things, and may think that that's how you want to play, too.

LET SLEEPING DOGS LIE Never disturb a dog who is sleeping, as he may instinctively defend himself if he is startled, and may snarl or even snap at his imaginary assailant. Even if a dog is awake, never approach and pat him if he has not seen you first. Again, he could be startled by the unexpected contact and may snap at you.

LET EATING DOGS LUNCH Don't try to pet a dog while he's eating food or chewing a bone. Dogs are naturally very protective of their food and may think you are trying to steal their dinner. Although not all dogs are protective of their food bowl, it's better to be safe than sorry.

DON'T STARE AT A DOG'S FACE Never put your face near a dog's face and never stare into a dog's eyes, even if you know the dog. Dogs can be very uncomfortable when people stare at them because that's one way dogs signal aggression to each other.

DON'T RUN AWAY Dogs growl when they are scared or angry. If a dog growls at you, fold your arms, turn your body so your side is facing the dog, and walk away slowly. Don't run. If you run away, you may trigger the dog's chase instinct.

038 UNDERSTAND EAR SIGNALS

Apart from Grandpa Joe who can wiggle his ears to amuse his grandkids, human ears are pretty useless for communication purposes. Dogs, however, have highly mobile ears that, like a couple of furry semaphore flags, send very clear messages to other dogs. Dogs with very long pendant ears have a disadvantage on this score, as their ear position often has more to do with wind direction than willpower, but all wild dogs and many domestic dogs have "pricked" ears that are erect and clearly visible from a distance. With a bit of practice, you too can learn to understand the basics of canine 'earsay.'

SIGNAL	Ears erect or slightly forward; head slightly tilted.	Ears pulled back against the head, expression apprehensive.	Ears erect or slightly forward; expression aggressive.	Ears pulled back against the head, teeth bared.
MEANING	"This is really interesting!"	"I'm not a threat. Please don't hurt me."	"I'm ready to fight, and I'm not afraid." This is a threat from a confident dog.	"I'm wary of you, but I'll defend myself if I must." This is a threat signal from a dog who's not so sure of himself.

ASK THE VET
MY DOG KEEPS SCRATCHING HIS EARS. WHAT MIGHT BE WRONG?

Don't just assume your dog's ears itch if he scratches them frequently. It may be a sign of a painful infection. Other symptoms include ear discharge, a strange odor, and head shaking. If you notice these signs, call your veterinarian.

Dogs frequently develop ear infections because of their long L-shaped ear canals that easily trap dirt and moisture. Breeds with long, floppy ears and pups who swim frequently are the most susceptible to ear infections. Parasites or allergies can also trigger an infection. The best way to prevent ear problems in your dog is to try to keep his ears squeaky clean and to check them regularly for any discharge or odor. Ask your veterinarian how to use cotton balls and an ear cleaner to keep your dog's ears clean.

BONE OF CONTENTION
CROPPED-EARS CONTROVERSY

Ear cropping, which is actually an elective surgery to remove a portion of a dog's ear, used to be performed on certain breeds of dogs to keep their ears from being injured while doing the work they were bred to do. For those dogs, that cropped ear look has become associated with the look of the breed, and many people don't realize this is not how the dogs are born. Since today it is mostly a matter of cosmetics, it is considered by many veterinarians to be a painful procedure that is cruel and unnecessary.

039 LOOK INTO THEIR EYES

Eye contact in humans sends powerful psychological signals, and steady eye contact shows that we are attentive and interested. Shifty sideways glances might suggest we are not being truthful, and averting our gaze can signal shyness, shame, or fear. Staring at strangers is considered rude and can be perceived as a threat or challenge. This last point is true for virtually all animals, and certainly all canines take eye signals very seriously.

	SIGNAL	MEANING
SIGNAL	Direct and steady eye contact	Eyes averted to avoid direct eye contact
MEANING	"I'm tougher than you!" This is an expression of dominance, and if the dog being stared at doesn't back down, the threat level will quickly escalate. Normally, however, one dog quickly signals submission and turns away.	"You're the boss! Peace." This is a clear sign of deference or capitulation from a dog confronted by a more powerful personality. The submissive dog will look away and may even roll over to signal complete capitulation. Size does not always matter, but dogs tend to quickly recognize when there's a mismatch.

040 RESIST THEIR GAZE

One common way in which dogs use their eyes to control members of their human family is by staring at people while they eat—often switching their gaze between the person and the food in a comical manner that is hard to resist. But resist you must: from the dog's point of view, she is asserting dominance. When you reward the behavior by giving her what she wants, you are reinforcing a behavior that can become irritating for you and your dinner guests.

BONE OF CONTENTION
OXYTOCIN RELEASE—THE LOOK OF LOVE?

In 2015, the prestigious journal *Science* reported that researchers in Japan had discovered that dog owners experienced a surge of oxytocin when their pets gazed into their eyes. Oxytocin is the same hormone released in a mother's brain when she looks into the eyes of her child; it drives maternal care and strengthens the bond between mothers and their babies. So, what's going on? Are we being hypnotized by our dogs? Well, yes and no; just as amazingly, the dramatic effect is mirrored in the dogs themselves, who also experience a spike in the same hormone when gazing back at their adoring owners.

The findings suggest that staring promotes a virtuous cycle that reinforces the bond that has existed between humans and dogs since the two first teamed up thousands of years ago. Which goes a long way toward explaining why dogs are commonly regarded as "man's best friend." When the researchers tried the same experiment with hand-raised wolves, the effect was nowhere to be seen.

So why do experts tell us *not* to stare at dogs? Well, it's important to remember that the experiments were carried out using dogs and their owners. The likelihood is simply that, just like with humans, it's only okay to stare into the eyes of your best beloved. If you stare at a stranger, you're considered rude and are likely to receive a cold stare rather than a warm glow in return—"Wanna picture, buddy?"

041 EXPLOIT YOUR LOOKS

Although people, and especially children, should be wary of staring directly into the eyes of an unfamiliar dog—even a small dominant dog may respond to this as an act of aggression—looking directly at your own dog can be used as an effective way of influencing behavior. A long, loving look can strenghten the bond between you (see left). A sharp and steady glare might be all that is needed to correct bad habits such as begging at the dinner table. Your dog should look away, perhaps with the odd furtive glance to check that he's appeased you.

042 BAT THOSE EYELIDS

In doggie language, blinking is a subtle signal of submission. Quite literally, when two dogs confront each other, the dog who blinks first is backing down. However, not unlike the human seductress who flutters her eyelashes to signal attraction, dogs also blink at each other to display friendship and affection. When a dog or wolf greets a higher-ranking pack member, he bows his head and then tentatively licks the face of the more dominant animal. If the greeting is accepted, the dominant animal will blink three or four times. The submissive dog completes the greeting ritual by blinking in return.

043 CLOCK HIS TAIL POSITION

Wild dogs, whether wolves, coyotes, foxes, or any other kind of canid, almost always have long bushy tails. A dog's tail is an important communication aid that allows him to signal information about his state of mind and status from a distance. It is important to note that human interference has led to a range of tail shapes and lengths, and that this must be taken into account when reading a domestic dog's "tail mail." A Border Collie, for example, will naturally hold his tail low, while a Husky will hold his tail high. Signals should be read in relation to the particular dog's default tail position. If you imagine a dog's tail as the hour hand of a clock, this default position is around 7 o'clock in a wolf-like dog, such as a German Shepherd. This tail position indicates that a dog is relaxed and happily going about his business.

❶ 10–12 O'CLOCK If a dog carries his tail high with the tip slightly curled over his back as he approaches another animal, he is full of confidence and expects other dogs to treat him with due respect.

❷ 9 O'CLOCK A tail held straight out indicates a mid-ranking dog (neither especially dominant nor submissive) approaching an unfamiliar dog. He doesn't necessarily feel threatened, only curious.

❸ 7–8 O'CLOCK If a dog's tail stays this low when he is approaching another dog, it indicates that he is unsure of himself. He's basically saying, "I'm no threat."

❹ 6 O'CLOCK If the tail touches the hind legs, or starts to move between the legs, it is a sure sign of a submissive dog who is wary of approaching another animal. Such a dog will probably stay still and wait for the more dominant dog to approach.

044
SPOT TELLTALE TAIL SHAPES

Information gleaned from a dog's tail position can be subtly or dramatically modified by the tail's shape. One of the most common changes in a dog's tail shape occurs when her hackles rise and her tail thickens all along its length. Even if a dog's tail is kept fairly low, this is a clear warning signal that she is no pushover and is prepared to defend herself if absolutely necessary. More dramatic still is the sharp bend that appears in the tail of many dominant wolf-like dogs, which heightens the threat level to "red alert."

BONE OF CONTENTION
IS TAIL DOCKING A NECESSARY EVIL?

Tail docking, or more accurately, surgically removing the portion of the lower spinal column that is the tail, was once routinely performed on many working breeds of dogs. Today, many veterinarians believe it is unnecessary and discourage the procedure unless it is required for medical reasons.

Not only does tail docking cause unnecessary suffering, it clearly inhibits a dog's ability to communicate with other dogs. In one experiment that studied how dogs interacted in a dog park, it was shown that dogs without tails were twice as likely to be involved in open hostilities when meeting and greeting other dogs. Their greeting ritual was more ambiguous and open to misinterpretation.

045 WATCH THOSE WAGS

Everyone knows that a dog's tail motion sends a clear-cut message—if the tail is wagging then the dog is happy. Right? Not necessarily! A dog uses tail wagging to send a range of signals and, depending on the circumstances and accompanying body language, a wagging tail can indicate a friendly greeting or an assertive warning. Generally speaking, however, higher speeds of tail wagging correspond to higher levels of excitement, and the broader the sweep, the more positive the tail signal. Slight movements or vibrations of the tail can signal uncertainty, distress, or aggression. Here are a few of the most common tail signals to watch out for.

SIGNAL	Tail relaxed and swinging in short sweeps.	Tail held erect and wagging or "vibrating" in very short movements.	Tail tucked between the legs, wagging rapidly with short sweeps.
MEANING	"Hi there!" This is a common signal to a respected pack member, and is what you would expect as a friendly greeting from your dog when you return home. As you greet your dog in return, the sweep and rate of tail wagging will increase accordingly.	"Back off or back down, now!" This is a common signal from a dominant dog to a lower-ranking dog (or human). You may notice this movement, which is often accompanied by a low growl, when your dog is eating and another dog approaches his food bowl.	"I'm scared. Please don't hurt me." Although this signal may be exaggerated in some dogs, such as Whippets that may naturally carry their tails very low, this is generally a clear indication that a dog is nervous and concerned for his safety.
	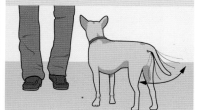		

046 SPOT A DOMINANT DOG

While the vast majority of dogs are friendly, some dogs are naturally more dominant than others, and their high self esteem is clearly signaled in their body language and assertive behavior. A dominant nature is more common in un-neutered male dogs. Dominant dogs may greet other dogs with tail held high and an unflinching gaze, and may be swift to resort to aggression if they are not given the respect they feel they deserve. Such dogs require careful handling, preferably by more experienced dog owners. It is important to note that size is not necessarily a factor when judging a dog's dominant nature: Chihuahuas and diminutive Jack Russell Terriers are notorious for their "supersized" characters.

EARS ERECT AND ALERT

DIRECT EYE CONTACT HELD

TAIL HELD HIGH

BACK STRAIGHT

LEGS RIGID AS DOG ADOPTS FORWARD STANCE

047 READ HER LIPS

When a dog wants to send a warning signal to another dog or human to back off, she does so by curling her lips to display her weapons, in the form of those impressive fangs. This display is usually accompanied by a low, menacing growl. It is important to be aware that if a dog stops growling but is still baring her teeth with lips trembling, this does not indicate that the dog is calming down. It is far more likely that she thinks that her warning has not been effective and that she has no alternative but to fight. It is important to note that growling is ritualistic signal—an attempt to change another individual's behavior.

WHY IS MY DOG
CONSTANTLY CHASING HIS TAIL?

It is not uncommon for dogs to chase their tails, and it is usually just a harmless expression of a playful temperament or a brief exploratory phase during puppyhood. It can also be a way for a dog to release excessive energy, and your dog may well stop tail-chasing when he is taken for longer walks or taught to play fetch. It can, however, be a sign that your dog has a tail injury, skin irritation, or a flea bite, which is causing him discomfort. More rarely, compulsive tail-chasing can be a sign of a psychological or neurological disorder. If you are worried, schedule a trip to your vet.

048 INTERPRET GROWLS

Everyone knows that a dog's growl can be a precursor to a bite, but did you know that dogs use growls to communicate many different messages? Below is a general guide to some commonly heard growls and their meanings. Please note that it can be difficult to distinguish between some of these signals; when in doubt, give a growling dog some space immediately to avoid exacerbating a stressful situation.

SIGNAL	A low-pitched growl that seems to come from the chest	Low-pitched growl that leads to a bark	Undulating growl with occasional high-pitched bark	Boisterous growl without lip curling, emanating from the throat rather than the chest
MEANING	"Back off!" This is an unequivocal warning that is accompanied by confident body language, such as a head held high, ears alert, and strong eye contact. A less-confident dog may emit a higher-pitched growl from the throat rather than the chest, accompanied by lip curling, which says, "I don't want to fight, but I will if I have to."	Although the growl is once again a clear warning, the accompanying bark is a call for support. This dog is less confident, but will defend himself if left with no choice. If the pitch of the bark rises, it suggests the dog is increasingly unsure of the situation.	"I'm scared and excited—leave me alone!" This is more of a fearful groan then a growl, and the dog is just as likely to run away as he is to stand his ground and deal with the conflict.	"This is great fun! Let's keep playing!" This playful growling is usually accompanied by those characteristic stutter-barks that are invitations to play. The sound may be scary to people who don't know the dog, but to his owner it's a cheerful sound associated with games such as tug-of-war and fetch.

049 PLAY TUG-OF-WAR (MAYBE!)

Dogs love to play tug-of-war, but if you're not careful, you could be training your dog that it's okay to take your possessions and not relinquish them. If taught correctly, though, you can use tug-of-war to teach him to drop items on command, which is a great lesson for him to learn. Hold a really enticing treat and, as your dog drops the item in his mouth, quickly (and belatedly) command him to "give," and then give him the treat to reinforce the behavior.

Work on this repeatedly, until you've trained your dog to stop in the middle of an exciting game of tug-of-war and drop the item on command. One thing to keep in mind during the tugging portion of the exercise: very determined dogs may hold on so firmly that you can lift them off the ground and they still won't let go. Experts warn that this is not a good idea, and that bones and teeth may be damaged if play gets too rough.

050 NEVER INTERVENE

Never reach in between two dogs to break up a dogfight, or you may be seriously injured. Squirt the dogs in the face with a water bottle or try to distract them by throwing something near them or making a loud noise. It's worth investing in a handheld gas horn, which fits neatly into your pocket or handbag, and can be very effective for breaking up a fight without intervening physically and risking injury.

051 LEAD THE PACK

Dogs evolved as pack animals and are highly social creatures that can work together as a team. It is crucial to recognize that a domesticated dog views its human family as its pack. In the wild, packs have a strong hierarchical structure and each individual knows where he or she stands within that hierarchy. Your dog should accept you as the pack leader, but not because you are bigger and stronger than he is (which may not be the case with a large mastiff, and won't necessarily cut the mustard with a dominant Chihuahua) even though he's a fraction of your size. Being an effective leader stems from good understanding, good communication, and good training. If a dominant dog is not properly trained and socialized, he may become aggressive to other dogs, to visitors, or even to you. Effectively he thinks that he's the pack leader and is responsible for protecting the pack. You must assert yourself as leader in order to prevent this behavior and reassure your dog that you are perfectly capable of protecting him and the rest of your family. Train your dog to obey at times, and lovingly reward and praise him for gentle behavior. If your dog shows signs of dominance, here are some tips to address specific behaviors.

DOMINANT DOG-AGGRESSION

A dominant dog that has not been properly socialized may try to protect you from other dogs by barking aggressively or even attacking them.

PREVENTION When you encounter other dogs, assert your authority by asking your dog to sit. He will soon realize that you do not feel threatened by the strange dog. Be sure to praise your dog for good behavior with other dogs.

POSSESSIVE AGGRESSION

A dog with a dominant temperament may challenge another dog or human—including his owner—over possession of such important items as favorite toys, comfortable seats, and of course food.

PREVENTION Keep all treats and toys as a reward for good behavior, and be sure to put toys out of reach when designated playtime is over. Remind your dog who's boss by making him execute a command such as "sit" or "stay" before receiving food, toys, or being allowed to go through the door when you take him out for a walk.

TERRITORIAL AGGRESSION

If a dog sees himself as the pack leader in a home, then he may aggressively defend his pack and its territory—effectively your family and home—against intruders, including the mailman and visiting friends.

PREVENTION Introduce your dog to new people gradually and ask them to play their part by not approaching your dog or making direct eye contact. Instead, ask your visitor to sit down and introduce your dog at the dog's pace. Again, reward your dog for being gentle with strangers. It's also a good idea to require your dog to sit and stay when a visitor enters your home until you give the release command.

052 SPAY OR NEUTER YOUR DOG

There are many benefits to spaying (female dogs) and neutering (male dogs) beyond helping to deal with the problem of overpopulation. Here are just a few of the reasons experts recommend getting your dog "fixed."

1 YOUR DOG WILL BE HAPPIER When you spay or neuter your dog, you remove the burden of his or her constant longing to find a mate. This longing can cause behaviors like aggression, pacing, obsessive behavior like chewing and shredding things, and even depression. When you remove the underlying hormonal causes, you're lifting a weight off your dog's shoulders, allowing him or her to be happy, affectionate, and relaxed.

2 YOUR DOG WILL BE HEALTHIER Medical evidence proves it: In females, spaying helps prevent uterine, ovarian, and breast cancers, which are fatal in about 50% of dogs. Females spayed before their first heat (4–5 months old) are the healthiest, but it helps at any age. For males, especially if neutered before 6 months of age, the procedure prevents testicular cancer and prostate problems.

3 YOUR PET WILL LIVE LONGER Because they are healthier, spayed and neutered pets have a significantly longer average lifespan. Also, neutered pets are less likely to roam or fight (see #5 and #6), both of which too often lead to fatal injuries.

4 YOUR SPAYED FEMALE WON'T GO INTO HEAT This means you don't have to deal with menstruation (yes, dogs do that!) and more-frequent urination—indoors as well as out.

5 YOUR MALE DOG IS LESS LIKELY TO ROAM An un-neutered male pet is driven by strong hormones to mate, and will often turn to Houdini-style escapades to get out of his home or yard, whether or not there's a female in heat close by.

6 YOUR MALE DOG WILL BE FRIENDLIER A fixed male is less likely to want to fight with other male dogs he sees as competition, or with female dogs who may not appreciate his annoying advances.

7 YOUR FEMALE DOG WILL BE FRIENDLIER When a female pet goes into heat, the hormones can make her behavior become erratic. A usually friendly pet who goes into heat can suddenly become aggressive with both people and other pets in the home.

8 HUMPING WILL BE REDUCED OR ELIMINATED This is true for both males and females, although it is most common in un-neutered males. Dogs will be much less likely to hump other dogs . . . or people's legs, or your couch cushions.

9 **IT WILL SAVE YOU MONEY** Fixed pets have fewer health problems, so vet bills are lower. These pets are less likely to bite, avoiding potential costly lawsuits (80 percent of dog bites to humans are from intact male dogs). They are less likely to try to escape and do damage to your home or yard, or cause a car accident.

10 **YOU'RE ACTUALLY SAVING PETS' LIVES** Nearly every city in the U.S. still deals with shelter overpopulation by directing shelters to humanely kill pets as cages and kennels are filled. Thankfully, this situation is changing as more and more communities launch programs to educate people about the importance of spaying or neutering their pets. Also, more people are learning how to care for and keep their pets, and more people adopting pets. Spaying or neutering your pet will improve the situation by helping to deal with the underlying problem of overpopulation.

DOES FIXING DOGS CHANGE THEIR PERSONALITIES?

Neutering or spaying dogs doesn't change their personalities, but it does change certain behavior patterns driven by their instinctive longing to find a mate. Imagine if you were constantly hungry and never able to eat. You'd spend all of your time obsessing about finding a meal, and you'd probably be pretty moody, right? Now imagine that a simple medical procedure could remove your hunger and set you free. That freedom is what you're giving your beloved dog when you alter him or her.

053 SEE THE SIGNS OF SUBMISSION

The submissive roll-over is perhaps the most distinctive of all doggie body-language rituals. In order to avoid aggressive confrontations, a submissive dog rolls over and raises a leg to expose his belly to a more dominant dog. The submissive dog generally averts his gaze, although he may find it tempting to glance at the dominant dog to check that his tactic is working its magic. If a submissive dog remains on all fours, he basically skulks before any dog or human that he recognizes as a high-ranking individual—his tail is low and may wag slightly, he holds his body low, his eyes make brief and indirect contact, and his teeth are hidden from view. He is likely to lick his lips or tentatively lick the face of the dominant dog, or to yawn conspicuously. In brief, his mission is to make himself as unthreatening as possible.

Submissive dogs, especially if they're timid, need to be trained in a way that offers them confidence. Only positive-reinforcement training methods, like clicker-training, should be used, as punishment-based methods can completely destroy these sensitive dogs' self-esteem and erode their trust in, and emotional connection to, you.

TAIL BETWEEN LEGS

LEG RAISED

EARS FLATTENED

MOUTH CLOSED

FACE AVERTED

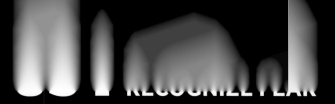

RECOGNIZE FEAR

The sight of a dog performing a submissive greeting ritual can be comical to human eyes, but the sight of a genuinely fearful dog, although not dissimilar, is always distressing. His tail disappears between his legs and his ears lie back against his head. His body tenses and leans away from the perceived threat. Unlike the submissive dog who thinks he can allay the danger by averting his eyes, the fearful dog may stare directly forward. Most importantly, his teeth may be bared, but this is only because his lips are drawn so far back in anguish. He may growl in an undulating tone that is more of a groan than a growl. Some dogs in shelters may display such fearful behavior, but in a patient and loving new home where they are continually reassured that they are safe, they can turn into visibly happy and confident dogs in a remarkably short time. No matter what, it is important to remember that fearful dogs are not necessarily dangerous dogs; they just need to be given some space, patience, and love to help them gain confidence.

BONE OF CONTENTION
TO BREED OR NOT TO BREED?

Don't breed your dog. Even if you do find homes for all the puppies, those are homes that could have adopted a pet instead. Can you be sure that all your puppies' new owners will never give them up to a shelter, will spay or neuter them, and will not breed more puppies? With so many shelters overpopulated and four million homeless pets killed each year in the U.S., fewer dogs need to be born, so please do your part.

ARTHUR'S TALE OF ENDURANCE AND DEVOTION

In November 2014, the extreme-sports team Peak Performance was representing Sweden in a 430-mile (690-km) endurance race through the Amazon rain forest in South America. During a brief rest periods in the grueling race, the team was approached by a local feral dog with a painful wound on his back. He was clearly tired and very hungry, so the team captain Mikael Lindnord gave the dog a piece of meat. With that simple act of kindness, the team of four became a pack of five—the dog refused to leave Mikael's side.

As the team trekked from village to village, they were met not only by local well wishers, but also by packs of less-than-welcoming feral dogs who barked and growled menacingly at their new teammate. Mikael was struck by the "proud and dignified" manner in which the injured dog stood his ground, calmly allowing the circling dogs to sniff him without showing any sign of fear or aggression. Mikael decided to call the dog Arthur, after the legendary king of Camelot.

Arthur continued to follow the team on their hazardous journey through dense undergrowth and, at times, knee-deep mud. Impressed by Arthur's stamina and loyalty, the team shared their food with him, and Arthur was still at their side when they reached the last leg of the race. Unfortunately, the final stage was a kayak race along a perilous stretch of the Amazon River, and the race organizers told the distraught team that they could not possibly take Arthur with them as it would not be safe for them or for him.

The team thought it safest to leave Arthur to return to his village. Too distressed to look back, Mikael was astonished to see the intrepid Arthur swimming alongside the kayak, trying desperately to keep up with the team. Deeply moved by the dog's unswerving devotion, Mikael heaved Arthur aboard. For a moment the sound of the river was drowned out by the applause of the delighted crowd still standing on the bank watching the drama unfold. On several occasions during that final leg, the team had to turn back to rescue Arthur from the treacherous water, but six days later, they crossed the finish line in an honorable twelfth position.

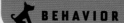

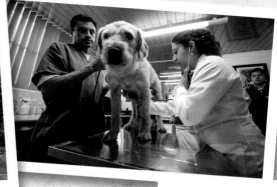

The team's celebrations were short-lived, however, as they immediately faced a new battle—getting Arthur's wound patched up by the nearest veterinarian and getting Arthur safely back to Sweden. At first, permission was refused both by the Ecuadorian and Swedish authorities, but the team pressed on undaunted and set up a Twitter campaign to promote their cause. The story became an Internet sensation and the authorities eventually relented. Just twenty minutes before their plane was due to leave Ecuador, permission was granted for Arthur to join the team on their journey home.

Mikael had one final challenge—convincing his wife that they should officially adopt Arthur. She was worried about how Arthur would behave around their one-year-old daughter Filippa, and was at first reluctant. However, she agreed to visit Arthur during his obligatory four-month quarantine and immediately fell in love with him. On March 20, 2015, Arthur was finally released from quarantine and was free to begin his new life in Sweden. Mikael has officially adopted Arthur, and the athletic dog and the dogged athlete are now permanent training buddies.

The story doesn't end there, however, as the adventure team has set up the Arthur Foundation as a charity that aims to help all stray dogs in Ecuador. Go team Arthur!

055 DEAL WITH SUBMISSIVE URINATION

Some dogs may leak a little simply because they get overexcited, for example when you return home from work or a friendly stranger pays a visit. Such leakages are particularly common with younger dogs, but may occur from time to time with a dog of any age. Depending upon where you are at the time, this can require a quick cleanup, but such behavior is perfectly natural and doesn't necessarily indicate a health problem (so long as there is a clear reason for the urination). Such accidents may also occur when a dog is frightened, perhaps by an overzealous greeting from that friendly stranger.

Urination can also occur when a dog is intimidated and lying on his back to signal submission to a more dominant dog. Such "submissive urination" is not an accident as such, but an intentional sign of appeasement to convey that the dog does not want to be seen as a threat.

Problems can arise when a dog is fearful of a family member (usual the dominant male) and is yelled at for what is mistakenly viewed as disobedience or even intentional peeing. This is a completely inappropriate and counterproductive response to submissive urination, which is, afterall just your dog indicating submission. Such dogs require reassurance and patience when they urinate indoors, and praise when they pee in appropriate places. They are effectively waving a white flag, and can do no more to show they respect you as their parent and protector.

056 GIVE A SHY DOG SOME SPACE

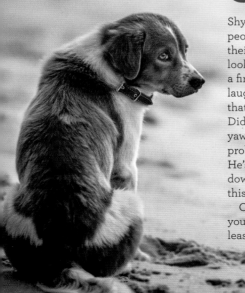

Shy dogs are often overwhelmed by how people show affection. People display their affection toward other people by looking them right in the eye, giving a firm handshake or big strong hug, or laughing loudly. For a shy dog, though, that kind of contact can be terrifying. Did you know that a dog licking his lips, yawning, or dropping his head low is probably trying to tell you he's nervous? He's effectively saying, "Hey, please slow down and give me my space. Let me take this meeting at my own speed."

One of the best ways to let a dog know you are a friend is by behaving in the least threatening manner possible and essentially ignoring the dog for a few minutes. That's actually a lot harder than it sounds. But if you can ignore the dog, he can then approach you at his own pace, sniffing you from behind and feeling safe, like he's not on your radar. Then, when you do want to engage, crouch or even lie down on the ground and calmly gaze away from the dog. Leave your arm and fingers outstretched to let him come to you at his own pace and sniff your hand. Once you are able to gently touch his head, the dog's fear will likely subside.

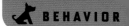

057 PET, DON'T PAT

For human adults, patting a child's head is a time-honored sign of affection, but this gesture doesn't translate well into doggie language. While it's so tempting to reach down and pat a dog on the head with light taps, this can be annoying to a canine, and if done too vigorously can even be misinterpreted as a slap or strike. In the wild, dogs rub against each other and groom each other to express their mutual affection, so it will feel much more pleasant and natural for a dog if you stroke him and scratch him lightly with your fingers instead of patting him on the head. Stroking or lightly finger-scratching your dog's head, neck, ears, back, belly, and rear end is a simple way to make your dog feel great. Just remember, when it comes to your dog's head, pet, don't pat!

DON'T PAT A DOG'S HEAD

DO STROKE A DOG'S HEAD

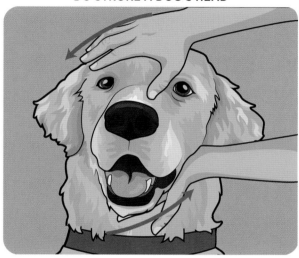

ASK THE VET
HOW CAN I HELP MY DOG LEARN TO PLAY WITH A TOY?

While playing with toys is a great way for a dog to work out his energy, you may be surprised to learn that not all dogs know how to play. While some dogs are just not interested in toys by nature, others were not given exposure to play as puppies and therefore might not know what to do with a ball or toy. Other dogs may have never been given proper socialization, and might be generally timid, uncertain, or fearful. Teaching your dog that it is okay to play with a toy can be a great experience both for you and your dog.

ROLL A BALL To get your dog to play with a ball, wait until you can both lie on the ground, and when you have your dog's attention, gently roll the ball toward her. If you see she is noticing the ball, praise her. Then take the ball and gently roll it again. By praising her attention on the ball, you are giving her permission to sniff and interact with it, which may draw her interest.

TUG A TOY Another way to elicit toy play is to purchase a soft chew toy and smear it with a tiny bit of wet food (just enough to transfer the scent onto the toy without tempting your dog to swallow it). Wave the toy slowly in front of your dog's mouth and, if she bites at it, gently and playfully pull the toy to encourage a tug of war. Inviting your dog into this type of playful competition is a great way to encourage her to engage with a toy and with you!

058 CALM SEPARATION ANXIETY

Some dogs, whether puppies or adults, just don't like being left at home alone. In more extreme cases, they can become nervous and agitated, and release their tension by chewing objects such as shoes or furniture, scratching and even damaging a door, barking constantly, urinating or defecating in the house, or trying desperately to jump a fence to go find you. If your dog exhibits these behaviors when left alone, it is important to remember that he is not intentionally misbehaving; he is experiencing real stress that he can't control, and he needs your help and loving understanding.

TAKE YOUR DOG TO DOGGIE DAY CARE If your dog experiences separation anxiety, minimizing the time you are gone is always helpful. Being gone for one hour is better than being gone for the whole day. If you must be gone for a long time, then a doggie day-care facility can be a great option for giving your dog care and attention while you are gone.

REASSURE YOUR DOG
A trainer can help you with many techniques to minimize separation anxiety in your dog, but the standard technique is to repeatedly leave your house for just a minute or two, and then come back in. The goal is to teach your dog that whenever you leave, you will return. Gradually increase the time you are outside, in the hope that your dog will come to trust that longer absences are not a problem.

CRATE TRAIN YOUR DOG
Another solution is to work with a trainer to teach your dog to be comfortable in a large crate or cage while you are gone. If your dog learns to like this cozy environment and feels safe there, this can give her reassurance when you are gone.

059 ADOPT A FRIEND

Some dogs, especially those with strong pack instincts like Huskies or Beagles, simply do not do well being left alone (Beagle types are particularly good at projecting their voices across the neighborhood). Consider inviting a friend's dog (preferably one your dog already knows) to stay at your house with your dog for a day and see if that helps. If it does, consider adopting another dog, not only to add more joy to your house, but also to keep your first dog company.

060 HELP YOUR DOG STOP CRYING

We all know that wolves howl to call to fellow pack members, and if you have a dog suffering from separation anxiety you may also have noticed that domestic dogs haven't necessarily lost that ancestral urge. Sad, lonely, anxious, or bored—dogs that aren't happy when you leave can make a lot of noise trying to let you know. Separation anxiety takes many forms, and has many different levels of intensity, but if your dog is crying, howling, barking, or otherwise vocalizing when left alone and is upsetting your neighbors, this is definitely something you want to fix—for your dog, for your neighbors, and for you! Here are some ways to calm her down and keep the peace.

❶ SET A RELIABLE DAILY ROUTINE Some newly adopted dogs may vocalize at first when they are left alone, as they are getting used to their new home. They might not be sure that when you leave you will actually return. Give them a very consistent, reliable routine of eating, playing, and exercise every day, including weekends. Even if your hour-by-hour schedule varies day to day, make sure your dog's stays exactly the same.

❷ GIVE REGULAR DAILY EXERCISE Unspent energy builds up in a dog (just like in a child) and needs to come out somehow. Better it be by running around the block with you, than by singing the blues while you're gone. Take your dog for a walk right before you leave, or engage in an intense play session (ideally at a dog park). Make it long enough to tire him out, so he'll be more likely to sleep while you are gone. Also, exercise releases serotonin rapidly and safely into your dog's brain, causing a happy, calm feeling without giving him any drugs.

❸ LEAVE THE TV OR RADIO ON A talk radio station or a news TV channel with people talking generally work well as a means of comforting your dog in your absence. Set the volume as loud as people would be talking in your home. Or, if your dog enjoys it, experiment with leaving on classical or other forms of music. Bach is an obvious choice, or she might feel more at home with the great Wolfgang!

❹ GIVE HIM A "FOOD PUZZLE" TOY A food puzzle is a toy with something yummy inside that the dog has to work to get. Give it to him right before you go, so he will be busy trying to get the food out while you are gone. Make sure you get the right size toy for your dog. Even better, buy four or five different toys, and rotate, so he gets to enjoy one "new" one each day, putting the "old" one away.

❺ DESENSITIZE HIM TO YOUR LEAVING Just go down the hallway to your front door, or down the driveway, then come back ... then go down the hallway or the block and wait 5 minutes, then come back ... then actually leave. Your dog will think that you are coming back right away, and will be less likely to cry.

❻ DON'T MAKE A BIG DEAL ABOUT LEAVING When you are getting ready to leave, gather up your things and leave as if you are coming right back—no overwhelming hugs, kisses, or dramatic farewells. Don't say "Goodbye, sweetie pie! It will be okay! Mommy will be back soon!" This just gives her a huge alert that you're leaving, possibly forever (an hour can feel like forever to a dog).

❼ CRATE TRAIN Consult with a trainer on this one. The idea is to get your dog comfortable in a small, confined space when you are gone, as long as you won't be gone for long. Once you've crate trained him, to help reduce crying, put your dog in his crate a few minutes before you leave, and leave without saying anything. You might want to try an airline crate, which is darker and more secure feeling than a wire crate. Don't use a blanket to cover the crate—a dog can pull a blanket inside and eat it. Make sure you only use a chew-proof crate pad, too.

❽ TRY NATURAL ANXIETY REMEDIES Many health-food and pet-supply stores sell herbal and homeopathic remedies that claim to calm pets. Some pets seem more affected by them than others, but it can't hurt to try. You can also try a DAP (Dog Appeasing Pheromone) collar or plug-in, available in many pet-supply stores.

❾ INVEST IN A SNUG SHIRT Many people have had success dressing their dogs in a snug shirt or vest, which keeps them feeling "hugged" and safe while home alone. Ask about this at your local pet-supply store.

061
UNDERSTAND JUMPING BEHAVIOR

It's natural for a puppy to jump up on other dogs to say hi, but some dogs jump up to make themselves taller than another dog, in an effort to show a higher status in the social pack. Similarly, dogs may jump on people either as a friendly greeting or as an attempt to establish dominance. People may think this is cute when a dog is small or a puppy, but for dogs that are (or will be) medium-sized or large, jumping up can scare people or even cause an injury.

062
KEEP PAWS ON THE FLOOR

Small children and elderly folk are especially vulnerable when larger dogs jump up, but even a small dog can get you into trouble by planting muddy paw prints on your neighbor's pristine white pants. Follow these guidelines to teach your dog to keep those paws on the floor—it's good doggie manners.

TURN AWAY Ignore your dog and literally turn away when she jumps up. For this to work, everyone must be on board, including family and visiting friends. Everyone must be told, "Turn and ignore her when she jumps on you!"

BE STILL AND QUIET Kids and people who squeal, make noises, or move around when a dog jumps on them are rewarding the jumping up. Kids sometimes understand this better when you tell them, "Be a boring tree."

LOOK AWAY Don't return her eager gaze when your dog jumps up; instead, turn away and look away, too. Just looking at her is a reward. Praise her when she stops jumping up and, if she jumps up again, return to being a boring tree.

REWARD FOR STANDING! Once she puts all four paws on the floor and keeps them there, greet her on your own terms: look at her, pet her, talk to her, and praise her. She'll soon realize that she shouldn't jump up to greet you.

COMMAND "SIT" If your dog has learned the "sit" command, then asking her to sit before she has time to greet you is a sure way to stop her in her tracks before she gets her front paws off the ground.

063
PLAN OFFICIAL JUMP TIME

If your dog just can't stop jumping for joy, you may want to allow her jumping outlets, when you ask for a jump and she can release that urge during structured play times. Turning "jump" into a specific command is a great way to let her know it's not okay to jump at other times. Just remember to give her appropriate jumping time—like on an agility course or out on a hike—so she can remember it's now become a command. And hey, you could always try jumping with her for fun!

 BONE OF CONTENTION
KEEP YOUR FEET ON THE FLOOR

Never use your knees, hands, feet, or legs to push into a dog that is jumping up. That type of physical attention can actually reinforce the unwanted behavior, and is therefore counterproductive. Ignoring your dog is the best remedy, and crossing your arms as you turn away will help keep your hands out of the mix.

064 LICK THAT LICKING HABIT

Some dogs won't lick or kiss you even if you ask, but others like to lick and kiss all the time. Young dogs especially love to lick your mouth, as this is their instinctive behavior—once weaned, wolf cubs lick their mother's mouth to encourage her to regurgitate a portion of her lunch for their consumption. You may think this licking is lovable, but others might view it as unhygienic and socially unacceptable. Here's how to "lick" the habit.

WALK AWAY If your dog licks your face at every opportunity, she's probably seeking your attention, much like a dog that jumps up on people. So don't reward the behavior with attention. Instead, get up and walk away when your dog licks you.

GIVE PRAISE Be very consistent and conscientious about ignoring the undesired behavior, and make absolutely sure everyone who meets her follows your no-attention-for-licking rule, too. When she comes over to you without licking, give her lots of verbal praise and positive treat reinforcement to let her know that's the behavior you want from her.

EMPLOY A TOY In addition, you can head off licking by redirecting your dog or puppy's mouth on to a toy. Just be sure you give her the toy before she starts licking, so it isn't mistaken as a reward for licking. Before long, she'll learn which behaviors get her the affection and attention she desires, and which don't.

065
MINIMIZE MOUTHING

Puppies test everything with their mouths and tend to mouth even more as they learn proper bite inhibition, which is when they experiment on their mother and littermates to discover how much jaw pressure is acceptable during play. However, left without proper training, mouthing can continue into adulthood and become a problem. Although it is not to be confused with biting or aggression (dogs that mouth do not bite down or apply any real pressure with the jaw), such behavior can cause someone to become uncomfortable with or even afraid of your dog. Mouthing commonly occurs during play, at times of excitement, or sometimes during a stressful situation. Follow this simple drill to curb this unwanted behavior.

STEP 1 Encourage your dog to gently lick your skin by smearing a little peanut butter or cream cheese on the back of your hand.

STEP 2 As your dog licks your hand, reinforce this gentle behavior by giving the command "soft."

STEP 3 If your dog starts mouthing and you feel any kind of pressure from his jaw, withdraw your hand. You don't need to say a word, just remove the thing that he wants (in this case your hand and the yummy peanut butter).

STEP 4 When your dog has thoroughly learned the lesson through repetitive drilling, you can use the word "soft" when he next starts mouthing and he will remember the command and adjust his behavior accordingly.

STEP 5 Reward your dog by saying "good boy" as he stops mouthing. Your soothing praise will be just as effective as the peanut butter in terms of positive reinforcement.

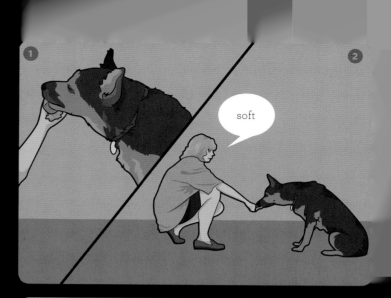

066 MEET THE RELATIVES

To understand deep-down doggie instincts, you need to know something about your pet's closest living relative—the wolf. The wolf is a highly accomplished predator capable of hunting in packs to bring down large prey such as moose. Most of the dog breeds we recognize today have been selectively bred to exhibit certain aspects of the wolf's behavior, and particularly the predatory sequence. The complete predatory sequence is eye, stalk, chase, grab-bite, kill-bite, dissect, and consume. Scent hounds, such as the Beagle, specialize in pursuing their quarry's scent trails. Pointing and flushing breeds, such as the Irish Setter, excel at stalking and flushing prey. Sight hounds, such as the Greyhound, have been bred to excel in the chase part of the sequence. Herding breeds, such as the Border Collie, are also accomplished chasers and stalkers, but they concentrate their efforts on controlling the movements of livestock. Terriers, such as the Jack Russell, outrival other breeds in their ability to capture and kill prey—usually mice, rather than moose. Today, the vast majority of dogs are friendly family pets, and the priority is to keep a lid on any unwanted wolfish ways.

067 UNDERSTAND YOUR DOG'S PREY DRIVE

Many dogs have a natural instinct to chase, capture, and even kill prey. This can be true for dogs of any size. That desire to chase and catch is called a prey drive. This drive can be the basis of a dog's desire to chase and find a ball, dig out a hidden toy under a pile of clothes, or to play tug of war with a toy and shake it violently once you let go. Toys that squeak are particularly gratifying for playful predators.

INDOORS For the most part, companion dogs' vestigial prey drive is not a problem in the home, where socialized pets as diverse as cats, dogs, and even rabbits, can get along perfectly well together. However, it certainly can become a problem if your dog has a strong instinct to chase smaller dogs or cats in your house and this is left unchecked. A game of chase is most often just that, but you do need to make sure your dog is not really trying to harm another pet.

OUTDOORS The prey drive can also be a concern when you are out on a walk or in a dog park. A dog with a strong prey drive might chase after a small dog in a dog park, or might pull hard on your leash trying to chase a squirrel or cat you encounter on a walk. That same desire might lead your dog to try to dart across a street to chase an animal without any regard for oncoming traffic. So it is crucial to understand the level of prey drive your dog has, and accordingly keep her and other animals safe.

068
STOP YOUR DOG CHASING RUNNERS

For some dogs, the prey drive that makes them instictively want to chase other animals translates into a desire to chase human runners. Your dog may just see it as a game, or in some cases, your dog may feel threatened by the fast movement and may think he is defending you by chasing a runner.

Whatever the reason, it can be a problem, causing fear in the runner, and forcing you to fight to control your dog on his leash.

An obvious way to cope with this problem is to walk your dog in places where runners are not likely to be. However, this is not always possible, and it is far better to free your dog of this behavior entirely.

To train your dog to avoid the chase, it is best to watch for when his attention turns to a runner, then immediately call his name and reward him with a treat. This will prevent your dog from becoming fixated on a runner, and will teach him to turn his attention to you. You can also try running with your dog so he learns to run by your side and grows more accustomed to seeing other people running.

069 PET A PIT

Pit bulls and pit bull mixes are some of the most common yet misunderstood dogs you'll see these days. So what's the truth about this infamous breed?

First of all, there isn't even much agreement on what a pit bull really is. The term "pit bull" is often used to refer to dogs with certain similar features including square heads and muscular builds. The majority of dogs called pit bulls are dogs who simply look a certain way. Because the term is used so imprecisely, it's important to be aware of misleading information about "all pit bulls."

Dogs thought of as pits and pittie mixes can make great family pets. They demonstrate all the love that man's best friend is known for. They're smart, social, and highly trainable. They develop strong bonds with their human family and are deeply loyal.

Contrary to myths about pit bulls, they were never bred to be aggressive towards people. Their jaws do not lock (as many believe). In fact, no breed of dog has a locking jaw; this is pure mythology.

As with all dogs, pit bulls and mixes are individuals and should be judged as such. Their high responsiveness to training and hard-working nature makes them great candidates for a dedicated home with people willing to provide the structure, training, and exercise these "love-a-bulls" need in order to stay happy and healthy. Ask anyone with a pit bull or mix, and they'll tell you that their pooch is loving, gentle, smart, and extremely loyal. Many with pit bulls even describe them as oversized lap dogs because they love to snuggle and be held. Stick to the facts about these cuddly canines, and you may get a new best friend.

BONE OF CONTENTION
HOW HEALTHY ARE PUREBREDS?

In nature, animals of the same species can freely interbreed to remain genetically healthy and diverse—the opposite of "purity"—and the practice of selectively breeding dogs for certain specific "purebred" visual characteristics has left many dogs with inherited genetic abnormalities, including tendencies toward blindness, hip dysplasia, and many other debilitating illnesses. Even some of the characteristics that people today find cute and endearing, such as a crushed-in nose or short stubby body, are actually physical traits that cause health problems for dogs. This is why many people prefer to get a mixed-breed dog. These dogs, sometimes called "mutts," tend to have fewer genetic health problems and are often unique in their looks. If you're seeking a dog of a specific breed, you should keep in mind that any dog can end up in a shelter, so start your search there, and if you do work with a breeder, you must find a responsible one who carries out strict genetic testing and takes full responsibility for finding all of their puppies caring homes.

Keep in mind that all dogs are individuals, and any two dogs of the same breed, even if from the same litter and raised in the same home, will have distinct personalities. This is why it is so important to not assume dogs of certain breeds are all the same. They aren't. That said, there are certain tendencies and characteristics that are more likely to be present in certain breeds of dogs.

070 GET TO KNOW BREEDS

All dogs belong to a single species, so they can all breed and reproduce. The term "dog breed" is not a scientific term, but is defined by hobbyists and dog clubs. Even the use of the word "pure" in purebred harks back to an early misunderstanding of genetics and a desire to create "purity" through selective breeding. There is no qualitative difference between a dog someone calls a "purebred" and one called a "mixed breed." They are all the same species and are all great dogs! It's just that over time, dogs have been selectively bred (and even inbred) for certain traits, and then there are dogs who are subsequent mixes of those breeds.

Dogs are thought to have begun living with people about 100,000 years ago. About 12,000 years ago, people began working with dogs in different ways, and that led to a tendency for dogs with certain traits to reproduce. Some breeds are ancient and were selectively bred for hunting, guarding homes and livestock, or fighting alongside soldiers. However, most of the dog breeds we recognize today are relatively modern (from the last 150 years or so) and were created initially to promote particular behaviors people found useful, such as pointing, and retrieving. However, for quite some time now, most breeding has been based solely on aesthetic considerations.

071 IDENTIFY TYPES OF DOGS

Since breeds are all creations of people and not nature, the groupings can at times seem random. No two national kennel clubs seem to agree on the categorization of all the breeds they recognize. Sometimes a dog that is accepted as a specific breed in one country is considered to be a "type" (perhaps varying only in coat type or color) of another breed by other experts in other countries. Nevertheless, it can be interesting and useful to look into the history of a breed if your dog is a purebred or has a very clear type, as this might explain certain aspects of your dog's behavior.

To understand the spectrum of breeds you find today, you can use the general categories listed below. Again, it is worth remembering that there are many breeds that do not fit into these categories, and that even the experts disagree on the origins of many dog breeds.

HOUNDS This group includes sight hounds and scent hounds that were bred for hunting, often in packs.

SPORTING DOGS This group includes spaniels and retrievers bred for hunting and swimming.

WORKING DOGS This group comprises a wide range of dogs bred for tasks such as guarding and hauling.

HERDING DOGS Herders are dogs, such as the various cattle dogs and sheepdogs, that drive and control the movements of livestock.

TERRIERS Dogs such as Jack Russells and Yorkshire Terriers, which were largely bred to hunt rodents, belong to the terrier group.

TOY DOGS Toys are tiny dogs, such as Pomeranians, that were bred to hunt rodents, and act as living hot-water bottles and companions.

072 TRACK DOWN A HOUND

Hounds were originally bred to assist hunters. There are two main kinds: those who hunt visually (sight hounds), and those who hunt using their highly developed sense of smell (scent hounds).

Sight hounds, like Greyhounds, tend to be extremely fast. They generally like to run in short bursts, but also can be quite content with just staying close by your side once they have released their energy.

As their name suggests, scent hounds—floppy-eared breeds such as Beagles, Bloodhounds, and coonhounds—have an incredibly well-developed sense of smell, often combined with a strong pack instinct, and boundless energy.

These traits in both types of hound can become problematic if your dog won't let you pull him away from a scent he is interested in, if he disappears into the woods in pursuit of some invisible quarry, or pulls hard on his leash to dart into the street to chase another animal. Additionally, some scent hounds have a loud and unrelenting bark, known as a "bay," which can make them extremely unpopular if they are left alone in a home to serenade the neighbors.

Like all dogs, hounds and hound mixes are individuals, so if you think you want one, you should go meet the dog and assess if he is the right fit for you and your lifestyle.

ASK THE VET

DOES IT MATTER IF MY DOG'S NOSE IS WET OR DRY?

If a dog is man's best friend, then a dog's nose is a dog's best friend. A dog "sees" the world through her nose, picking up scents that humans cannot smell, so it is important that her nose remains healthy. Generally, a healthy dog's nose is cool and moist, but can occasionally be dry as well. If your dog's nose is dry and warm, it does not mean she is ill. Temperature and wetness can vary from day to day and even within the same day. Appetite and energy level are more reliable indicators of your dog's general health. If, however, you notice a discharge from your dog's nose, that is something that a vet should take a look at. It could be an infection, or perhaps a foreign object, such as a piece of grass, lodged in a nostril.

073 MEET TEN TYPICAL HOUNDS

As hunting with hounds has declined in popularity in many parts of the world, some of the more obscure breeds of hound are now extremely rare even in their homelands. Others, however, have made the transition from hunting dog to household companion with consummate ease. Built for speed, sight hounds tend to have streamlined features, with deep chests, and long, powerful legs. Greyhounds, Borzois, Salukis, and particularly Afghan Hounds have long been prized for their elegant looks and calm temperaments. Scent hounds are more varied in appearance, but are typically characterized by their long floppy ears and, of course, their large noses. Short-legged scent hounds tend to pursue smaller prey into burrows, while long-legged hounds pursue faster quarries.

GREYHOUND

The archetypal sight hound, Greyhounds have a deep chest, long, powerful legs, and a barely perceptible forehead (or "stop").

WHIPPET

Looking like small versions of a Greyhound, often with a similar calm nature, Whippets are known for their high speed and low maintenance.

SALUKI

Salukis look a lot like Greyhounds with feathers. This elegant, ancient breed has been around since the time of the Pharaohs.

AFGHAN HOUND

Another ancient sight hound, the Afghan's luxurious coat protected it against the harsh climate of its high-altitude homeland.

BORZOI

Also known as Russian Wolfhounds, Borzois were bred to hunt wolves, and combine typical sight-hound speed with great strength.

BEAGLE
Beagles and Beagle mixes can be hard to train and, like many pack hounds, are more inclined to follow their noses than instructions.

BLOODHOUND
The most ancient and distinctive of the scent-hound breeds, Bloodhounds are still used by some law-enforcement groups.

BASSET HOUND
Basset Hounds and mixes have similar droopy features to the Bloodhound. The Basset was originally bred to hunt rabbits.

BLACK & TAN COONHOUND
This native American breed is a mix of the Bloodhound and foxhounds, originally bred to hunt.

DACHSHUND
Despite their comical looks, Dachshunds were originally bred in Germany to hunt badgers and are renowned as spirited characters.

074 RECOGNIZE A RETRIEVER

Retrievers and other sporting dogs, such as the highly distinctive poodles, were originally bred for hunting, but are now seen as family dogs. The truth is that just about any dog is a great family dog, but retrievers and retriever mixes tend to have lots of energy, like to chase balls, and often love to jump into water. These types of dogs are fairly large, so you'll want to make sure you have room in your car (and in your house).

OODLES OF POODLES Poodles are famed for their unique and highly recognizable haircuts. Of course, their hair doesn't naturally grow into those fluff balls that we immediately associate with this breed. That haircut harkens back to when poodles helped hunters retrieve game from water—patches of shaved skin and thick spots of hair enhanced their swimming ability. Poodles tend to have hair, rather than fur, the distinction being that hair grows without shedding and needs to be cut, just like a person. Poodles and poodle mixes tend to be better for people with allergies.

LOADS OF LOVABLE LABS For decades now, Labrador Retrievers have hung around the top spot on the list of the world's favorite dog breeds. Bred to work closely alongside their owners, they tend to be naturally friendly and fun loving. They also famously love their food and have a tendency toward obesity if their diet is not carefully controlled or they are not given adequate exercise to match their voracious appetites. Labrador Retrievers can be black, yellow, or chocolate in color. Whatever their color, Labs and Lab crosses are invariably sweet natured.

075 PLAY BALL TO RELEASE ENERGY

Does your dog get crazy excited when you come home? Does he jump all over you and, though it's adorable, would you rather he took it down a notch? Next time you come home, consider playing ball with him right away, to redirect the excitement and eagerness away from you and onto the game. Keep a basket of tennis balls right outside your front door so you'll be ready for a toss as soon as the door opens. This way, you'll have an activity for him to focus on when you come home, and you can help burn off a little of his excess energy, too (he's been waiting all day for you). Take it outside to the backyard if you have a good deal of space and he seems like he really needs to run.

076 MEET TEN TYPICAL SPORTING DOGS

Sporting breeds and mixes are typically medium to large dogs that tend to respond well to training. However, their need for lots of mental as well as physical stimulation can lead to problematic behavior if their needs are not met (although this is true to a large extent with any dog). These are typically boisterous and energetic creatures, and they are probably best represented as a group by the long-coated Golden Retrievers and the ubiquitous Labrador Retrievers. Often masters of the game of fetch, Labs and other sporting-breed mixes are still employed in a range of professions, as guide dogs for the blind, search-and-rescue dogs, and detector dogs for drugs and explosive devices.

GOLDEN RETRIEVER
Perennially popular, "Goldies" and mixes are renowned for their friendly natures and beautiful golden coats.

LABRADOR RETRIEVER
Most Labs love water, so if you're worried about mud on your upholstery, you should look elsewhere for your perfect pet.

ENGLISH SPRINGER SPANIEL
Bred to flush or "spring" birds for their owners to shoot, Springers and mixes are highly energetic.

POODLE
Standard, Miniature, and Toy Poodles are usually smart and active. They can excel at obedience and can be excellent swimmers.

POINTER
Pointers tend to be energetic sporting dogs, and were bred to point out hidden prey to hunters. They tend to have a very strong prey drive.

VIZSLA

Even if raised as a pet from puppyhood, Vizslas often instinctively adopt the typical pointer stance, with one front paw raised.

WEIMARANER

Renowned for their gorgeous and highly distinctive "gray-ghost" coats, Weimaraners and mixes tend to be friendly and obedient.

ENGLISH COCKER SPANIEL

English or American, "Cockers" and mixes are generally fun-loving and gentle.

NOVA SCOTIA DUCK-TOLLING RETRIEVER

The canine instinct to swim to arouse the curiosity of waterfowl is exploited in the Duck Toller.

IRISH SETTER

Irish "Red" Setters and mixes tend to be big dogs with big characters. They make good-natured family dogs for an active family.

STAND BY A WORKING DOG

Many dogs are referred to as "working-dog" breeds. These dogs were bred to perform diverse roles, including guarding people, property, and livestock; aiding law enforcement; and pulling small carts and sleds. Consequently, this group includes breeds as varied as Rottweilers, Dobermans, Boxers, Huskies, Chow Chows, and Saint Bernards. Working breeds tend to be large dogs, but they can be just as obedient and friendly as any breed or mix. Dogs bred for protection, such as Rottweilers and Dobermans, can still inspire fear in some people just by their look, but they can be among the most friendly and loving of dogs.

BONE OF CONTENTION
BEWARE OF DOG?

It's important to remember that although there are a lot of good reasons to bring a dog into your home, having a guard dog is not one of them! While any dog might certainly alert you to an intruder by barking, and might even come to your aid if needed, dogs should not be relied upon to be aggressive to an intruder. Never train your dog to be aggressive to people, because that training itself can cause dangerous situations—for you, an innocent person, or your dog. Sure, a "beware of dog" sign might provide an effective deterrent against an opportunist burglar, but if you feel you need further protection, take other steps to protect yourself and secure your property; a dog's only responsibility should be to be your loving companion.

BEWARE of DOG

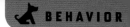

078
GET PAST RESOURCE GUARDING

Resource guarding is exactly what it sounds like. Your dog believes he has something of significant value, which he feels defensive about, and he growls if you try to take it away. Usually the higher the value of the resource, the more your dog might guard it. A dead bird, for example, or a bone from the neighbor's barbecue, might be a very high-value object because dogs are hardwired to protect their "prey." However, the treasure could just as easily be a prized toy or a slipper. So even if your pup has had a good life and has all the food and love he needs, his instincts may kick in to prevent certain things from being taken away. If your dog displays such unwanted behavior, enlist the help of a certified, professional, positive reinforcement-based dog trainer. A professional trainer can teach you how to read your dog's body language, and knows how to teach your pooch the "drop it" command. Your dog will learn that dropping a resource is in fact a good thing by receiving a treat for backing away and letting go of the resource. Of course, this treat must be of higher value than the item your dog is protecting. Eventually your dog will not feel the need to defend something he wants, and will trust you to give and take his resources, no matter what they are.

ASK THE VET
WHY WON'T MY DOG STOP BARKING?

When dealing with excessive barking, take into account that it's often a symptom of another problem, such as anxiety or boredom. The symptom will not go away until the source is addressed. Watch and listen to your dog. What is causing him to bark when you're home? The same things may be causing him to bark when you're not home. Figure out how can you alleviate these triggers for him and set him up to succeed!

079
BEAT BOREDOM BARKING

Keep in mind that your dog might be barking simply because she is bored when she's left alone for too long. Ask yourself the following questions.

QUESTION	Is your dog getting enough exercise?	Is your dog getting enough mental stimulation?	Is your dog lonely?
ANSWER	Give your dog a good long walk before you leave her alone for any length of time and you may find that her barking magically stops (due to the fact that she's sleeping contentedly). If your time is limited, teach her to play fetch, so she gets the maximum energy release in the shortest time.	Give your dog a chew treat as a project to work on just before you leave to keep her busy in your absence. Only give her these special treats when she's home alone, so she associates your absence with a positive event. If you have more than one dog, however, do not leave them unsupervised with chew treats—this can lead to fighting.	If you spend a lot of time away from home, then a more permanent solution may be needed. Hire a dog-sitter or, if your dog is good with other dogs, consider adopting a second dog so they can keep each other company and play while you're gone. Or try fostering a pet from a local rescue group to see if that helps relieve the boredom and barking.

080 MEET TEN TYPICAL WORKING DOGS

It's hard to pin down a "typical" working dog, but many share a large size and formidable appearance. Mastiff types were originally bred as dogs of war to fight alongside human soldiers and to provide entertainment by fighting each other. Consequently, some of these breeds retain a strong natural aggression toward other dogs and a mistrust of strangers, although they can often be very gentle with their human pack members.

HUSKY
These stunningly beautiful, wolflike dogs are tireless runners equipped to survive in freezing conditions. They typify the spitz-type dog.

CHOW CHOW
Known for their instinctive mistrust of strangers and devotion to their owner, Chow Chows and mixes can make wonderful pets.

ROTTWEILER
Too often used as guard dogs due to their strength and formidable appearance, well-cared-for "Rotties" are usually gentle and loving softies.

DOBERMAN PINSCHER
These handsome creatures are generally highly intelligent and obedient dogs that move with the agility of a deer.

BOXER
The archetypal bulldog type. Although Boxers were originally bred for fighting, they are generally intelligent and friendly animals.

SAINT BERNARD

The original moutain-rescue dogs, St. Bernards are hugely powerful but famously laid-back characters.

ENGLISH MASTIFF

These archetypal mastiffs and their mixes are true colossi, and are generally loyal, sweet-tempered, and protective.

DOGUE DE BORDEAUX

Made famous by the movie *Hooch* in 1989, Dogue de Bordeauxs are typical mastiffs with massive heads and good natures.

DOGO ARGENTINO

These distinctive white-coated mastiffs were bred to hunt large animals such as wild boar and mountain lions.

GREAT DANE

Giants of the dog world, with correspondingly huge appetites, Great Danes are generally friendly and enjoy gentle exercise.

081 ROUND UP A HERDING DOG

Any dog can be smart, but herding dogs and their mixes have a reputation for being some of the smartest—as anyone who grew up watching "Lassie" knows. For a dog, smart means being attentive, interactive, and eager to learn. Herding breeds, such as the Border Collie, Rough Collie, and German Shepherd, tend to need high levels of activity and human interaction, since they were originally bred to follow the commands of a shepherd and keep livestock together while moving the flock or herd from place to place. Herding dogs often have luxurious coats that were originally designed to protect them from the hostile elements, or from the jaws of large predators such as wolves that might threaten the livestock. These breeds and their mixes are generally good with kids, and can even have the instinct to round up children and keep them playing in one area. On the down side, some herders are notorious for ankle nipping and, needless to say, require particularly careful handling around livestock.

082 DISCOURAGE ANKLE BITING

Some herding dogs, notably Border Collies, are notorious for their instinctive impulse to nip at ankles, whether those ankles belong to a sheep or a mail carrier. This is not bad behavior, as it is actively encouraged in working dogs and is how they goad particularly stubborn sheep and other reluctant livestock to do their handler's bidding. However, even if the action is gentle and unlikely to break or even bruise the skin, it can be very disconcerting and occasionally painful for the person being nipped, and it is most definitely to be discouraged in your pet. It is best dealt with in puppyhood, but if the habit continues into adulthood then the assistance of a professional, positive reinforcement-based trainer might be required to resolve the issue.

083
WHISTLE WHILE YOU WORK

In many countries, sheepdogs are traditionally given commands with a special whistle, which has the advantage of being audible from a considerable distance above the bleating of sheep. Variations in the number, duration, and pitch of whistle blasts are immediately understood by a well-trained dog, and it is magical to watch a master handler and his dog guide an unruly flock of sheep around various obstacles and into a pen at professional sheepdog trials. A few typical whistle commands are listed here. Most of us will never do more than learn a single whistle in order to get our pets to return to us, but it is certainly worth experimenting with your dog, no matter what his breed or mix, to see how well he responds if you can add one or two extra commands to your whistling repertoire!

COMMAND	SIGNAL	ACTION
Come here!	Three short blasts	Dog returns to handler
Stop!	One long blast	Dog immediately lies down and awaits the next instruction
Walk up!	Two short blasts, even tone	Dog moves directly toward livestock
Come by!	One short, one long blast	Dog moves around livestock in a clockwise direction
Way to me!	Two short blasts, rising and falling	Dog moves around livestock in a counterclockwise direction
Slow down!	Four short blasts with brief pause after first two	Dog works more cautiously to calm the livestock

084 ENJOY AGILITY

Okay, so most of us aren't going to be trying to control our dogs among a herd of unruly livestock (at least not intentionally!), but it is worth remembering that herding dogs and mixes have tremendous energy and intelligence, and that needs an outlet. Agility training is the perfect pastime for a hyperactive superpooch, no matter what breed or mix, and the combination of obstacles—including jumps, weave poles, tunnels, and teeter-totters—will keep even the most intelligent dog stimulated. Here are a few of the major benefits of agility training.

INSTINCTIVELY CHALLENGING

In the wild, canines pursue their prey across—over, under, around, and through—all kinds of terrain, and agility obstacles are designed to mimic such natural challenges.

GREAT EXERCISE FOR YOUR DOG

Agility courses are physically taxing as well as mentally challenging. Completing a course will help to strengthen your dog's muscles, increase his stamina and endurance, and improve his coordination.

GREAT EXERCISE FOR YOU

Your dog doesn't get to have all the fun (or do all the work!). Your job is to run alongside him and encourage and assist him as he flies over jumps and burrows through collapsed tunnels. It'll soon get you in great shape.

BRILLIANT FOR BONDING

In agility training, you and your dog are a team and he relies on you to help him negotiate the various obstacles in the quickest possible time. You'll find that agility training reinforces obedience training and builds an even stronger bond between you and your best buddy.

085
MEET TEN TYPICAL HERDING DOGS

There are two types of dogs used to work with livestock herds: herding dogs such as the Border Collie, which control the movement of livestock; and guardian dogs, whose principal role is to protect livestock from wolves and other predators. Herding dogs, also known as stock dogs, are energetic, nimble, and highly intelligent, working closely with their handler to manage the movement of the herd with a quiet authority. Border Collies are generally regarded as the world's premier sheep-herding dogs, noted for their tendency to be intelligent and energetic. Border Collie mixes may share those tendencies, making them great pets. Guardian livestock dogs, typified by French Briards, are generally bigger than herding dogs and usually have heavy protective coats.

GERMAN SHEPHERD
German Shepherds are one of the most popular dog breeds and are known more for their use as police dogs than as herders.

BELGIAN SHEPHERD
These dogs are generally alert and intelligent. There are different types that are sometimes recognized as separate breeds.

AUSTRALIAN CATTLE DOG
Australian Cattle Dogs were bred as crosses between Australian Dingoes and collies to create agile and intelligent herders.

ROUGH COLLIE
Made famous by the *Lassie* movies, Rough Collies are popular pets for active families ready to put in the work to maintain those coats.

BORDER COLLIE
This classic collie most commonly has a black and white coloration, but other colors exist, especially in mixes.

BEARDED COLLIE
Most bearded collies and bearded collie mixes are natural herders that tend to excel at agility and obedience.

OLD ENGLISH SHEEPDOG
Known for their intelligence and gentle natures, Old English Sheepdogs were bred to move sheep over long distances.

BRIARD
Big and powerful, Briards were originally bred to protect livestock against wolves and poachers. They can be black, gray, or tawny.

BERGAMASCO
Originating in Italy as independent and intelligent flock guardians, Bergamascos are famous for their thick coats with long "dreadlocks."

KOMONDOR
With their mop-like coats, Hungarian Komondors are difficult to distinguish from the sheep they were bred to protect.

086 DIG A TERRIER

The first terriers were bred to dig in pursuit of rodents and other small animals, including rats, moles, and even foxes. But like virtually all breeds, they are generally just bred for their looks today. Terriers and terrier mixes are known for being high-energy lapdogs with way more personality than you might expect. Terriers and terrier mixes tend to have hair that is more coarse or wiry than other dogs, a feature that originally protected them from thorny undergrowth. They often retain a strong instinct to dig, and some terrier types have a reputation for being more vocal than other dogs.

087 UNDERSTAND WHY DOGS DIG

If your dog likes to dig in dirt or grass, there can be a number of reasons. For the most part, it is perfectly natural behavior related to a wild dog's need for food and shelter.

DIG MY DEN! Some dog relatives (foxes, for example) dig to create small dens to provide protection from other animals and the elements. Many dogs display vestiges of this behavior, pawing at the ground and circling before lying down, which is how some wild dogs flatten an area of long grass to prepare a bed that is both comfortable and concealed. A dog may also paw at the ground to dig up cooler dirt to sit in on a hot day.

DIG MY DINNER! When a dog really starts digging a hole in earnest, she is usually in pursuit of something—perhaps the scent of a small animal, or perhaps something that has become buried in the ground. A dog might be digging to hide or retrieve a toy or a bone, which is another vestigial instinct inherited from ancestors who would store excess food underground for consumption in leaner times.

088 DEAL WITH DIGGING

In the majority of cases digging is a minor irritation for dog owners; however, a determined digger can present a real danger to herself and others.

DIGGING PROBLEMS

- It can cause frustration if your dog destroys garden features such as a flowerbed or a lawn.
- It can be dangerous when holes and indentations create a tripping hazard for people in the area.
- It can be fatal to your dog if she digs under a boundary fence to escape from your yard.
- Digging itself can actually be a neurotic behavior due to boredom or stress.

If you are having a problem with your dog digging, call a professional dog trainer who can help you evaluate the cause of the digging, and find the best solution for your dog and for you.

089 DESIGNATE A DIGGING AREA

If you find it virtually impossible to discourage your dog from digging, try to provide him with a "digging area." This is a corner of your yard where digging is allowed. This could be a dirt area, or even a sandbox you create especially for your burrowing buddy. When your dog digs in this designated area, praise and reward him with attention or a treat. If your dog digs outside this area and is caught in the act, a firm "no" is usually sufficient as a deterrent.

AMERICAN PIT BULL TERRIER

Although Pit Bulls have gotten a bad rap due their exploitation as fighting dogs, they are usually friendly and loyal.

WELSH TERRIER

Bred to hunt badgers and otters, Welsh Terriers tend to be solid, wire-haired dogs who are friendly and fearless.

FOX TERRIER

Another classic terrier type, Fox Terriers tend to have the fearlessness and curiosity that typify terriers. They can be smooth or wire-haired.

JACK RUSSELL TERRIER

Feisty and full of character, "Jacks" are stocky and athletic. The Parson Jack Russell Terrier is a longer-legged version.

BEDLINGTON TERRIER

With a distinctive woolly coat, the Bedlington Terrier is often compared to a lamb. However, this tough dog was bred to hunt badgers.

090 MEET TEN TYPICAL TERRIERS

From stocky bull terriers to the agile Manchester Terrier, terriers and terrier mixes come in a range of shapes and builds. They are small dogs with big dog attitudes, and are particularly tenacious, willful, fearless, and independent. They tend to be loyal, in a independent terrier way, and very protective of their families. They can make excellent watchdogs, although some are a little too vociferous. Although they are small dogs, terriers and terrier mixes are energetic and love to explore.

MANCHESTER TERRIER

Tenacious and agile ratters, Manchester Terriers look like miniature Dobermans and tend to be equally fearless.

SCOTTISH TERRIER

With distinctive beards and long eyebrows, "Scotties" have a feisty look. They tend to be spirited and confident.

WEST HIGHLAND WHITE TERRIER

Often loyal and friendly, "Westies" are popular pets that tend to be the classic big dog in a small dog's body.

STAFFORDSHIRE BULL TERRIER

Bred to bait bears and bulls in the 16th century, "Staffies" are stocky dogs that are renowned for being gentle with humans.

DANDIE DINMONT TERRIER

These distinctive looking dogs with low-slung bodies and fluffy heads of hair were bred to hunt otters.

091 PLAY WITH A "TOY"

Tiny dogs are hugely popular, and with good reason. For practical purposes, miniature mutts win paws down when it comes to minimizing mess and cutting costs. However, even though their care may be cheaper and easier (who wouldn't prefer to clean up poop from a 10-pound dog rather than a 100-pound dog?), they nevertheless need just as much care as their larger compatriots. And cuteness can be a curse when it leads people to purchase a dog simply because it's convenient or, far worse still,

fashionable. However, pocket-sized pooches are not a modern phenomenon; the Pekingese was used to warm the hands of chilly Chinese aristocrats over 2,000 years ago, and Renaissance art is littered with lapdogs doing what they do best—looking adorable. But be warned, most diminutive dogs come with king-sized characters, and although many toy breeds would fit in the average slipper, they can be as tough as old boots.

? BONE OF CONTENTION
BAG A DOG?

In recent years toy dogs have been increasingly subjected to a new trend in canine transport: tiny toy dogs are carried around in "must-have" handbags and, more recently, "pooch pouches," which are effectively shoulder bags stripped down to the straps, from which a dog is suspended with limbs dangling. Although they are growing in popularity in the U.S., such contraptions are not without their critics. A bag can be genuinely useful—if you're worried about leaving your dog tied up outside a store while you do a little shopping, having a bag to carry him in will mean he is safe while you are hands-free to browse for fashion accessories at your leisure. However, wearing a dog *as* a fashion accessory is another matter; the dog is prevented from socializing and exercising, and likely feels extremely vulnerable,

as he will be unable to respond to any perceived danger. The long-term danger is not difficult to imagine: fads, by definition, are fleeting trends, and when this fad fades, the rate of dog abandonment is all too likely to rise.

092 PAMPER A POOCH

Tiny dogs can have affectionate natures and seem to enjoy nothing more than being petted and pampered (but then, don't we all?). It's great to spend time pampering your pooch and showing her off to friends in the neighborhood or online. Pet stores are packed with products to take grooming to new levels, from buckles, bows, and booties to fancy dress and designer doggie outfits. Products range from functional fun (small dogs do need extra layers to stay warm in winter, so why shouldn't she have a personalized hoodie?), to foolish fun (that tutu is strictly for photo shoots), and on to the downright dangerous (excessive clothing can restrict a dog's natural behavior and cause her to overheat). It's worth repeating: toy dogs are not toys! Always put their care and comfort above all other considerations.

093 MEET A MIXED BREED

They're smart, healthy, unique, and some of the best pets around. Call them mixes, mutts, hybrids, or even be cool and say "My dog is a Pet X!"

THE MIXED BREED A mixed-breed dog is simply a dog whose lineage spans various breeds, rather than descending from a single breed of dog. Just as a person might be a descendant of people from different regions or groups, a mixed breed is a dog with diverse lineage.

HISTORY OF MIXED BREEDS All dogs are thought to be descendants of wolves or some early canid. At some point, dogs began living alongside humans, and, more recently, people began to selectively breed dogs for certain traits. However, dogs of various breeds have frequently interbred (either intentionally aided by humans or not) and so there are lots of dogs that are not of one specific defined breed. For centuries, the typical family dog has been a loyal mixed breed (or "mutt") of some sort. Very common mixes include terrier mixes, shepherd mixes, Chow Chow mixes, pit bull mixes, and even Chihuahua mixes. A mixed-breed dog can include any number of breeds in his lineage because all breeds are the same species and, therefore, all dogs can interbreed.

THE TRUTH ABOUT "MUTTS" The term "mutt" refers to a mixed-breed dog and is sometimes used in a derogatory manner. Recently, however, the term has been reclaimed, as pet lovers realize there is nothing wrong with having a diverse lineage. Some might believe that because a mixed-breed dog is not a "purebred," they are somehow not as good or not as "pure." Purebred simply means of a line of dogs selectively bred for certain traits. This has resulted in a wide variety of dogs (from Great Danes to Dachshunds) with distinct and wonderful looks and attributes. But it can also lead to inherited genetic problems associated with inbreeding, as a smaller pool of dogs are bred with each other to isolate certain physical or behavior traits.

ROBUST AND RELIABLE PETS Mixed breeds on average have fewer genetic health issues than their purebred relatives. Mixes come in all shapes and sizes, and often have very unique body types and markings that make them a really attractive-looking pet. Animal shelters are great places to find mixed-breed dogs of all kinds. Just ask anyone with a mutt—these lovable pooches are a top-quality addition to the family.

TRAINING

> ❝ Don't walk behind me;
> I may not lead. Don't walk in front of me;
> I may not follow. Just walk beside me
> and be my friend. ❞

ALBERT CAMUS (FRENCH AUTHOR AND PHILOSOPHER)

Training is vital if you want to keep your dog socialized and safe. The vast majority of dogs enjoy training because it involves mental stimulation and lots of praise and treats. Obedience training helps to prevent bad habits from forming in the first place, and makes it easier to change unwanted behavior.

All dogs should be given at least basic obedience training, including teaching your dog his name and to reliably return to you when called. Potential lifesavers, such as "come" or "drop it," can keep your dog out of harm's way in a situation where he poses a potential threat to himself or others; for example, if a gate is left open and he decides to bolt into a busy street, or if he picks up a harmful object. Basic commands, such as "sit" and "lie down," come very naturally to most dogs. While not necessarily lifesavers, these commands help your dog enjoy human society and receive praise rather than reprimands. Even if you don't mind when your dog jumps up on you, he will have a happier life if he understands when this behavior is acceptable and when it isn't. Walking well on a leash is another important part of good basic training that makes time with your dog safer and more enjoyable for both of you.

Tricks like "speak" and "shake hands" are great for dogs who really enjoy the attention and treats they get when they become performers. This type of training can help to stimulate your dog mentally and reinforce the bond between you. Games such as fetch can be great fun, too, and are particularly useful for high-energy dogs who need extra physical exercise. Remember, though, not to get your ego involved in your dog's training. He should perform tricks only because he likes to play and be rewarded. If he isn't interested in performing, you should respect that. Make training a positive and fun experience for both of you.

094
ALLOW A LITTLE BREATHING ROOM

After you bring home your new dog, he'll need a few days to get his bearings. It's not unusual for a dog to be a bit out of sorts for a while. Sometimes dogs will hide, and sometimes they won't eat for a couple of days. Put yourself in your dog's shoes: He's been through a lot of changes, and he doesn't know if more are coming. Give him four or five days just to get used to the idea that this is his new, wonderful home, and then begin obedience training sessions.

There are, however, a few things you can try right off the bat.

Be consistent about ground rules. So, for example, if your dog is not allowed on the furniture, gently remove him from the couch or lure him off of it every time he jumps up. Set a schedule for feeding and walking and stick to it. Create a routine around waking up and going to sleep, so your dog knows he'll be taken out to do his business as soon as he wakes up and right before he goes to sleep. Look for, and reward, good behaviors, such as lying on the floor quietly during family mealtimes, urinating outdoors, and calmly meeting new people and other dogs.

095
TAKE AN OBEDIENCE CLASS

Many people, especially first-time dog owners, wonder if they need to take their dog to obedience classes or if they should train their dog themselves, with the help of the Internet, books, and videos. The answer? Both! It's true that there are many resources out there to help you train your dog, and it's also true that you'll most likely do a great job of home-schooling your pup. Obedience classes can be an important part of the process, however. These classes, which you and your dog attend with a group of other dogs and their owners, provide a safe space where

you can observe your dog socializing with other dogs. If there are any conflicts, the trainer is equipped to handle the situation. Also, because there are other dogs and other people in the class, your dog gets valuable practice performing commands in the face of distractions. The instructor will give you feedback on your own training style, which can be invaluable. Finally, obedience classes give you the opportunity to meet and make friends with people with whom you have something in common: a love of your dogs.

096 STOCK UP ON TREATS

The way to most dogs' hearts is definitely through their stomachs; make sure you stock up on plenty of tasty tidbits to reward your dog for hanging on your every word at training time. To have your dog, quite literally, eating out of your hand in no time at all, select tiny snacks that don't satiate her too quickly, but keep her keen and coming back for more. Visit the pet store to test a few of the huge variety of treats out there, and find out which are her favorites. Make sure you know how many calories there are in the treats you buy, however, since they must be included in your dog's calorie count to keep her from getting overweight. Of course, treats won't work so well if your dog isn't hungry, so be sure to schedule training sessions before her mealtimes.

KNOW YOUR BISCUITS Dog biscuits can be high in fat and carbohydrates, which is why your pooch finds them irresistible! They are correspondingly high in calories, so they should be saved for special treats at the end of a successful training session, or as a post-bath bonanza.

CHOOSE CHEWS Chews generally contain few calories, are good for your dog's teeth and gums, and can keep him occupied for hours. They, too, are best left as high-value rewards after a successful training session. As long as they don't present a choking hazard, chews are an invaluable aid for crate training.

097 LEARN THE TEN TRAINING COMMANDMENTS

Dog training is as much about training yourself as teaching your dog. Again, just reading this book is a sure sign that you want to do the right thing and you're on the right track. Here are ten golden rules to bear in mind before you begin your training regimen, which we'll go over in a lot more detail over the next few pages.

1. Never hurt or frighten your dog.
2. Be consistent.
3. Be patient.
4. Use positive reinforcement.
5. Teach the "lifesavers" first.
6. Start slowly and safely.
7. Keep sessions short.
8. Know your dog's learning style.
9. Keep going.
10. Have fun!

098 NEVER HURT OR FRIGHTEN YOUR DOG

Training is an important part of the bonding process between you and your canine best buddy. It's amazing what happens when you start to figure out how to communicate with your dog in a way he understands, and he starts to figure out what you're asking of him. This should be a very positive experience that cements your relationship. When you introduce hitting, yelling, or fear into that equation, the relationship you're cementing is one of mistrust and suspicion. Not only are hitting, yelling, and throwing things at or near your dog cruel, but these also don't work nearly as well as positive-reinforcement training methods. Be kind to your dog, and you'll gain his unconditional loyalty.

099 BE CONSISTENT

The biggest gift you can give your new dog is the knowledge of what to expect, and what is expected. Consistency is vital; it allows your dog to know what's coming and what behavior to expect from you, and helps him to relax into his position in the "pack." Be consistent in everything you do. Choose a training method and stick to it. Set your ground rules (that is, what is and is not allowed in your home) and never waiver from them. For instance, if you choose to make your dog sit and stay before you give him his dinner, do it every single time, and never give him his dinner until he's done what you expect. A dog without a consistent schedule and a consistent leader is an insecure dog. And a good leader is a consistent leader.

100 BE PATIENT

Training your dog is a process and, as with any process, it takes time. Often your dog will make fantastic headway only to have a temporary setback. It's tempting to get impatient and discouraged, but there's no need to worry. Just remember, you're teaching a member of a different species to do what you want him to do, and often these things are very foreign to a dog's natural behavior. Along the way, you can absolutely expect to procede by fits and starts. Sometimes your dog will pick up a new behavior right away, and you'll feel like a genius. Other times, you might spend days or even weeks working on something without much progress. Stay the course, have patience, and you'll both succeed. When you start getting frustrated, it's time to end the training session and go for a walk or play a game of fetch with your dog's favorite toy. Take a deep breath and recognize that training is a challenge, and you're both doing great!

101

USE POSITIVE REINFORCEMENT

What's the difference between positive-reinforcement and correction-based training methods? With positive reinforcement, you reward your dog for doing what you want him to do. With correction-based methods, you punish him or physically correct him (using choke collars, startling noises, or verbal admonishments like "no!" or "bad dog!") for doing what you don't want him to do.

We are firmly in the camp of positive reinforcement, not only because it works, but also because it helps forge a wonderful bond between you and your dog. There are many effective training methods, including the increasingly popular clicker training. This method uses a small clicker (and lots of treats) to help shape desirable behaviors and teach commands. It's fun for you and your dog, it's easy, and it really works.

102

TEACH THE "LIFESAVERS" FIRST

There are so many fun things to teach your dog: shake hands, roll over, say please—the list goes on. Before you go for the fun commands that will impress people at parties, make sure you teach the three commands that could save your dog's life in an emergency situation. The three main lifesavers are "stay," "come," and "drop it." "Stay" can keep your dog from running out the door. "Come," which is perhaps the most important of all commands, can protect your dog from any potentially perilous situation by bringing him back to your side. "Drop it" can prevent your dog from ingesting a toxic substance. Train these three commands and you'll officially have a well-trained dog.

103 START SLOWLY AND SAFELY

Start to train a command or behavior indoors, and when your dog is executing it reliably every time, introduce some distractions. Practice in your backyard, and then in your front yard. Then, when you are confident that your dog is sufficiently well trained and socialized, go to an off-leash dog park—the ultimate distraction—and practice there until your dog can perform the command at any time, regardless of what's going on around him.

104 KEEP SESSIONS SHORT

Training should feel like a game, and should never become tiresome. As soon as your dog's attention starts to wander, or he stops making progress, that's your cue to wrap it up. When clicker training or practicing other types of positive-reinforcement training, aim for one or two short sessions each day. Always wrap up a training session on a positive. Rather than persisting with something your dog just isn't getting right now (he will feel your frustration), shift to practicing something that he already knows. Keep sessions short and sweet—and always end on a high!

105 KNOW YOUR DOG'S LEARNING STYLE

Sometimes you spend a whole session working on one trick or command, and it seems like your dog just isn't getting it. Then, a day or two later, you come back to the same trick or command, and your dog absolutely nails it on the first try! A dog's brain works in much the same way as ours; it continues to process information even when the active learning session is done. Once you figure out the way your dog learns, you can apply that to future lessons. If you know that your dog needs some time away to process a new trick before he grasps it, you'll know that you should keep your session short and give him a day or two before you come back to it.

106 KEEP IT GOING

Learning is a lifelong endeavor and training is not something you only do for a few months when you first bring your dog home. Even once you feel like your dog has an impressive repertoire of commands and tricks under his belt (collar?), that's no reason to stop training. Training and learning together with your dog is a lifelong exercise in communicating, bonding, and growing. Keep it going!

107 HAVE FUN

Having fun while training your dog isn't just a nice add-on, it should be a requirement. In fact, the minute a training session stops being fun and starts feeling like hard work, it's time to wrap it up. Why? First, because dogs love games, and love to having a job to do. When that job is figuring out what you're asking them to do, and then doing it (and earning praise and treats in the process), it stimulates the pleasure centers in their brains. Positive-reinforcement training methods are especially wonderful for this game-like training experience.

The second reason training needs to be fun has to do with you. Dogs are extraordinarily sensitive to their people's moods and emotions. When you're relaxed, your dog feels safe and secure, and finds it easy to focus on the task at hand. Conversely, when you're stressed or frustrated, your dog will sense these feelings. When you stop having fun, you'll notice your dog stops learning as quickly and may indeed seem to forget a trick he appeared to master just minutes before.

So, next time you're working with your dog, kick up the fun and reap the rewards.

108
PAY ATTENTION TO WHAT YOU WANT

Here's an odd concept: When we scold, push, look at, talk to, or touch our dogs when they're misbehaving, we're actually reinforcing their less-than-desirable behavior. In other words, correcting a behavior can actually cause your dog to keep doing it. For example, when your dog is jumping up on you—a behavior most of us don't condone—by yelling "no" and pushing her down, you are giving your pup words, eye contact, and attention when she's jumping! She loves attention from you—any attention at all—and she will do her best to keep that attention coming. So, by giving her a correction, you're actually reinforcing the jumping.

The solution is to withhold that attention until she's exhibiting a behavior you approve of. Back to the jumping-on-you example: Instead of correcting her when she jumps, try instead to stop interacting with her completely. As she jumps, turn your back and ignore the behavior. The moment your pooch sits down and stops jumping on you, that's the moment to give her attention and let her know what a good girl she is! Pay attention to what you like; ignore what you don't.

Then, catch your dog doing the right thing. When your canine pal is resting calmly on her dog bed, remember to give her praise and let her know that is exactly the behavior you enjoy. In short, focus on what you want, not on what you don't. In the end, your relationship with your dog will only get better for it, and you'll both enjoy each other's company a little more.

109 TEACH YOUR DOG HIS NAME

When you adopt a dog, often you'll need to give him a brand-new name. Many pets in shelters were found as strays, and the shelter personnel have no way of knowing what their former names might have been. This gives you an opportunity to give your dog a whole new identity, along with a whole new wonderful life. Of course, until he learns his name, your dog will just stare blankly at you, or ignore you completely, when you call him.

Start to teach your dog his new name when you're alone together in a quiet room with no distractions. Have a pocket full of small, yummy treats ready as rewards. Wait until he isn't looking at you and then, in a really upbeat tone of voice, say his name. If he looks at you, toss him a treat. Wait until his attention wanders again and then repeat the exercise. Next, try it when you're out on a walk with plenty of distractions. Gradually increases the amount of time between when you say his name and when you toss the treat. Soon, you'll notice that his attention stays on you after you say his name, which is what you want.

SAY IT STRATEGICALLY...

Your dog's name is more than just the word on the ID tag he wears to help you find him if he should ever get lost. It's also a magic word you can use to get your dog's attention. Many trainers believe you should say your dog's name before you give a command (for example, "Woofy, sit"). Using his name in this way signals that you're about to give him a directive, and that he should focus on you.

In fact, it's crucial for your dog's safety that he looks to you promptly anytime you say his name. In an emergency situation, this kind of name recognition could save your dog's life if he slips his leash and heads toward traffic. Or perhaps you are enjoying your daily trip to the dog park when a new neighbor arrives with her dog still on his leash. Friends have warned you that the dog is nervous around other dogs and prone to aggression, but your friendly dog doesn't know this and bounds toward the newcomer to say hello. To prevent the two dogs from getting off to a bad start, you call him and he stops and looks back toward you. Now you can ask him to "sit" and "stay," while you walk over to introduce him properly to his potential new buddy.

...BUT DON'T NAME AND SHAME

Your dog's name should be a happy thing. When you say it, he should look up at you, or even come over to you, anticipating that something fun or interesting is about to happen. Your dog should associate his name with rewards, affection, and important alerts.

So, here's where things can break down: imagine your dog jumps up on a visitor. "Dudley!" you shriek. Your dog steals a waffle out of your toddler's hands at breakfast. "Dudley!" you bellow in a threatening tone of voice. Your dog starts to pee on the floor. "Dudley!" you thunder, menacingly. Now, your dog thinks "Dudley" means "bad dog!" Next time you say, "Dudley! Come here," how do you suppose your dog will respond: with enthusiasm, or with trepidation? You can see how important it is to use your dog's name wisely and to make sure that he equates his name only with the positive. If you catch your dog in the act of doing something you don't want him to do, a simple "no!" is usually sufficient to reprimand him and let him know that you are unhappy with his behavior. Again, always focus on and reward the things you want.

110 USE A TEAM NAME

Training a houseful of dogs can be a challenge. How can you communicate that you want just one dog to follow a command, or that you want them all to follow suit? Here's an easy way: Come up with a collective name for your pack. When you want them all to come, sit, or stay, use your team name. Fun team names include "Gentlemen," "Troops," "Fellas," and "Friends." Reinforce the name by saying it loudly and in a cheerful tone of voice, and rewarding your dogs with treats when they all come to investigate. Next, try telling them all to sit, using the team name, and rewarding them again when they all comply.

111 TRAIN YOUR PUPPY

If you adopt an adult dog, she will most likely have already learned basic obedience, but with a puppy you have to start from scratch. You should begin training as soon as your pup has settled in to her new home. Train your dog from as early an age as possible to obey your commands and play games—that way, you will be far less likely to have to deal with undesirable behavior later on. Informal training can start immediately, as you capture any natural behavior that you want your dog to be able to perform on command, such as sitting, lying down, or even fetching. This simply involves saying the command as soon as your dog adopts the position or performs the desired action, and then reinforcing the command word with gentle praise. Be consistent with the command you use for each action from the start. If you find that difficult at first—you're learning this job, too—it might be a good idea to invest in a clicker, which can initially take the place of a command word.

112 KNOW WHEN TO SAY "NO"

Only use the command "no" when you actually catch your dog in the act of doing something you want to prevent, such as chewing a slipper or, inevitably, peeing on the carpet. If you reprimand your puppy even a couple of seconds after the event, he will already have forgotten what it is he's done wrong. Again, always try to focus on the positive, and pretty soon you'll find you rarely or never have to say "no" to your dog. If you do say "no," say it firmly but calmly—never yell.

113 INVEST IN TRAINING EQUIPMENT

You don't need to invest in very much equipment to start training; just stock up on plenty of treats to reward your dog as he progresses. A clicker can be a powerful training aid if used correctly. There are a wide range of clickers out there to choose from, including battery-powered "bleepers" and simpler mechanical models. A leash is a must for certain training exercises, and a whistle can be useful for recalling your dog from a distance. Muzzles and other tools may be advisable for correcting unwanted aggressive behavior, but such items should only be used under the guidance of a training professional.

TREATS Find out which treats your dog particularly enjoys. Keep them small for training, as they will quickly lose their effectiveness if your dog is not hungry. Larger treats can be saved for special rewards—following bath time or during crate training, for example.

TREAT POUCH Any small shoulder bag will do the trick, but specially designed pouches are available to carry treats. These attach to your belt or have a built-in shoulder strap so that you can keep your hands free to hold a leash or other equipment. Such bags should allow quick access and have pockets for other small training products, such as clickers or whistles.

CLICKERS The simplest clickers are plastic with a stainless-steel clicking mechanism. A lanyard may be supplied with the clicker so that you can secure it to your wrist. Other noise-producing products are available to serve the same purpose, including small bells and, of course, whistles.

TOYS Balls and other throw toys are useful as rewards and to teach your dog to fetch. They are available in a range of sizes to suit all types of dogs.

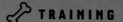

WHISTLES Whistles are useful for recalling your dog from a distance. Special "dog whistles" are designed to emit a blast at a high frequency that can be heard by dogs but not by humans.

LEASHES Leashes can be useful when teaching your dog the "come" and "stay" commands, and are a must for any outdoor training session when you are not yet 100 percent confident that your dog will return when called. Special long lines are available, which range between 15 and 50 feet (4.5—15 m) in length.

PUPPY TRAINING PADS Highly absorbent pads are very useful for toilet training. They are available in a range of sizes, depending on the size of your dog.

CRATES A crate can be a useful aid for a number of training purposes, but dogs should never be locked in a crate for long periods. Don't use a crate to punish your dog for bad behavior. He should learn to love the crate as a comfortable retreat—not fear it as a prison.

114 INTRODUCE YOUR DOG TO OTHER PETS

Be extra vigilant when you introduce your dog to other pets. Keep control of the situation by arranging the meeting in a specific room, or on a walk while your dog's on a leash. Give them an opportunity to see each other and to sniff each other, too, without yanking back the leash, which could alarm your dog. Keep tension out of it, and keep the first encounter short and sweet. Slowly increase the length of time the new friends spend together and allow the relationship to grow organically. Regardless of who your dog meets, stay calm and even-keeled so that both animals sense a relaxed, safe energy. Avoid treats, toys, or excitable play, which can cause competition and confusion among animals who don't know each other well yet.

WALK BEFORE YOU RUN If your dog is getting to know another dog for the first time, consider meeting on a walk. Walking is a natural bonding activity for canines, and reduces the likelihood of miscommunication, such as hard stares or overexcited energy. Try going on a long walk together before letting the two new dogs sniff and check each other out.

TREAD SOFTLY If your dog is meeting a cat for the first time, consider putting him in a crate so that the cat can walk around the crate. Watch your dog's reaction to make sure he doesn't have feline aggression. Alternatively, try leashing your dog (as long as you can control him) and walk into a room where the cat is. Be sure your cat has an easy escape route and does not feel cornered. Even a dog that does well with cats may want to chase if the cat runs—if your dog chases your cat, this does not necessarily mean your dog does not like cats, as long as the chase seems playful and not aggressive.

115 SOCIALIZE YOUR PUP

Just as with children, you cannot control exactly what your puppy's personality will turn out to be when she grows up. Similar puppies raised in the same way will still have different personalities. But one of the best things you can do for your pup to be sure she is well-adjusted is to expose her to new places, animals, situations, and people as often as you can (especially once she's up to date on vaccinations).

STAY POSITIVE When introducing your dog to new people, make it a positive experience. Offer the stranger a treat and ask him to give it to your dog when your dog approaches. Your dog will be curious and will go up to the stranger to smell and assess him. If your friend offers your pup the treat, avoiding direct eye contact (which can be seen as a threat), your dog will have just had a positive experience meeting a new person.

THE MORE, THE MERRIER Consider practicing this introduction with whoever you can wrangle to help you. The more new people, faces, scents, and energies your dog encounters, the more well-adjusted she will be out in the world. Just remember to keep all experiences positive and calm, reinforcing good behavior and positive meetings with a treat or praise—soon your dog will be a social butterfly!

116 INTRODUCE YOUR PUPPY TO CHILDREN

Introducing your puppy to children is a wonderful way to ensure he is exposed to all sorts of people. It's important that your dog knows how children behave and what their energy level is like, so he isn't shocked or nervous about it when he becomes an adult. Puppyhood is a perfect time to set up positive encounters for your dog with kids. Bring treats with you, ask the children to be gentle with your puppy, and always supervise your dog to ensure that the meeting goes well. You wouldn't want a well-meaning child to handle him in a way that could spur future fears. Keep meetings short, sweet, and fun for your puppy and the kids involved. You may want to play a game or encourage gentle, soft petting. Praise your puppy for doing such a good job, and give yourself a pat on the back, too—you're teaching your dog to love children!

117 CHOOSE THE RIGHT TIME FOR CRATE TRAINING

A crate is just a cozy kennel or carrier designed for a dog. Some dogs like to stay in them while left home alone, or use them as a retreat when Auntie Emma visits with her six kids. To a dog, it should feel like a small, safe den. It must have lots of ventilation, fresh water, and soft, nontoxic bedding. Crate train your dog as early as possible, as it can be a useful aid when toilet training a puppy, or to help deal with destructive behavior or separation anxiety. Most of the time, though, leave your dog's crate door open so that he can come and go as he chooses. Never leave him locked in a crate for too long—that's the surest way to make him loathe it.

CRATE AID FOR TOILET TRAINING Teaching your dog to enjoy the comfort of a crate or kennel is useful when he is not yet housetrained. Dogs prefer not to soil an area they have to remain in, so unless your dog has lost this inhibition by being kept too many hours in a small space before you got him (for example, at a puppy mill or pet store), he will want to hold it in and wait until you get home from your errands so he can go outside.

CRATE AID FOR SEPARATION ANXIETY A cozy crate is also useful if your dog has anxiety and prefers the comfort of a small space when you are out of the house. Again, a crate is not a tool for punishment of any kind; in fact, for a crate to work for your dog, your dog must appreciate it as a home within his home and always feel happy when there.

CRATE AID FOR DESTRUCTIVE CHEWING Destructive chewing happens for a number of reasons. If your dog is less than a year old, destructive chewing is an unfortunate common side-effect of puppy cuteness. Your puppy might benefit from being left in a crate with lots of chew toys when you are not home (for a limited number of hours) to prevent her from chewing your valuable possessions.

118 CONSIDER HOW LONG TO CRATE

Since a very young puppy won't be able to hold it in until his muscles learn to control his bladder, his first night's sleep might only last four to five hours, which can gradually be increased to eight hours. Puppy bladders and bowels are just not mature enough to hold it much longer than that. Remember, just as with babies, mornings come very early with young puppies. At around four months old, the puppy's bladder should start to mature and he will sleep for longer periods. Once you have put your puppy in his crate, don't go back to him for at least two hours. If you do, you are teaching him that making lots of noise will get him what he wants— your company. Your puppy must learn that nights are for sleeping and his sleeping place is the crate. Once he learns this lesson (and it will take about two to four nights) he will begin to see the crate as his special place. One day, you will look for your puppy and find him curled up in the crate, where he went on his own for a nap.

119 SELECT THE RIGHT CRATE

A crate should be large enough to allow your puppy or dog to lie down and turn around in a tight circle. If it is big enough to lie down in, it should be big enough for your dog to sit in without her head hitting the top, too. It is also important not to choose a crate that is too large to provide a cozy "den" feeling. If you have a puppy that will grow into a large dog, buy a full-size crate that will fit her as an adult, and use chew-safe material (like cinder blocks) to block off a section just big enough for your puppy's current size. Then the crate can be expanded as your puppy grows. Canvas indoor kennels can perform a similar role to crates from your dog's perspective; they provide all the snugness and sense of security, without appearing too cage-like.

TYPE There are many models of crates, including fancy wooden ones that look like furniture, steel-wire folding styles, ultra-portable and cozy canvas numbers, and the molded plastic airplane-travel variety. Make sure to select a crate that won't allow your pet's paw to squeeze through and get stuck.

STRENGTH Many puppies and large breeds are very strong chewers. Pick a material that matches your pet's chewing strength. Steel-wire strength varies between brands and models. Wood or wicker is not advised for a puppy or dog that is not already crate trained.

120 DECIDE WHERE TO PUT THE CRATE

Many people put the crate in their bedroom, where they can reassure their puppy during the night. Some people prefer to put the crate where they won't hear the puppy crying. There is nothing wrong with either plan. However, it's going to be easier for the puppy to get used to being in the crate if he's sleeping with his new family (next to the bed) like he was when he was sleeping with his mom and littermates. It's best to place the crate where you can hear if the puppy's complaining cries turn into "I got my paw stuck in the wire" cries.

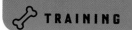
121 GET YOUR PUPPY USED TO HIS CRATE

Ideally, you will never force a puppy into his crate. Just place him inside with one or two of his favorite toys, leaving the door open. Try to budget at least a full day to get your puppy used to the crate. How you get him inside will depend largely on his age; as a general rule, the younger the puppy, the easier it will be to get him into his crate, and the sooner he'll start to see it as a home within a home.

VERY YOUNG PUPPIES (3 MONTHS AND UNDER)
Very young pups can usually just be gently picked up and placed inside the crate, or lured directly inside by throwing in a tasty treat. Give lots of verbal praise when the puppy is in the crate, such as, "What a good puppy in the crate! Good puppy!" Use a calm but happy voice. Even if the puppy leaves right away, you should have time for at least one "Good puppy!"

OLDER PUPPIES (4 MONTHS AND OLDER) First try luring your puppy in by throwing in a treat or toy. If the puppy will not go all the way into the crate, you may need to create a trail of treats leading into the back of the crate. If regular treats are not enough of a lure, you might need to try special treats, such as bits of hot dog or chicken. If that fails, you may need to wait, withhold treats and food for the next few hours, and then try again. Then at feeding time, put the bowl in the middle of the crate, close the puppy with you in the room, and sit and wait. Even one paw in the crate is a step forward. Verbally praise this step. At the next feeding time, try the trail of treats again, and place the food bowl in the back of the crate; then sit and wait. At this point, you are hoping the puppy will go into the crate, eat, and leave, so do not close the door. Then, in a few hours, try tossing the treats in again.

122 CLOSE THE CRATE DOOR

Once your puppy goes willingly into the crate when you toss in a treat (or to get to her food bowl in the back) a few times in a row, you're ready to try gently closing the door for a few short sessions. Fill a hollow rubber toy with wet and dry dog food. Let the puppy smell the food in the toy, and then place the food-stuffed toy in the back of the crate. Don't use a rawhide or any other toy she can't have safely when unsupervised. If the puppy doesn't go in to get the toy, toss the treats in the crate and softly close the door once the puppy is inside. Give lots of praise, then calmly walk away. Walk out of the room and peek in to see how she's doing. Attempt this when you have a whole day free, so you can feed her all her meals in the toy inside the crate. So on the first day, you'll close your puppy into the crate for 10–15 minutes at a time (depending on how good a toy-destuffer she is), and let her out just a few minutes after she finishes the food in the toy.

123 TRAIN YOUR CHILDREN

Hey, Moms and Dads! You guys can prevent dog bites (and make your dog's life a lot more pleasant, too) by teaching your kids some very basic safety rules. Although they seem like common sense to an adult, children need to be taught these top-ten tips.

❶ NEVER TOUCH OR PAT A DOG ON THE HEAD OR REACH OVER HIS HEAD Reaching over a dog's head is a very intimidating gesture. Teach your kids to pet your dog on his side or his chest. Don't worry—if your dog wants to be petted on his head, he'll let you know by offering it and rubbing it against your kids' hands.

❷ NEVER PULL TAILS OR EARS, OR POKE AT YOUR DOG Even a friendly dog can become annoyed and snap at a child who is prodding at him in this way. Demonstrate how to pet the dog gently by taking the child's hand, running it softly along the dog's body, and saying, "Niiiice" in a soothing tone of voice.

❸ DON'T RUN NEAR A DOG Chasing is an instinctual response in most dogs. If your child runs, your dog will most likely chase him or her. Chasing can lead to jumping, which can lead to knocking a small child down.

❹ DON'T CHASE A DOG Many puppies are afraid and will retreat if approached quickly. Toddlers seem to love to run after animals, which may frightens your dog. And if cornered, a normally gentle pet may resort to nipping to protect himself.

❺ DON'T WAKE A DOG WHEN HE'S SLEEPING Teach your child that the puppy likes to be approached slowly, and that when the puppy is sleeping, not to wake him.

❻ NEVER TAKE FOOD OR TOYS OUT OF A DOG'S MOUTH Taking food or toys out of a dog's mouth is simply not safe. If your dog tries to prevent his possession from being taken, he can inadvertently bite your child's hand.

❼ DON'T TREAT A DOG LIKE A TOY Dogs do have the most squishable little faces, and it is tempting to pull their ears into approximations of funny human hairstyles, but kids should be taught that dogs are living beings, not toys.

❽ ALWAYS BE GENTLE Dogs don't like to be touched in certain ways; some are sensitive to being touched on their feet, their ears, or other areas of their bodies. Teach your children to be gentle with dogs.

❾ UNDERSTAND A FEARFUL DOG'S BODY LANGUAGE Most of the time, your dog clearly communicates his needs via his body language. If a dog is backing away with his tail between his legs and his ears folded back, he's clearly saying, "Please don't touch me."

❿ UNDERSTAND A FRIENDLY DOG'S BODY LANGUAGE Conversely, if a dog is doing the full-body wag, with ears relaxed, and confidently looking at your child, it's a full-on green light for petting and playtime.

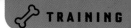

124 COPE WITH A PUPPY AND A YOUNG CHILD

Maybe you're pregnant and worried about how your puppy will react when the baby comes. Maybe you already have a baby and want to adopt a puppy. Or maybe you just want to teach your new dog to interact safely with any young child, or you want to teach your child to interact safely with any young dog. No matter what your particular dog and child setup is, here are some tips you can use to help make all puppy and child interactions safe and happy.

LEARN AT A DISTANCE It takes a lot more time and effort to overcome a bad experience than to create a safe setup for ongoing positive ones. While you are training your new dog or puppy, keep her safely separated from your child using baby gates, playpens, and/or a crate. That way they can safely get used to seeing, smelling, and hearing each other.

BE SUPER-WISE AND SUPERVISE The two should be introduced to each other for short periods of time, and very gradually. Never leave them alone together until you are sure that your ground rules will be followed. This will only work after both your new puppy and your child are old enough to understand, remember, and follow those rules.

CONSIDER THE "6-6" RULE Many dog experts recommend following a "6-6" rule: only when the puppy has been trained and socialized with your child for six months, and the child is at least six years old, is unsupervised time together safe.

125 CREATE A CHILD-PUPPY BOND

You can help build a relationship between your puppy and your child by encouraging them to play together under your supervision.

PLAY BALL Teach your child how to throw a ball for the puppy, and teach your puppy to bring the ball back and drop it for the child.

GO FOR WALKS Go on walks together where you attach two leashes to the puppy's collar, so you each can hold one.

PLAY HIDE-AND-SEEK Hold the puppy back while your child hides the toy and then let the puppy go find it (see item 171).

TELL STORIES Spend quiet time reading together. Puppies and dogs make especially wonderful, non-judgmental listeners for new readers.

126 NIP NIPPING IN THE BUD

Puppies will try to play with babies and toddlers by jumping on them and grabbing hold with their teeth. After all, this is how canine babies play with their canine brothers and sisters. Puppies must be taught that human children are not their littermates. If this isn't taught, a growing puppy's behavior will become increasingly rough, and the odds increase that a small child will be hurt during play. Never allow your child or any adult to use their hands, fingers, feet, or clothing (like pant legs, or shirt sleeves) for play, and do not play tug-of-war games: That kind of play can lead to aggressive behavior. It's tempting, because its cute and fun when puppies are little, but will it still be fun when your 70-pound (32-kg) adult dog comes running at you, grabs your pant leg with his teeth, and pulls?

127 SURVIVE TEETHING

Puppy teething usually lasts until four to five months of age. As with babies, teething is painful for puppies. Chewing is natural and helps to relieve the pain, and puppies will chew on anything they can get their mouth on, including small hands and fingers—especially since those things often smell like the delicious food they were just holding. Puppies have baby teeth, which are as sharp as needles, until around four months of age, and they can do serious damage to a baby's soft skin. Make sure your pup has plenty of suitable toys to chew on. Even then, you will need to very closely supervise your young puppy and restrain her with a leash to prevent her from teething on or play-biting a young child.

128 TEACH TABLE MANNERS

Practice, practice, practice! Whenever your dog eats, ask for a "sit" before putting the food bowl on the ground. Consider gradually reaching a hand in there to move the food bowl away, touch it, or pick it up, and immediately give your dog a treat with your other hand for allowing you to do so. The goal is to teach him that it's safe when people touch his bowl, and that good things come from it (like mushy treats!). This helps him see human hands not as threats, but as part of the feeding process, and to trust that he'll always be provided for without needing to set up a defense mechanism to protect his food.

Make this a fun, regular, and easy part of his eating experience, and in no time at all you'll have a dog who isn't possessive of his food or his bowl.

129 KEEP YOUR DOG OFF THE FURNITURE

To keep your dog from jumping on the furniture, it's best to start by never letting him up there in the first place. It is much easier to allow a privilege later than it is to curb a behavior that's ingrained. If you're adopting a new dog, consider not letting him on the furniture until you've decided for sure that you'll want him there.

If your dog is already accustomed to jumping up on the couch, here are a few tips for encouraging him to jump down.

DO DRILLS Consider using an "off" command and invite your dog off the couch in an excited tone of voice. Every time you do, give him a treat. Start to pair positive associations with the floor or his dog bed, such as food, praise, and petting. If you caress your dog while he's on the couch, he's going to want to be on the couch more. But if you ask him "off," and then caress him while he's on his dog bed or rug, he'll naturally want to be there more.

DENY ACCESS Don't give your dog access to furniture when you're not around. Your dog could then practice getting on the furniture without you knowing it, which means the behavior will become more of a habit. To break this, don't keep him in a room with furniture when you're not home. You need to be there to invite him off the furniture, and then to reward him for listening.

MAKE "OFF" A WONDERFUL PLACE TO BE Whether you choose a dog bed or the rug, begin to make this place magical. Treats fall from the sky here! Love and kind words rain down on him. Good things randomly happen when he's "off." But when he's on the furniture, he's ignored and promptly requested to come down. If you make the furniture a less desirable destination for your dog than his bed or the rug, you'll find he's less interested in jumping up.

130 PRACTICE "ON" AND "OFF" THE SOFA

If you decide you would prefer not to have your pets on your furniture—most of the time—set up a dog bed in your living room so that Fido can be near you, enjoying your company. If he has a comfy bed of his own and you have practiced your "on" and "off" commands, he will be happy enough resting in his own place.

STEP 1 Invite your pooch onto the sofa by sitting on it and patting the cushion, saying "on." The couch is intrinsically rewarding because it is soft and comfortable, therefore your dog will not need a treat or petting to reinforce the command "on."

STEP 2 Give the command "off" by using a treat in your hand to lure him off the couch. Once he jumps off, release the treat and praise him with affection, perhaps reinforcing by saying "good off!" Your goal with the treats is to make your pet believe that being "off" is just as fun as being up on the couch.

STEP 3 Repeat steps one and two, practicing "on" and "off" drills for ten minutes each day. When you are not able to keep an eye on him, leave your dog in another room where he will not have access to the couch and won't be tempted to jump up without you being there.

131 HOUSETRAIN YOUR DOG

Unfortunately, dogs don't come with a manual. It takes patience and time to housetrain your pup, but it's simple and very doable. Dogs are naturally clean creatures who do not like to soil their living areas. Since they like to poop in the same place, the trick is simply to show them where that place should be. Praise and reward your dog each time she gets it right (you'll need to keep plenty of treats handy). Your pup is most likely to relieve herself first thing in the morning when she wakes up, after she eats, after she drinks, and after she plays. Here are some tips to help you along the way.

SET UP A POOP PATROL Keep your dog under constant supervision while she's inside. If you can't watch your pooch, put her in a crate (but only for limited amounts of time) in a room with a hard-surfaced floor where accidents can be easily cleaned up, or outside in a secure area. Be alert to telltale signs, such as your puppy sniffing the ground before she pees. You can also keep your dog on leash beside you, ensuring that you catch any mistakes in the act.

DON'T YELL! If you see your dog about to do her business indoors, or in the middle of relieving herself, you can say "no" firmly or clap loudly. There's no need to yell. Instead, immediately take her outside and reward her for being there so she has a positive association with the outdoor potty area. Do not scold or punish her. If she happens to finish going about her business when you take her outside, make a big deal out of it with lots of rewards.

SCHEDULE REGULAR "BUSINESS TRIPS" The more often you go to the same potty spot, the better your chances of success. Put your dog on a daily bathroom schedule. For example, take her out first thing when you wake up, again after breakfast, then at set intervals throughout the day. You might want to start every three hours and work up to longer stretches, depending on your dog's age (both very young and very old dogs need more frequent chances to go outside).

INCREASE THE INTERVALS When you're outside, praise your dog while she's doing her business, and then reward her right afterward with a game or treat. If she doesn't go, keep up the supervision until you try again. Continue with the routine, and once she's going when you take her out, gradually increase the time between visits. When you're on a schedule you like and she's had no accidents inside for a few weeks, you've housetrained your dog!

CLEAN UP THOROUGHLY If your pooch has an accident inside your home, thoroughly clean it up and keep your dog away from the area until training is complete. Dogs learn where the restroom is based on smell, so don't blame your dog if she keeps having accidents in the same spot. And don't use ammonia-based cleaning products, which can smell a little like puppy pee. Aim to prevent her from having access to accident spots, and let your outside time together be the focus.

132 PAD TRAIN YOUR POOCH

Many people work eight-hour days or spend chunks of time away from their pets. Most dogs need a midday potty break, so if you're not able to hire a dog walker or enroll in doggie day care, or if you don't have a secure yard for your dog to stay in, pad training might be a helpful solution to deal with the long hours away. Pad training is especially helpful if you have a puppy, as puppies cannot be expected to hold their bladders for more than three hours. Newly adopted dogs or senior pets with weaker bladder control can also benefit from pad training.

SECTION OFF A POTTY SPOT To start, pick a room with linoleum or easy-to-clean flooring. Section off that area of your house with a gate, and place a dog bed, toys, and water at one end of the room, with your training pads at the other end of the room (dogs do not like to do their business near where they eat or drink). You can try using newspaper, or buy specialized potty pads at pet stores, which are thick and easy to clean up.

PRAISE AND BE PATIENT When you first leave your dog in this closed-off area, you'll want to watch and wait until he relieves himself on the pads. Be there to praise and treat him for it so that he gets the message. It helps to put him in his potty area about three hours after he took his last pee, when you know another's due shortly. Repeat this for a few days until you can trust he knows where to go. This might be something you can do over a weekend—once he knows the new system, you're set to try it out during your workday.

133 GET YOUR PUPPY TO GO ON COMMAND

When you're housetraining your dog, pick a command like "go potty" and use it while your dog is doing her business. Saying it two or three times is enough—you don't want the term to lose its meaning. Keep your tone happy, and then immediately praise or treat your dog when she's finished, repeating the phrase one more time while you pair it with the reward. Make sure to use the same command, since she's likely to be confused if you change it.

"GO POTTY" Continue to escort your pooch every time she goes outside, and make sure you say the command each time she pees or poops. When you go on walks, don't forget to use it as well, so that she learns "go potty" as a consistent term for going to the bathroom regardless of where she is. In a few weeks (or days, depending on the dog), your dog should know exactly what you mean when you use this command. It's all about consistency, patience, and reinforcement, so make sure you keep it fun. She's learning something new, and she's doing it for you. That's exciting.

134 TEACH YOUR DOG TO SIT

Teaching your dog the simple command of "sit" goes a long way. "Sit" is a useful way to get your dog focused on listening to you. It's helpful to ask your dog to sit before going on a walk, and to practice sitting at the front door so as to curb the desire to dash out should it ever be left open by accident. Saying "sit" before placing a food bowl on the ground is also a good idea, to reward calm behavior before feeding.

STEP 1 To teach your dog to sit, go to a quiet, controlled room where he won't be distracted. Bring yummy, smelly treats and as you sit on the ground, gently lure your dog with a treat, by placing it just above his nose, and then moving it slowly up and over his head and behind his eyeline. The goal is to get his eyes honed in on the treat, which will naturally require him to look up and to (hopefully!) sit his bottom down as the desired morsel moves behind his head.

STEP 2 As soon as your dog sits, reward him by excitedly saying "sit!" and giving him the treat he's earned. It may take a few tries or sessions for your dog to offer you the sit without you even asking, and the more patient you are, the better it will go. No need to force your dog's bottom down with your hand or shove him into a sit. This is a natural position for your dog to get into, and the the trick is simply to catch him in the act and reward him for it. Once he understands that's what you want—and you pair it with the command word—he'll start showing off his sits to you all the time!

135 TRAIN YOUR DOG TO LIE DOWN

Once your dog knows how to sit, it's easier to teach him how to lie down. Again, pick a quiet, controlled room without distractions and place a yoga mat or carpet on the ground. This ensures your dog has some traction as he learns to lie down, and won't slide on the floor, which might make him want to pop back up. There is no need to shove or force your dog into a down position; he will naturally offer you this very natural position as long as you stay clear and patient. The "down" command signals to your dog that he may be expected to stay in that position for a while, perhaps so that you feel secure while waiting to cross a busy street.

STEP 1 Begin by asking your dog for a "sit." You can add a hand signal to reinforce the verbal command. The classic signal for a sit is to hold out your hand, palm upward, and simply raise your palm toward your chest.

STEP 2 Next, hold a treat in front of your dog's nose, and then lower it down and away from him, toward the ground in front of him. You'll be luring near his chest area. Your dog may start to offer versions of a "down" that aren't quite the sphinx-like posture you're looking for. That's okay, reward him for it anyway! Any movement toward lying down is progress, and by rewarding the behavior you are gradually shaping him into a full down position.

STEP 3 Pair the movement with a happy "down!" command, and little by little your dog will lower into a full down position. Soon, you can pair the "down" command with a hand signal. The classic signal for "down" is the same as for "sit" except with the palm facing down. Simply lower your hand a couple of inches toward the floor and give the signal. Be there to give him treats when he lies down, as that will drive home the point.

BASIC TRAINING HAND SIGNALS

SIT	DOWN	STAND

136 USE HAND SIGNALS

You don't want to have to lure your dog to sit or lie down every time: pretty soon the verbal command alone will be enough to get your dog to adopt the required pose. After a while, you should be able to ask calmly and quietly for a "sit" and get it without any fuss, treats, or excessive praise. A simple "good dog!" will do the trick. However, dogs are visually oriented creatures, and can read your body language more easily than they can understand spoken words. By adding a hand signal to the command you will soon be able to drop the verbal request, and communicate with your dog using hand signals alone.

SIGNAL FROM A DISTANCE You can signal to your dog to lie down as he waits patiently outside the store for you simply by giving him the "down" hand signal through the store window. It can be easy for him to understand from a distance. So, for example, once you are are on a roll with your training and you are practicing "come" from a distance, you can try asking for a "sit" and "stay" then calmly walk 50 feet (15 m) or more away from your dog. Then turn to face him and before asking for him to come—usually with a more dramatic gesture such as slapping your thighs, clapping your hands, or opening your arms wide—you can test his obedience by asking for a "down" instead. Simply lower your down-facing palm to the floor and your dog should spot the command and respond to it even from that distance.

SIGNAL TO OLDER DOGS Visual commands are also particularly helpful for older dogs who are going deaf and, of course, for those dogs who actually are deaf.

BE CONSISTENT You don't have to use the hand signals shown here. You can use any signal that feels comfortable for you, as long as you use it consistently and your dog clearly understands it. However, the advantage of using standard or universal commands is that they are often based on the actual visual cues used when teaching a particular behavior. So, when you teach your dog a basic command like "sit," "down," or "stand," you're using a luring technique holding a treat in the palm of your hand and moving it—and then that hand movement becomes the actual dog-training hand signal.

STAY

HEEL

COME

137 STAY!

When teaching your dog to stay, she should already know the "sit" command. Once your dog is seated nicely, have a few treats on hand and start to get her attention. Get her interested in working with you, but not overly excited. The "stay" command is all about learning self-control and building up the ability to wait patiently. Follow these steps:

STEP 1 Stand close to your dog and put out a "stop-in-the-name-of-love" hand (your arm straight out in front of you, with your palm facing toward your dog). Ask her to stay, and then give her a treat if she doesn't move at all.

STEP 2 Now take a tiny step back and repeat. Slowly and gradually, one step at a time, increase your distance from your dog, and each time ask for a "stay" and use your hand gesture. The repetition will start to make sense to your dog. The most important thing is to only give your dog a treat if she actually stays put and does not move at all. If your dog does move—whether lifting a paw, shifting, standing up or walking toward you, take it back to the step before. You've found her threshold and need to work at that distance for a bit before increasing it further.

STEP 3 Little by little, even if you need to take half-steps, you'll begin to add to the distance between you and your dog with her remaining in a nice sit-stay position. With repeated sessions, your dog should be able to stay seated even if you briefly step out of the room.

138 STAY A LITTLE LONGER

Once you've worked on distance and practiced regularly using the "stay" command, you can begin to work on the length of time. Ask your dog to sit or lie down and stay (she will understand the command and hand gesture by this time) and increase the time you make her wait before you treat and release her by five or ten seconds at a time. With repeated drills, your dog should be able to stay for a full minute. This is a great game to play with her and keeps her mind working and tuned into you. This skill is useful if your dog has to wait for you for a couple of minutes outside a store or at the school gates, for example.

139
TEACH YOUR DOG TO COME ON COMMAND

A simple and effective way to teach your dog to come to you is to hold a piece of treat in your closed fist and give the verbal command "come" or "here." The fist helps you avoid training your dog to come to you only when he sees a treat in your hand. Instead, he'll learn to focus on this very specific hand gesture—the fist—and he'll learn that sometimes when it opens there's food in there. Sometimes there's not, but he still gets petting and positive reinforcement anyway. For his own safety and the safety of others, never allow your dog off his leash in a public place until you are completely confident that he understands (and will respond to) the "come" command.

STEP 1 When your dog is outside, or indoors on the opposite side of the room, practice enthusiastically calling him to "come!" and showing him your fist. At first, you should open your hand to reveal a yummy piece of treat. Give your dog the treat and praise him enthusiastically.

STEP 2 Repeat this drill several times in different areas of your home. Work particularly on getting him to target on your fist when he's outside smelling the yard. Once you can get his attention immediately despite grass-sniffing, you'll know he's paired your new hand gesture and the command with all things wonderful (food and praise).

STEP 3 Once he is coming back every time you call him, you can open your fist without revealing a treat. Give him plenty of petting and praise. As you practice over the coming weeks, gradually reduce how often your dog gets a treat, until you are confident that he will always return to you regardless of whether or not there is a food reward.

140
PLAY "HERE BOY!"

A fun alternative way to teach your dog to come when called is to make a simple game out of it. In your living room or fenced-in yard, stand in a circle with all family members at a distance from one another. Let your dog come up and sniff one of you, and while he's doing so, the person across the circle should call your dog to come in a happy voice. Use your dog's name plus the command of your choice (such as "here" or "come"). Your dog will likely make a beeline for this new, excited voice, and as he comes to the caller, she should praise him wildly for listening and then give him some petting or a treat once he's arrived. While he's engaged with this new person who just called him over, somebody else in the circle should call him and similarly reward him. Continue around the circle until everybody's had a chance to practice calling your dog to come a few times. Use enticing, smelly treats, clap, and make it fun for him to learn to come to you.

141
TRY A WHISTLE CALL

If you intend to take your dog to outdoor areas where he is allowed off leash, it is also good to first teach him to come using a whistle instead of the word "come." A whistle can be heard from a longer distance (such as across a dog park or field) and will save you from yelling. Whether you call your dog with a verbal command or a whistle, you can add a clear visual signal by opening your arms wide, slapping your thighs, or clapping your hands.

142 ROLL OVER, ROVER

To teach your dog to roll over, start with her lying down on her belly (best to teach this after you've worked on "down!"). Stand over your dog or kneel beside her, and use a treat as a lure over her nose. Slowly move the treat around her snout and behind her, so that she lies on her side and then (eventually) rolls over. Any movement in the direction of a roll over deserves your praise and reward. By paying attention to every bit of progress, you will slowly shape the behavior into a full-on roll over. That's when you can pair the behavior with the command "roll over!" and practice this trick, using treats to make her love it. Soft surfaces like carpets or grass are best for rolling over so your dog doesn't hurt her back. And if your dog doesn't seem to like this trick (some dogs find rolling over scary), choose another fun one to work on instead. Never force your dog to roll over, as it can teach her to be afraid of you.

143 SAY PLEASE!

To get folks sighing and cooing over your dog, there's no more effective trick than teaching your dog to "say please!" The begging posture is irresistible to adults and children alike, and it's amazing how quickly some dogs will adopt it to ask for all sorts of things—going outside, being fed, going for a walk—once you have released the genie from the bottle by teaching this very simple trick. Again, the only qualification your dog needs in order to master this super-cute pose is the ability to sit on command.

STEP 1 Ask your dog to sit, then hold a treat between your thumb and forefinger and place it just above your dog's nose. Just like with the down command, you are going to lure your dog into the desired posture. This time, of course, the bait is headed up, not down.

STEP 2 Now, simply move your hand up and slightly behind your dog's head in a smooth and deliberate movement. As your dog follows the tasty treat, trying desperately to keep it in his sights, he will naturally roll back onto his haunches, and up he goes! Give the command "say please!" at precisely the moment your dog sits in the begging position. With a few repetitions, your dog should adopt the begging position directly from a stand.

144   TEACH FETCH AND DROP!

You may or may not have a dog who fetches (runs after a ball and brings it back to you) naturally. If you don't, you can teach him. In return, you will have a great way to give your dog the maximum amount of exercise with minimal effort on your part. Most importantly, it's a fun way to teach your dog the potentially lifesaving "drop it" command. But a word of caution: Once your dog learns this trick, be ready for endless repetitions, as he tirelessly returns and drops the prized object at your feet with a look that says "Again!"

STEP 1 For starters, carefully cut a tiny slit or hole in a hollow rubber ball. And make sure you don't choose a ball that could be a choking hazard for your dog. Now put some treats inside the ball by tucking them into the hole, and show your dog where the treats are hidden. Get your dog excited about it, and feed him a tiny piece of the treats so he can taste how yummy they are.

STEP 2 Wave the ball around his snout and then throw it happily, encouraging him to "go get it" or "fetch." If he retrieves the ball, even if he doesn't bring it all the way back to you, praise him wildly for picking it up and for fetching at all. Run with your dog to get the ball and throw it again. He'll start to understand the game and to enjoy it because of your engagement, and the thrill of chasing.

STEP 3 Over time, instead of retrieving the ball with him, you can start to clap and cheer for him to bring it back to you. Even if he only comes two steps closer, reward that! The behavior will progress over time if you reinforce each step of the way, and pretty soon he'll be bringing the ball back to you. Now you can remove the treat from inside the ball and keep it in your hand, instead.

STEP 4 Throw the ball and give the command "fetch." This time, offer him a really tasty treat when he brings the ball back to you. As he inevitably drops the ball to get the treat (even if it isn't yet exactly at your feet), capture the action by saying "drop." Some dogs will get this quickly, and some might take more time. Try to have a good time and be patient with your pup as he learns.

145

PLAY FETCH FROM WATER

Once your dog is able to fetch on land, it is often a simple process to teach him to fetch something out of the water. Many dogs naturally love swimming and won't need an excuse to take the plunge. Other dogs, however, are far more cautious about the idea of dipping a toe in. First and foremost, check that your fetch toy floats; it'll be a short and disappointing training session if the toy sinks. Then, the trick is simply to find a safe, clean body of water where the depth increases gradually from the bank, so your dog can easily walk out and not get trapped in the water. Throw the toy a short distance at first—short enough to wade in and retrieve the toy yourself if Rover is reluctant. Then gradually increase the distance until your dog is obliged to swim a little out of his depth. Don't ever be tempted to "throw him in the deep end," which is dangerous, as the shock of plunging beneath the water could send your dog into a panic. It could also leave you with a dog that's terrified of water and won't trust you near water ever again.

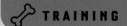

146 SWIM SAFELY

Swimming is great exercise for dogs just as it is for humans, and some dogs just love to swim. With any body of water, stop and consider the possible dangers before allowing your dog to enter. As ever, obedience training is crucial. When called, your dog should return to you from water just as obediently as he does on land.

RIVERS AND LAKES Check out rivers carefully before allowing your dog to leap in. Currents can be strong and fast and, in tidal rivers, can increase to dangerous levels in a matter of minutes. In any natural area of water, conditions can change from one day to the next: currents can be stronger, water can be deeper, and underwater (often unseen) hazards may appear overnight.

SWIMMING POOLS Dogs that love water will jump into a pool without batting an eye, but getting out of a pool with steep sides can be fatal if a dog panics when he finds he can't escape. Even pools with a clear escape route (where one side has steps leading down into the water) can be fatal for dogs who may swim to the wrong side and exhaust themselves trying to escape. Never leave your dog unsupervised near a pool.

PONDS Large ponds can present the same hazards as swimming pools, in that dogs may be able to get in but struggle to get out. Algae on the top of standing water can be poisonous, and can be a problem in the summer months. Even small ponds can be dangerous if thick mud or silt has accumulated over the years. If a pond isn't fenced off, it's best not to leave your dog unsupervised nearby.

SEAS Waves can present the same hazards for dogs as they do for young children, pulling them away from shore and hurling them around. If they become disoriented, they could aggravate matters by swimming in the wrong direction. Seas can have strong currents and dangerous riptides. Make sure you know the area well before allowing your dog to swim. And, if in doubt, keep him out!

147 EQUIP YOUR SEA DOG

Special flotation devices and life jackets are available for dogs. If you plan to take your dog on a boat, then it's best to give him a life jacket even if he is an excellent swimmer, as most dogs are. Canine life jackets have many of the same characteristics as those designed for humans. They are usually brightly colored so that your dog is clearly visible if he falls overboard in choppy seas, and they may have reflective strips for increased visibility in dim light. Dog life jackets are usually equipped with a handle to make it easier to hoist the dog out of the water if necessary.

148 UNDERSTAND CLICKING

Clicker training is a positive-reinforcement training method. It uses a clicker—a small, noisemaking gadget—to help teach your dog by reinforcing desired behaviors. Clickers can be purchased at a low cost online and at most pet-supply stores. The clicker-training technique is basically very simple: when your dog does what you want him to do, you click the clicker, and then you praise him and give him a treat. The clicker functions as a very precise marker of the exact moment your dog does what you want. Clicking is always followed up with a treat; in fact, at its core, a click is really just the promise of a treat. It says, "This is the very second you're doing what I want, and a treat is on its way." There are a few ways to use your clicker: you can capture a behavior, you can lure a behavior, or you can shape a behavior.

CAPTURE A BEHAVIOR
Dogs naturally adopt certain postures and behaviors—for example, sitting, lying down, and barking—without us needing to teach them. The trick is to get them to do these things when we ask for them. By clicking when a dog naturally behaves in a certain way, we can "capture" that behavior, reward it, and turn it into something we can control.

LURE A BEHAVIOR To lure a behavior, you effectively entice your dog into performing the desired action. You use a treat as bait to tempt your dog to sit, lie down, etc. The moment your dog successfully follows the command, you click your clicker and then give him a treat. You may need to repeat the process several times, or just a few.

SHAPE A BEHAVIOR Some tasks involve more than one step; for example, fetching a ball involves sitting or lying down until the ball is thrown, chasing the ball, bringing it back, and dropping it at your feet. By teaching and rewarding each small step toward a particular behavior, you can shape a far more complex command.

149 START CLICKER TRAINING

You'll need two things to get started: a clicker and a bowl of very small, very delicious treats, like chopped bits of hot dog or cheese. Make sure they're small enough that you can give your dog a lot of them without upsetting her stomach.

STEP 1 Sit in a chair with your bowl of treats in your lap or on a table next to you. Hold the clicker in one hand; you'll use your other hand to serve treats.

STEP 2 Click your clicker, and then immediately give your dog a treat from your treat hand. As soon as your dog finishes the treat, click your clicker again, and give your dog a second treat.

STEP 3 Repeat the first two steps until your dog starts looking expectantly at the clicker, rather than at the bowl of treats. Congratulations! Your dog now understands that she must hear the sound of the clicker in order to receive a yummy reward.

150 ADD A VERBAL COMMAND

When you're absolutely sure that your dog understands what she needs to do in order to earn a click, and you see her offer it over and over again on her own, it's time to associate the behavior with the verbal command. You can do this in two simple steps.

STEP 1 Watch your dog, and when she begins to perform the action you want to train, give the associated verbal command, and click-and-treat when she's performed it successfully. Practice this several times: give the verbal command, click, and treat.

STEP 2 Now limit your click-and-treat response to the times when you've actually given a verbal command. In other words, stop clicking and treating any time your dog offers the behavior; only give the click-and-treat reward when you've asked for the behavior.

151
GET A BARK ON COMMAND

Having your dog "speak" on command is a real crowd pleaser, and a good way to entertain your kids and their friends. Start to teach this trick by getting your dog riled up to play with his favorite toy. Although you can't force a dog to bark, by encouraging him to be his most joyful and playful, he will likely offer up this natural reaction. If you have dog that barks when you don't want him to, don't play this game, as it stimulates a behavior you're probably trying to curb.

STEP 1 Show your dog his favourite toy and let him know that you have really tasty treats. Dance and jump and pump up the energy. If your dog offers you a bark at any time, say "good speak!" in a happy tone and hand him a treat or the toy as a reward.

STEP 2 Keep practicing, and say "good speak!" each time your dog barks. Just remember it's your excitement that will get him eager enough to let out a sound. As usual, timing is everything, so be sure to reward him the moment he barks—you might find a clicker particularly useful for this trick.

STEP 3 This time, ask for a speak before he barks. Chances are he'll have gotten the idea and will bark. Don't reward him if he starts barking continuously; only reward single barks. As ever, be patient: you might need to practice the trick over a few days before it sticks, but it'll be worth the effort!

152
STOP YOUR DOG FROM BARKING AT HOME

Although it's natural for dogs to bark to show their enthusiasm, to alert you to strangers at the door, or to ask for some attention and playtime, some characters like to bark a little too often around the house, and teaching the "quiet" command is particularly useful for them. If you've checked out the Behavior section, you know that incessant barking can signal boredom or anxiety issues, so if after teaching the "quiet" command your dog still barks too much, consult a behaviorist. Quieting your dog on command is most easily taught as a captured behavior. Your clicker is a useful tool here. Don't encourage your dog to bark in order to teach him to stop; you have to be ready with your tasty treats when he decides to bark.

STEP 1 When your dog starts barking, just ignore him until he's quiet, even for a couple of seconds. Then, capture that quiet behavior by clicking or saying "good boy," and give him a really tasty treat. You may need to repeat this step several times over several days to really capture the quiet behavior.

STEP 2 When you're confident that your dog understands that he's being rewarded for being quiet, add the verbal command. When he starts barking, say "quiet" or "hush," and when he stops barking—even if it's not until ten seconds after you give the command—give him a treat and lots of praise.

STEP 3 Now it's time to raise the bar, or rather decrease the amount of time between your command and the end of the barking. Only reward your dog if he stops barking within eight seconds of your giving the "quiet" command. Keep reducing the time until he is quiet as soon as you give the command.

STEP 4 Finally, work on extending the time that your dog remains quiet by only giving him a treat once he's been quiet for ten seconds. When he succeeds, up the stakes and reward him after 20 seconds. Pretty soon you'll be able to give the "quiet" command without needing to give a reward every time.

153
KEEP THE PEACE AT THE FENCE

A big, fenced-in yard is a playtime paradise for a dog, but it can turn into a canine version of barking brimstone if another dog walks by outside the fence, or a squirrel family starts using the fence top as a freeway. We wouldn't let our human children scream and yell at neighbors, and the same should go for our dogs.

SUPERVISE First and foremost, if possible, don't leave dogs in the yard unattended. When your dog or dogs are out in the yard, you should be there—and be in charge.

BE A GOOD NEIGHBOR AND KEEP A GOOD FENCE Check your fences regularly. As fences age, gaps can appear between the wooden planks. A solid fence is the quickest fix: if you can't install a block wall, install a solid fence covering on chain link and iron fences.

TAKE CONTROL Some dogs will listen if you intercede before they've gotten all the way to an aroused state. Use the "quiet" command and call the dog to you before he charges the fence. If you miss the moment, go and calmly retrieve your dog, leashing him if necessary. If your dog will not come when called in the yard, you need to go back to basic training and reinforce the "come" command.

154 FIT A COLLAR

Too big, too tight, or just right? Finding a collar for your dog is like Goldilocks tasting porridge! In order to check that you have the right size for your dog's collar, try slipping two fingers comfortably between the collar and her neck in order to assess that she has enough room, but not sot much that she could pull back out of it. You can always take your dog to a pet store and ask an attendant to help you measure. Puppies should be introduced to their collars from eight weeks of age.

Put the collar on your pup for just a half hour or so at first, and distract her with a little playtime. Don't leave her unsupervised with her new collar in case she gets it caught on something—possibly her own paw, in a Houdini routine gone wrong. Once again, it is very important that you include a tag on your dog's collar with all of your information, even if she has a microchip. Some people only know to look for tags should your dog escape.

155 TRY A MARTINGALE COLLAR

If your dog is a flight risk or a leash puller, you might want to consider using a no-slip or martingale collar. This collar is composed of two loops, one larger than the other. The larger loop slips over your dog's head and adjusts to fit her safely, yet not too snugly. The leash is then clipped onto a D ring on the smaller loop, which is known as the control loop. When your dog pulls on the leash, or tries to pull her head out of the collar, the tension pulls the small loop taut, which in turn closes the larger loop.

LOOSER FIT When not engaged by a tight leash, a martingale fits more loosely than traditional collars, potentially reducing fur tangles and skin irritation.

GENTLE CONTROL Martingales are recommended by some professional trainers for their use as a gentle form of correction—not to be confused with the more brutal choke chain.

EVEN PRESSURE A martingale avoids the pressure on the trachea that results from a dog pulling on a traditional collar. With a martingale, a pull on the leash translates to a more even pressure around your dog's neck.

156 CHOOSE A LEASH

ROPE

When it comes to selecting the right leash for your dog, other than the aesthetic considerations of color and style—plain or patterned, studded with metal or diamonds—you need to consider the size and strength of your dog. A typical nylon leash is usually fine, but if you have a very strong or rambunctious dog, you may want to try something thicker and sturdier, which offers a bit more hold. Chain leashes can be a good option for more powerful dogs. If you have two smaller dogs, you might choose a leash with a splitter, so that you can hold one leash handle yet still keep both dogs connected to you. An extending leash is a great option if you want to retain control of your dog but give her a little more freedom to wander. Have fun shopping for your dog!

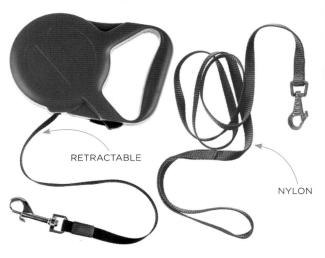

RETRACTABLE

NYLON

157 LEASH-TRAIN YOUR DOG

Not all dogs have been exposed to leashes since puppyhood. If you've adopted a dog who doesn't know how to walk on a leash, don't worry—you can still teach him! Experiment with walking your dog inside your home and get him used to the leash before taking it outside. As he grows more comfortable and confident, you can try out a walk! Just remember to let him stop if he needs to take a time-out, and to gently coax him toward you with food or soft praise if he gets nervous while on the longer walk. This might indicate that you need to take it back a notch and review earlier steps, or try walking when there is less traffic, fewer dogs out, and fewer overall distractions. Soon your dog will love the leash, because he will know that when the leash comes out, a walk is coming next!

STEP 1 Start by hooking up a leash to your dog's collar and giving him a treat just for that. Snap the leash on—treat. Take the leash off—no treat.

STEP 2 Next, clasp the leash on and let him drag it around the house (under supervision of course—you don't want him to get caught on something and hurt himself).

STEP 3 Once he's used to seeing and feeling the leash, pick up your end and gently hold it. If your dog freezes up or pulls back, don't fight him. Instead, try luring him with a piece of treat in your hand, letting it dangle by your side and encouraging him to follow next to you. Don't pull him along; slowly move together as much as possible.

STEP 4 Walk through different rooms, and keep treats on hand so that he can have a positive association with being on leash. Once indoor leash walking is comfortable for him, take it to your backyard, front yard, or another small, contained outdoor area. Start over with the treats, the luring, and with getting him adjusted to being on leash.

158 KNOW WHEN TO USE A HARNESS

A harness is a wonderful tool for full-body control of your dog. It slips over your dog's shoulders and around his chest below his collar (which should be left on with the tag intact).

SAFETY There are many reasons to use a harness. If you have a dog with any sort of neck or trachea injuries, or if you are concerned about preventing those types of injuries, a harness is easier on your dog's body and prevents pulling on his head.

CONTROL If you have a high-energy or large dog who is challenging to handle, a harness might offer you extra control and support. Dog harnesses can often be sturdier and offer extra assurance, removing the fear that your dog could slip his head out of his leash.

CONFIDENCE A harness is also good for training purposes. Because it provides you with a greater ability to manage your dog's body, it will give you the confidence needed to remain calm and collected on a walk. This is essential if you want a well-behaved dog, because he needs to feel that his leader is taking care of him. It also allows you to focus on his training, and to sink into the beautiful dance of communication between you and your furry friend.

159 AVOID RETRACTABLE LEASHES FOR TRAINING

Retractable leashes have clear advantages in certain situations: for example, if you want to give your recently adopted dog a little freedom on her walk, but you're not yet entirely confident that she will come back when called. In general, however, retractable leashes are not the best tool when it comes to training your dog. Because they offer a variety of distances and allow your dog to constantly test how far she can go, retractable leashes make it difficult for your dog to stay focused on you. When you're walking and working with your dog, the goal is to keep her engaged with you. The retractable leash is counterproductive in this respect, as it allows your dog to explore in an uncontrolled and unpredictable manner. By using a standard leash when training, your dog will understand her limits and boundaries, and you won't have to fight for her attention. When training, it's always best to take out the competition of smells and sights, and keep things between the two of you as consistent and bonded as possible. A regular leash will help you achieve this goal far more easily.

BONE OF CONTENTION
CHOKE CHAINS: CORRECTION OR CRUELTY?

There's a pretty big clue in the name: choke chains are archaic correction devices that have no place in modern training methods. They are dangerous devices that can damage a dog's trachea. If you really can't stop your dog from pulling without resorting to a choker, you should think about calling in a professional positive-reinforcement trainer to help you.

TRAINING

160
PREVENT PULLING ON THE LEASH

Training your dog to stop pulling on the leash has a ton of benefits. Since you'll both enjoy walks more, you'll likely go on more walks, which has health, behavioral, and emotional benefits for your dog—and for you. Physically, you'll avoid potential injuries to your hands, arms, neck, shoulders, back, and more. Your dog will avoid possibly injuring his neck, throat, and back too. Even if your dog is off-leash trained and you live in an environment where you almost never need to use a leash, you never know when good leash skills will come in handy—on a trip to the vet, on visits to friends or family, or in any new environment. If you adopt a new dog who's a strong puller, it can seem like an impossible task to get him to stop. Here's an easy-to-follow exercise that, with patience and persistence, can teach your dog not to pull on his leash, and instead walk happily at your side.

STEP 1 Hold the leash with your hand firmly behind your back or at your side. This is so every time your dog pulls, he doesn't get the reward of an extra couple of feet of slack from your arm stretching out.

STEP 2 Now, play red-light-green-light. When your dog pulls, red light! Stop and stand still—and what he wants (moving forward) ends.

STEP 3 As soon as he does anything that creates some slack in the leash (stops pulling, backs up, looks at you, etc.), green light! Give lots of praise and immediately start walking again.

STEP 4 Gradually you'll increase the distance your dog walks without pulling. It's a patience game; if you want your pooch to stop pulling, be consistent with this practice and "red light" every time he pulls, "green light" only on a slack leash.

161
CONSIDER USING A HEAD HALTER

A head halter can be an effective tool to help decrease pulling, especially if you have a leash-aggressive or extremely muscular dog who is difficult to manage on walks. The head halter works like a horse's head halter—it goes around your dog's snout, and if your dog pulls on his leash, the halter pulls his head down and shuts his jaws. Although these halters are somewhat controversial in terms of neck safety and impulse denial, many trainers do recommend them in order to offer guardians a gentle and workable solution to walking their hard-to-handle dog. Make sure your dog's halter fits snugly but not tightly. You don't want it to slip off, but it shouldn't be leaving marks on your dog's face. Manufacturers almost always provide a how-to video or pamphlet to help with fitting. Never pull on a halter to punish your dog, which could result in a serious injury.

STEP 1 Your dog will most likely resist and dislike the halter to begin with. Start by putting your dog's snout through the loop and giving him a treat for allowing that to happen.

STEP 2 Repeat step one as often as necessary. Then work your way up to snapping the halter behind his head, offering another treat for this major step forward. Once your dog keeps the halter on without trying to paw it off, you can snap its loop to the leash and try walking around your home so he gets used to the new feeling.

STEP 3 It will usually take some time for your dog to be comfortable with the head halter, but once he gets there you can use it on a short walk. Slowly increase the length of your walk so that he gradually gets used to wearing the halter for a longer period of time.

162 CREATE A GREETING RITUAL

Leash aggression, where dogs bark or lunge at other dogs while out on walks, is a common problem that is often caused by fear or insecurity about interacting with other dogs while constrained on a leash. Creating a greeting ritual for you and your dog can make all the difference. By having a consistent routine for your pooch, you can teach him how to greet other dogs on leash, and offer him a safe and positive experience. Once dogs meet one another, their curiosity is usually quenched and their reactivity quickly subsides. Best of all, since the ritual comes from you, it reinforces the human-animal bond.

STEP 1 When you see another dog on leash, stop and ask your dog for a "sit." As the strangers approach, ask if the dog is friendly with other dogs. If the owner doesn't seem certain that her dog will be friendly, keep your own dog seated or ask for a "down," and let the strangers pass.

STEP 2 If the other dog is friendly, signal to your dog that it's okay to say hello. Keep the meet-up short and sweet, let the dogs sniff each other, then carry on with your walk. By controlling the situation, you have given your dog the structure he needs to feel safe and calm.

163 PLAN SOME TIME OUT

The fact is, your dog is going to want to explore and enjoy life on her terms. That means smelling, smelling, and more smelling! Remember, generally the walk is for the dog and not for you, so it's good to let your dog walk on her own terms for at least some of the time. You can meet her instinctual needs in a structured way by creating a "time-out" or "free-time" command. If you give your dog the freedom to do what she is meant to do, on command, as determined by you, then she won't have to fight for it or force her will onto your times together. Everybody wins.

This strategy is simple: Pick a command and/or hand gesture, and use it every time you give your dog a break to do her thing. For example, if you're out on a walk and she's been heeling beside you for the past ten minutes, it might be a good time to give her a time-out. Tap her chest or excitedly say "time-out!" and point to a fresh patch of grass. Let your dog smell and roll and enjoy her surroundings for a couple of minutes before you end her

session and get back to the business of walking. Consider building a few of these breaks into every walk or outdoor activity time you spend together.

You'll soon have a happier dog who knows she can get everything she needs from you. She'll choose to listen to you—and she'll respect you more for it.

164 HAVE A SAFE TRIP!

It's essential to take it slow when it comes to introducing your dog to new things. If you'd like to make your pooch your travel companion or errand buddy, you need to get her used to the car first. And why wouldn't you? Your car can take you and your pooch on exciting adventures in the wide-open spaces outside of town, and it can get you directly to the dog park. Having your dog associate getting in the car with these super-exciting outings will go a long way toward making her see the car as a portal to doggie paradise rather than a scary, noisy prison.

STEP 1 Start by practicing getting your dog in and out of the car, whether you have to carry her or let her jump up and down on her own (perhaps with the help of a treat or two). Consider repeating this step a few times just to get her used to entering and exiting.

STEP 2 Next, sit in the car with your dog, but don't go anywhere. Just spend a few minutes in your driveway letting her get used to the new environment. Give her a treat, praise her, pet her, or bring her a favorite toy, so that she can have a positive association with being in the car. Again, you may have to repeat this step several times before moving on.

STEP 3 Once your dog gets into the car and sits with ease, strap her into her safety harness or put her in a crate, depending on what travel system you'd like to use to keep both your dog and yourself secure. You don't want a dog jumping into your lap while you're on the highway, so find a safe way to keep her buckled in. Then drive around the block.

STEP 4 Repeat step 3 while slowly and gradually increasing the length of your trips. Move on to driving around a few blocks, then around the neighborhood, and so on. You'll want to work up to traveling longer distances, and always make the car a happy, positive, and calm place to be.

165 NEVER LEAVE YOUR DOG ALONE IN THE CAR

It is never a good idea to leave your dog unattended in the car. Temperatures rise suddenly and drastically in a car, even if you leave a window cracked. Also, dog thefts happen quickly, and if you leave your dog alone, she is vulnerable to this sad reality. It can be a fatal mistake to leave your dog unattended in the car, so make sure you only take her with you when she will be part of the activity once you arrive at your destination.

166 HEAD FOR THE GREAT OUTDOORS

To keep your dog in sync with you, keep in mind what you're competing against! When you take your dog to a new, exciting environment such as a new neighborhood, hiking trail, or vacation destination, your dog will be overwhelmed with fun, unfamiliar smells and sights. He may have a harder time than usual focusing on you and listening to you. This is normal. Remember the rule of thumb: the greater the distraction, the greater the rewards should be. This means that if your dog has more to look at and sniff than ever before, you should prepare treats of higher value than usual to combat the sensory overload. For a training session at your house in the same kitchen he's used to, a plain dog biscuit should do the trick. But for a walk around a lake, with other dogs and new people around, not to mention unknown grasses and dirt, you will need to step up your game. Invest in some high-grade treats or figure out your dog's favorite foods beforehand. Then only use these highly valued treats when you go on extra-special outings like this, in order to keep his focus on you. Of course, you'll give him plenty of opportunities to explore the great new world, but you must be able to get his attention back when necessary.

DOG TALES

SAM AND BERTIE, "MEAN AND WILD" MINIS

Based in Lancaster, Kentucky, No Kill Central KY Regional Humane Society is a nonprofit organization whose mission is to "foster the well being of all animals through C.A.R.E.S.: Compassion, Adoption, Responsibility, Education, and Spay/Neuter." Their volunteers work every day throughout the year to care for abandoned animals in the Kentucky area.

One of the shelter's most extraordinary adoption cases involved two Miniature Dachshunds, Sam and Bertie. Sam and Bertie were surrendered to the shelter by their owners because they were deemed to be "mean and wild." But on the contrary, the two tiny "minis" were so terrified that they hunkered down in their pet carrier, not wanting to come out.

Many dogs are taken to shelters because they are lost, or because their owners move home and find they are not able or not allowed to take their pets with them. However, all too often dogs end up abandoned because their owners misunderstand them, and then make matters worse by mistreating them with the intention of correcting this perceived "bad behavior."

Happily, the volunteers at the KY Humane Society were able to win Sam and Bertie's trust, and with love and patience were able to undo the damage that had led to the two tiny pooches being so fearful around humans. In fact, the dogs were so transformed by their positive experiences at the shelter that they were chosen to be the featured dogs for a "Smooch the Pooch" event

at an outdoor festival in Lexington, KY. The two irresistible cuties helped to raise a very impressive $1,316 for their shelter, so that many more abandoned animals could be helped.

When two animals have been through so much together, it can be painful to separate them when one is adopted without the other. It is often the lesser of two evils, though, and is sometimes simply unavoidable. Fortunately for this pair of bookends, at that same outdoor festival where they raised such a huge sum for their shelter, Sam and Bertie met Belinda Tarpley, who fell in love with the two pups instantly. Belinda adopted them together as a bonded pair and their new life came complete with new names—Priscilla and Elvis!

167 RUN WITH YOUR DOG

Running has fantastic health benefits both for you and your pet, and can add some spice to the otherwise mundane task of regular exercise. If you have an energetic dog, chances are he will love the exercise. And if you find your dog bouncing off the walls and getting into trouble, burning off that extra energy will help give you a little more quiet time. But before you rush into your sneakers and out the door, here are a few things things to think about.

HAVE A HEALTH CHECK Consider your dog's overall physical condition before embarking on an exercise plan with him. If he's older or overweight, the stress of running may be too much pressure on his joints or his heart. You might want to check with your veterinarian prior to starting.

TAKE IT ONE STEP AT A TIME Just like you, your dog needs to build up his endurance and strength over time to prevent injury and burnout. Start out slowly and watch him for signs of fatigue and overheating.

PAWS FOR THOUGHT Since your dog doesn't wear cushy sneakers, choose grass and dirt trails that are easy on his paws, and check his pads periodically for cuts or injuries.

168 BIKE TOGETHER SAFELY

If on a cool spring day, you're biking through the peaceful, open countryside with an obedient and superfit canine companion running happily alongside you, then congratulations—you're both clearly living the dream. First, though, there are a lot of important points to consider before you venture out on a bike with your dog. Above all, you need to keep you and your pet safe. Ever see those clips of a dog running away from a rollerblader or biker? Don't be that person.

CHECK YOUR DOG'S HEALTH As with running, don't even consider biking with your dog if he's out of condition or overweight. Get him into shape first with a regular walking or jogging routine. Even if your dog appears to be in great shape, organize a health check with your vet to rule out underlying conditions that could be aggravated by strenuous exercise.

GET GEARED UP Invest in a non-tangle leash designed especially for biking, and a baton, which attaches to the frame of your bike to keep the leash (and your dog) away from the wheels. This is far safer than attaching a leash to the handlebars. Attach the other end of the leash to a fitted body harness; connecting it to a collar could lead to serious injury. Attach reflective materials and even lights to your dog's harness if you are likely to be out in poor light. Be sure to bring a water bowl and extra water for your dog, and most importantly, always bike slowly, and regularly stop to check in on your dog and give her a chance to rest.

169 ACCLIMATE YOUR DOG TO RIDING

Hitching your dog's leash to your bike's handlebars and heading off into the sunset is a recipe for disaster. Only attach your dog to the bike using specialty equipment, and introduce him to this strange and unsettling experience gradually. If you haven't cycled with a dog before, you are going to be nervous yourself, and your dog will pick up on that.

STEP 1 Start out by walking alongside the bike with your dog on the opposite side. Praise and reward her for staying calm. Keep the first few trips short, walking alongside the bike and turning only to return to where you started. Gradually introduce more changes of direction and, even at this stage, give your dog verbal cues to let her know your intentions, such as "turning left," "slowing down," or "stopping."

STEP 2 When you feel she is ready for your first test cycle, start out really slowly and keep praising her calm behavior. Keep her attention focused on you. Although in a way it's a good sign if she's relaxed enough to pay attention to anything other than the bike at this stage, don't take any chances, and bring her attention right back to you if she gets distracted. Stick to quiet paths with soft surfaces, and don't attempt any turns at first—just head off slowly in a straight line, and let her know when you are going to stop.

STEP 3 Repeat step 2 for as long as you need to, and be prepared to get off and walk if your dog seems frightened. Once she's relaxed, introduce the first turns—preferably on a clear path that bends, so that she's not taken by surprise. Only go for a short distance, and continue cycling at walking pace until your dog's confidence grows and she gets used to the new commands. If possible, cycle to a nearby field where you can set your dog free and play a game of fetch so that she associates the bike ride with a fun destination.

STEP 4 As your dog gets used to the routine over the first few weeks, gradually build up to a trotting speed. Early on, you might want to return to her fun destination for that reward play, but soon she will start to enjoy running alongside the bike as a fun experience in its own right. You can gradually increase the distance, but keep a close watch on your dog at all times for signs of fatigue, such as heavy panting or excessive drooling. Stop regularly so she can rest and drink water.

170 CONSIDER OTHER CYCLING OPTIONS

If your dog is too old or unfit to join you on your bike rides, there are one or two other ways you can bring her along. Small dogs can be trained to travel happily in a specially adapted shopping basket, and older dogs can learn to travel in an adapted baby carriage that is pulled behind the bike. Small dogs have even been seen happily riding in an adapted backpack, but sensible precautions have to be taken against overheating.

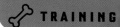

171 PLAY HIDE-AND-SEEK AT HOME

This classic game can be a lot of fun for you and your dog because, for dogs that enjoy it, the challenge of seeking a hidden object appeals to their instinctive prey drive. To play these two variations of hide-and-seek, it helps if your dog knows the commands "sit," "stay," and "fetch."

HIDE-AND-SEEK Have your dog sit and stay in one room while you (and any roommates or family members) go into another room. Hide in relatively easy-to-find places, like a closet with the door cracked open or behind a couch. Call your dog in a happy, excited tone, but try not to give away your location by laughing. Have a party when she finds you—celebrate with praise and petting, and let her feel proud for using her intrinsic gifts. Kids in particular will love to play this game with the family dog.

FIND THE HIDDEN TREASURE Try playing an alternative version of hide-and-seek with your dog by hiding a ball or one of her favorite toys. You might want to warm her up by playing a short game of tug or fetch so that she knows which toy you're going to hide. Ask your dog to sit and stay outside of the room while you find a hiding place, then open the door and command "fetch." Make the hiding place easy at first, then gradually more challenging as her skills improve. Reward her each time with enthusiastic praise or a treat. Some dogs get so good at this game that it can be amazingly difficult to outfox them.

172 FREEZE LIKE A STATUE

The statue game is an easy and fun way to burn off excess energy and reinforce the commands "sit" and "stay." It can be played indoors or out in the yard. The goal of the game is simply to get your dog wound up and then have her immediately stop and be calm (or at least appear calm). You can also practice the command "quiet," in the likely event that your dog starts expressing her excitement vocally. This teaches her valuable obedience skills that will be useful in any real situations when she becomes overly excited.

STEP 1 Start dancing or jumping around with your dog to get her energy level up.

STEP 2 Freeze in place and command your dog to "sit" and "stay."

STEP 3 Hold the freeze together, then give a treat and praise.

STEP 4 Repeat!

173 PARK YOUR POOCH

Dog parks can be a great place to socialize your dog and meet other dog owners in your area, who collectively can be a fount of knowledge about the best local vets, grooming facilities, places to walk, and dogs to steer clear of. However, dog parks can also be unsafe if you don't take proper measures, especially during your first few visits. Here are some tips to help you keep your dog safe and happy at the park.

KNOW YOUR DOG Not all dogs enjoy meeting new dogs. Don't let your dog get overwhelmed by meeting too many dogs at once. If your dog has not interacted regularly with other dogs, find out how he will react by testing him in a controlled environment before you go to the dog park. For example, introduce your dog to a friend's dog that you know interacts well with other dogs.

KEEP YOUR DOG HEALTHY Be sure your dog isn't vulnerable to picking up infections from other dogs by keeping him up to date on his vaccinations and deworming medications.

CHECK OUT THE PARK Consider visiting the park without your dog for the first time to familiarize yourself with the park itself and the dogs that play there. Before bringing your dog inside the park, spend a few minutes watching the other dogs and how they interact. If the dogs seem too rough for your dog, come back at another time or try a different dog park.

START OUT SLOW Your first few visits to the dog park should be short, no longer than 15 minutes. Slowly increase the length of your stays as your dog becomes more comfortable with the dog park atmosphere and makes a few friends.

AVOID PEAK TIMES Weekday evenings are peak, high-traffic times at dog parks, and weekends and holidays tend to be busy all day long. Acquaint your dog with the dog park when it isn't as crowded.

CLOSELY SUPERVISE YOUR DOG Don't get distracted while talking to other owners. Keep an eye on your dog at all times to make sure his interactions with other dogs are safe. Watch his body language to avoid any trouble before it begins. This also enables you to quickly clean up after him.

UNLEASH YOUR HOUND Let your dog off leash as soon as you enter off-leash areas. Mixing leashed and unleashed dogs can create a hostile situation. Leashed dogs, and their owners, often display body language and behavior that is threatening to unleashed dogs and may encourage them to be aggressive and defensive in return. A leashed dog doesn't have the freedom to choose between "fight or flight," and since he can't take flight, he may decide he has to fight.

LEAVE THE KIDS AT HOME Don't bring children with you to the dog park. You will not safely be able to watch your kids and your dog at the same time. Many dogs have not been socialized to children. Dogs and young children both frighten and excite easily—and react differently—creating a dangerous atmosphere. It's simply too easy for a child to get hurt at a dog park.

LEAVE SMALL PUPPIES AT HOME Puppies less than four months old aren't fully immunized yet, and run at higher risk of contracting diseases. They are also very vulnerable to being traumatized by another dog's aggressive behavior.

DO NOT BRING TOYS OR FOOD Most parks are already littered with balls and toys that other people have brought. Rewarding your dog with treats or giving him toys in front of other dogs can lead to jealousy and aggression.

KNOW WHEN TO LEAVE You should remove your dog from the park if he is being threatened or bullied and seems fearful, if he begins to display aggressive behavior by becoming overexcited or threatening toward other dogs, or if he is panting heavily or seems overly tired. Keep your dog's welfare the top priority.

CARE

> ## 66 The better I get to know men, the more I find myself loving dogs. 99

CHARLES DE GAULLE (FORMER PRESIDENT OF THE FRENCH REPUBLIC)

Essentially, dogs are like young children who can communicate only their most basic feelings, such as hunger, severe pain, and happiness. So it is up to us to understand them and know how to keep them healthy, comfortable, and safe.

Dogs are at once rather simple—needing the basics of life such as food, shelter, clean water, and companionship—yet also highly intelligent and social creatures, with complex personalities that require nurturing, too. They cannot speak to us to tell us how they are feeling and what they need. They do not complain when they are in mild pain, and often we do not know there is a problem until it has become serious.

You need to know what and how much to feed your dog, how to keep her healthy and safe, how to keep her clean, how much exercise to give her, and even what toys and bedding she needs—all this, all year round, throughout her entire life with you. The good news is that, much like having a baby, there are many resources and people available and willing to give advice and support.

You are your dog's benevolent guardian—responsible for providing her with a happy and comfortable life, and in return, she will provide you and your family with companionship and love. Think of her as part of your team, where you are part leader, part parent, and part coach. There is a time when firmness is needed, but most of the time, what is required from you is empathy and thoughtfulness. Do your best to make good decisions for the team, and your dog will be there to support and stand by you through all of life's ups and downs.

174 PREPARE FOR A PUPPY'S ARRIVAL

If you adopt a puppy, be prepared for a lot more work than you'd be facing if you'd adopted an adult dog (often obedience-trained, house-trained, and a known size and temperament). More than ever, being prepared can mean the difference between getting a good start, or getting off on the wrong paw. A puppy needs a safe, warm environment with lots of human interaction. Here are some tips for preparing your home for your new puppy.

PUPPY-PROOF A PLAY AREA Puppies will chew everything, from electrical wires to socks and shoes! You need a secure, puppy-proof, enclosed area, and a crate for those times when you cannot directly supervise your puppy. Note that puppies typically are not house-trained, and should be kept in an area where it is okay to have accidents.

ESTABLISH YOUR HOUSE RULES If you do not want an adult dog who gets on the furniture or jumps up on people, do not allow your puppy on the furniture or to jump up. Once a puppy learns that you allow a behavior, it can be difficult for you to change it. Ask all visitors (and family members) to follow your house rules. No matter how cute he is when he's tiny, most people do not want their full-grown dog jumping on everyone.

PREPARE YOURSELF Be ready to deal with crying, whining, and barking. Puppies make noise, just like babies, but there are ways to guide your puppy through this stage of his life without establishing permanent bad habits. The worst thing to do is to let the puppy cry and bark in his crate for a long time, and then go get him out or give him attention. When you do that, you teach your puppy to persistently make noise in the crate, because you have shown him that persistence pays!

175 VACCINATE YOUR PUPPY

Puppies need a series of DHLPP vaccines, typically at 8 weeks, 11 weeks, and 14 weeks. One of the Ps in the DHLPP stands for parvovirus, or "parvo" for short. Parvo can live on the ground for up to a year, and your puppy can step on it, lick his paws, and contract the virus, which, sadly, can be fatal. Do not put your puppy down on the ground outside (on your street, in the park, etc.) or inside public places like vet offices or pet stores. Your home, your enclosed yard, and your friends' enclosed yards and homes (if their pets are all vaccinated and healthy) are the only safe socialization areas until your puppy is fully vaccinated.

176 VET A VET

One of the first things you should do after adopting your dog is make an appointment for a checkup with a veterinarian. In addition to making sure your dog is healthy, a first vet visit gives you the opportunity to scope out a new vet while your pet is healthy, so that when your dog isn't feeling well, you'll have the comfort and confidence of knowing you have a veterinarian you trust. Here's a checklist of questions to ask at your first vet visit, both about your new dog and about the veterinarian's policies and philosophies.

WHAT DO I NEED TO KNOW ABOUT MY DOG'S BREED OR BODY TYPE?

Some dogs have special health or safety concerns that you need to be aware of. For example, dogs with a deep chest cavity are often prone to a life-threatening condition called bloat, wherein the stomach twists after gastric distortion. For these types of dogs, your vet may recommend a special feeding schedule, rest for a period after feeding, or preventive medication. Or, if you've adopted an Italian Greyhound, your dog's doctor will tell you that the breed is prone to broken legs, and they'll give you some tips for prevention.

WHAT VACCINES DOES MY DOG NEED, AND HOW OFTEN DOES HE NEED THEM?

There are a variety of vaccines for dogs, but each vet may recommend a different set of shots on different schedules. To complicate matters, the rabies vaccine is required by most states in the U.S., but each state's policies are different. Your veterinarian can tell you exactly what is required by law and which other vaccines are medically necessary in your geographic area, or are necessitated by your lifestyle (especially if you travel a great deal or regularly visit dog parks). Your veterinarian may recommend titer testing—a blood test that checks your dog's immunity to certain diseases—to determine which vaccines are essential and which ones your dog can safely skip.

DO I NEED TO PROTECT MY DOG FROM HEARTWORM? WHAT OTHER PARASITES ARE COMMON IN OUR AREA?

There are a variety of parasites that your dog may be at risk for, ranging from certain types of intestinal worms to common fleas and ticks. Perhaps the most serious parasite is heartworm, which, as its name implies, are worms that infest the heart, causing death. Heartworm is caused by the ingestion of a certain type of flea, common in some areas of the United States. Your veterinarian can answer your questions about whether or not dogs in your region are at risk for heartworm and other parasites and, if so, what you can do to protect your pal.

DOES YOUR OFFICE PROVIDE AFTER-HOURS EMERGENCY CARE?

This is an important question. If your pet sustains an injury or becomes very ill outside of normal office hours, where should you take him? Does your veterinarian offer after-hours emergency care, or is there a nearby emergency clinic he or she works with and recommends?

WHAT LOCAL RESOURCES DO YOU RECOMMEND?

Your veterinarian, and especially the veterinary technicians (the nurses of the canine world) in his office, can be a wealth of information about local resources. Don't hesitate to ask for advice about local obedience classes, private trainers, groomers, dog parks, and boarding facilities.

177 PLAN FOR VETERINARY EXPENSES

Pets can get sick or injured, just like people, and sometimes they need veterinary surgery, which can be very expensive. No one wants to be in a situation where a pet needs medical treatment, but can't get it due to a lack of funds. So as you plan your budget for everything else you need for a pet (food, accessories, day care, etc.), be sure to set some money aside each month to save for future unexpected vet bills. In fact, using that monthly amount to pay for pet health insurance is a very smart thing to do.

178 BUY PET HEALTH INSURANCE

There are now many companies that offer pet health insurance, which is exactly what is sounds like— health insurance for your pet should she become ill or be injured in an accident.

CHECK WITH YOUR VET To get started, insurance companies usually require some sort of records from a recent veterinary exam to rule out preexisting conditions for your pet.

DECIDE ON YOUR POLICY Then, for a monthly fee, insurance companies will cover some or all of the medical expenses your pet might incur in her life, so long as you keep the policy current and pay the monthly fee.

CHECK FOR DISCOUNTS Many companies offer multi-pet discounts for people with several animals.

179 GET HELP WITH VET BILLS

Veterinarians are regularly faced with owners who, when confronted with a pet's medical emergency, sadly end up choosing to euthanize their pet simply because they can't afford a costly veterinary surgery, and their pet is suffering too much to live without it. No one wants to find themselves or their pet in this situation, but sometimes a financial crisis occurs and the funds just aren't available. Perhaps you didn't have pet health insurance or it was a preexisting condition, or perhaps you just found the pet you wish to help. If you don't have extra money you can spend for this purpose, you are going to have to figure out a way to fundraise to cover your pet's expenses. Here are some tips on how to lower or get help paying for your vet bill.

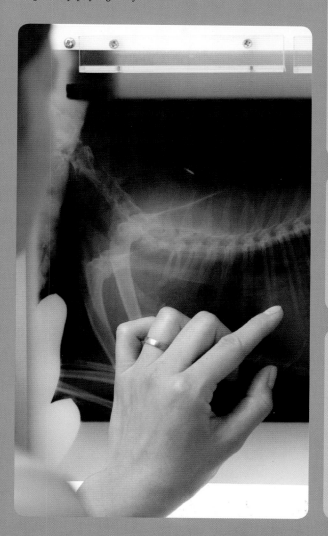

TALK TO YOUR VET Veterinary hospitals are businesses that, like any other, need to make money to survive. It may seem like they are making a fortune, but the cost of insurance, staffing, supplies, rent, etc., makes for a huge overhead. That said, they sometimes can offer you a discount or deferred payments if you can prove you qualify for low-income assistance. Alternatively, they may know of a local charity that offers financial support to people who can't afford vet care. Or, they may have a new vet-in-training on staff who can do a procedure for a much lower cost, especially if the only other option is euthanasia.

GET A SECOND OPINION Sometimes all you have to do is speak to another vet, and she may be able to offer a less expensive treatment option to try first—for example, a course of medication instead of a surgical procedure. The alternative to surgery might take longer or not be quite as effective, but it may still help your pet live comfortably and happily. The second vet may confirm that there is only one treatment possible for your pet, but you don't know until you ask.

LOOK FOR A LESS EXPENSIVE OPTION Call other veterinary hospitals to ask how much they charge for the treatment your pet needs. Explain in advance what your budget is, and see if they can offer a treatment within that budget. You can also see if there is a veterinary college near you, which may offer discounted care.

FUNDRAISE If your pet's vet-care need isn't urgent, you can try fundraising to cover each month's payment. Have a yard sale; offer your services (whatever skills you have) to friends, coworkers, and neighbors in return for a donation; set up an online fundraiser and ask all your friends on Facebook, Twitter, and in your e-mail contact list to donate. This is how pet rescuers pay their vet bills, and you as an individual pet owner can certainly try this too. You may have to swallow your pride to ask friends and family to help, but isn't your pet worth it?

180 ESTABLISH A ROUTINE

A puppy feels secure having dinner, playtime, lessons, and walks at the same time each day. Also, being left alone all day on Monday after having spent his entire first weekend with you can cause lots of anxiety. If you do bring him home on a weekend, get him used to being on his own by leaving him alone for progressively longer periods of time. Put him in his safe area and walk out of the room for one or two minutes, and then come back. Later on, leave the room or the house for five or ten minutes. Increase

the period of time until you can be away for an hour or more at a time. Schedule your puppy's feedings so that all meals are eaten by 5:00 to 6:00 p.m. (if you go to bed at 11:00 p.m.), so your puppy drinks very little water after that. Be consistent about your (and your puppy's) bedtime and morning wake-up time to help him learn to hold it through the night. Remember, you won't always have to be so structured, but the effort you make now to train your puppy will pay off in the form of a happy adult dog.

181 MAKE YOUR HOME SAFE

Before you bring your dog home, you should make a slow pass through your house to make sure it is safe for a new dog (just like you would for a baby). For any dog (young or old), you need to make sure that all your doors and windows are secure and there is no way your dog can escape your house.

HIDE HOUSEHOLD TOXINS

There any many things in the average house that can be dangerous or even fatal to your dog if swallowed. Some seem pretty obvious when you think about it, but others may surprise you (see the list below). If you have these things in your house, either remove them or make sure they are always safely stored in a place your dog can never get to.

STORE FOOD SAFELY

Be sure you have fresh water in a bowl that your dog can always get to, but if you have bags of dry dog food, store them in a place where your dog cannot get to them—otherwise, she may indulge in a potentially dangerous overeating session while you are gone. If you have cats and you feed them on the floor, you will either need to only feed them when your dog cannot enter the room, or move their food bowls up onto a counter where your dog cannot reach.

RECOGNIZE COMMON HOUSEHOLD TOXINS

PESTICIDES AND POISONS

Products designed to attract and kill bugs or rodents can also attract your dog—with lethal consequences.

CLEANING PRODUCTS

Household cleaners and soap products, such as shampoos and conditioners, can have enticing smells that may attract your dog, but can be harmful if ingested.

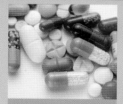

HUMAN DRUGS

Many common pharmaceuticals can be deadly if ingested by your dog—keep them stored out of reach, just like you would for a child.

CANINE DRUGS

If your dog has been prescribed medications by your vet, make sure you store the products away safely every time. Medications can be flavored to be attractive to dogs, to make it easier to administer treatment.

HUMAN FOOD

Certain common foods that are fine for you can be very bad for your dog. Never feed your dog chocolate, onion, garlic, raisins, grapes, avocado, macadamia nuts, seeds, or pits. Chewing gum can be dangerous for your dog.

182 CREATE A DOG-FRIENDLY BACKYARD

If your dog will be spending any time in your yard, whether supervised or unsupervised, it is important for you to make it a fun and safe place. Remember, though, that no matter how big your backyard is, your dog will still need plenty of time to interact with you and other dogs on frequent walks or dog-park visits. Here are the three essential keys to a dog-friendly backyard.

SECURE

ESCAPE-PROOF YOUR BACKYARD

Dogs are good at finding escape routes you can't see, so you really do need to do a close inspection of every foot of the perimeter. Make sure your gate and fence are high enough (A) and there is nowhere your dog can climb or jump over. Don't forget that dogs can dig. Check that the fence extends all the way to the ground, and there is no place where your dog could push, dig, or burrow under the fence (B). Your gate should latch shut (locked is best, so strangers cannot accidentally let your dog out). Place a sign on the outside of the gate informing everyone that there is a dog present. Be sure that your dog can't jump on the gate in a way that might unlatch it.

| SAFE | SUPPORTIVE |

REMOVE POTENTIAL DANGERS

Yard chemicals such as mulch or herbicides must be locked away (C). Plant fertilizers are often manure-based, and can be particularly alluring to canines. Sharp objects, which could be anything from old tools to other construction materials, can cut or injure your dog. Water features, such as ponds and pools (D), should be enclosed or covered. Trash bins should be stored in a shed or locked away (E), so that your dog cannot ingest dangerous food items that you have thrown away. Barbecues should never be left unattended when cooking food in your yard (F). Remember, too, that many plants can cause stomach upset if ingested by your dog. Some notable examples are oleander, rhododendrons, cyclamen, amaryllis, and chrysanthemum.

PROVIDE SUN PROTECTION

Trees or large shrubs can provide welcome shade (G). A doghouse, which itself can become very hot in the sun, should not be your dog's only protection from the sun. If you live in a colder area, your dog needs a place to be protected from ice or snow when it falls (keep in mind that certain products designed to clear ice from your yard can be harmful to pets). You must also make sure your dog has access to fresh water at all times. Never use a pool or pond for this purpose—this water is not fresh and often has chemicals that are harmful to your dog. Fresh water means a bowl of water that is kept full of clean drinking water (H). It's great if your yard has a place where it is acceptable for your dog to dig (I) if he likes to. Lastly, each day, take a walk around your yard and remove any dog waste. Dogs don't like to exist in their own waste any more than we would.

183 BEWARE OF WATER HAZARDS

Some dogs love to swim and can't resist water, but even if they are superb swimmers, they can drown if they fall or jump into a pool and panic when they find they are unable to exit. If you have a pool, the safest option is to enclose and gate the area so that your dog cannot enter. If that is not possible, you must bring your dog into the pool to be sure he knows how to swim, and guide him to the steps so that, if he were to accidentally fall in, he knows where to swim to be able to get out. You must do this repeatedly until you are absolutely confident that your dog can swim to safety. Similarly, garden ponds should be enclosed, covered, or designed so that they have an easy escape route if your dog should fall in. Ideally, you should never leave your dog in a yard with access to a pool or pond unless you are there watching.

184 BUILD A DOGHOUSE

If your dog is ever in your yard, it can be nice to have a doghouse where she can go inside and feel secure. Note that this is not a substitute for a fully shaded area in your yard. A dog in a doghouse, even though she's out of the direct sun, can quickly become overheated as the doghouse itself heats up.

WHAT MAKES A DOGHOUSE A DOG HOME?

1 Make sure the house you build or buy is made of a material that will not rot away over time, such as plastic or red cedar. Don't use metal, which gets too hot in the sun, and don't use pressure-treated wood, which can contain arsenic. Use rust-proof screws, nails, and brackets.

2 The house should be raised on short legs just off the ground to keep it dry if rain creates a puddle. It needs to be big enough for your dog to turn around, and should have an open doorway (not a door that swings open or closed, like the doggy door to a house).

3 Place the doghouse against your own house, ideally near your door, so your dog can look out of the doghouse and see your door, as well as the rest of the yard. Place soft bedding and a fun toy or two inside the doghouse.

185 UNDERSTAND CANINE NUTRITION

Dogs require a wide range of nutrients if they are to remain healthy and happy, with a well-muscled body, healthy teeth, and strong bones. And all that effort you put into grooming your dog will come to nothing if he doesn't get the essential nutrients that keep his skin healthy and his coat shiny. Meat, which provides essential proteins, should never constitute more than 50 percent of your dog's diet. Your dog's diet should also be rich in carbohydrates,

which can come in the form of dry dog meal, cereals, rice, or vegetables. It should contain fats, which are the most concentrated form of food energy. The easiest way to ensure your dog is getting proper nutrition at every stage in his life is to feed him store-bought dog food that has been specifically created with dog nutrition in mind. Consult with your vet to ensure that your dog is enjoying a diet that is right for his size, age, and energy level.

PROTEINS, FATS, AND CARBOHYDRATES
Proteins provide the basic building blocks for cells and are essential for growth, tissue repair, and the maintenance of vital metabolic processes. Fats from either animal or vegetable sources provide energy and promote healthy skin and coats. Carbohydrates also provide energy and, as a source of bulk, help to maintain regular bowel movements.

VITAMINS AND MINERALS With a well-balanced diet, your dog should obtain all the vitamins and minerals he requires, although there will be occasions when he may need supplements, perhaps as he gets older or when he's recovering from an illness. However, these days more dogs are diagnosed with problems caused by the overuse of vitamin supplements than with vitamin deficiencies.

186 KEEP WATER ACCESSIBLE

Water is the most essential nutrient for your dog—it accounts for up to 70 percent of your dog's body weight. Dogs lose water by passing urine and feces, and by panting. Your dog needs to have clean, fresh water accessible at all times to help replenish the liquid she loses during the day. Although canned food is usually three-quarters liquid (and even dried food has up to ten percent moisture), it is not sufficient to satisfy your dog's requirements. Dogs are just as dependent upon water as we are, and can suffer irreversible damage due to dehydration—a fifteen percent decrease in body water can be fatal.

ASK THE VET
MY DOG HAS DIARRHEA. WHAT SHOULD I DO?

It is not uncommon for a dog to occasionally have very loose stool or even diarrhea. Dogs occasionally get sick, just like people. Or it may be that your dog ate something while out on a walk that you did not see. Foods that are rotten, or even too high in protein, like pure meat or cat food, can cause a dog to have diarrhea. Diarrhea, if it continues untreated, can be very serious and even life-threatening. It can be a sign of a much bigger problem, and it can itself lead to a dog becoming dangerously dehydrated. If your dog has diarrhea for more than a day, call your veterinarian. It may be a sign that your dog is having a more serious problem, and even if not, it may be best to get your dog on some medicine until the problem resolves itself.

187 LEARN THE TEN COMMANDMENTS OF FEEDING

1 Your dog's water bowl must be kept full of fresh water at all times, and must always be accessible to your pet.

2 Provide your dog with well-balanced prepared foods from a reputable manufacturer.

3 Feed your dog only in the quantities advised by your vet.

4 Never feed your dog spoiled or stale food.

5 Do not feed your dog cat food; it is too high in protein.

6 Keep a close watch on your dog's weight, and avoid feeding her too many treats or scraps.

7 Do not give your dog cooked bones, especially chicken bones, which can splinter and become a choking hazard.

8 Always serve your dog's meals at room temperature. If you keep dog food frozen, make sure it is thoroughly defrosted before presenting it to your dog. If you cook your dog's food, make sure it is cooled sufficiently.

9 Throw away any food left uneaten.

10 Contact your vet if your dog gains or loses weight unexpectedly, or if she refuses to eat for more than 24 hours.

188 PROVIDE SEPARATE FOOD BOWLS

Although some dogs living in the same household may be happy to eat from the same bowl, this is generally not a good idea. You should always provide separate food bowls so that you know both dogs are getting the nutrition they need, and to reduce the risk of your dogs squabbling over their food.

189 CHOOSE THE RIGHT PREPARED FOODS

The easiest way to ensure that your dog enjoys a healthy, balanced diet is to choose from the wide range of complete prepared foods available from reputable pet-food manufacturers. Such foods provide all the nutrients required to satisfy your dog's feeding requirements (which makes it a lot easier than feeding your human family).

WET FOOD "Wet" dog food comes in cans. Some dogs prefer wet food, but it can be messy and attracts flies in the summer if your dog leaves a portion uneaten. If your dog is small and you are not feeding an entire can, it helps to buy some plastic lids to keep canned food fresh once opened. Canned food tends to have less carbohydrate content than dry food (kibble), which can be a factor for overweight dogs, but canned food is also heavier to transport from the store, and leaves you with a lot of cans to recycle.

DRIED FOOD Dried food (kibble) is convenient in that it is comparatively odorless, lighter to carry home than canned food, and easier to store once opened. It is also easier to clean up any spills. However, it may have as many as five times the amount of calories per gram as canned foods, so be sure to serve smaller quantities if you are switching from canned to dried food. Also, some dry foods need to be mixed with water, so check the instructions. Be sure to store dry food in a place where your dogs cannot get at it.

MOIST FOOD Some owners like moist food, as it has the convenience of dried food and yet appears more "meaty." Most moist foods have more calories than canned food, so adjust the quantities accordingly. Remember, however, that it doesn't really matter which type of complete food your dog has as long as it is from a reputable manufacturer and your dog enjoys it. And if for some reason you want to switch the type of food your dog is eating, make the change gradually to avoid stomach upset.

190 COUNT CALORIES

Wild dogs take their food where they find it and sometimes have to live for several days off a single meal. Consequently, wild canines gorge down their food and, when meals are scarce, retain food in their stomachs for a long time to slow down the digestive process. Although some domestic dogs are positively picky about their food, many still retain the gorging instinct, which can lead to obesity. Be aware of the amount of food your dog is consuming and check that his calorie intake corresponds to his size and energy consumption. The chart shown below is an approximate guide only, so be sure to feed your dog according to the food manufacturer's instructions and/or your vet's recommendation.

DAILY FEEDING GUIDE					
	TINY	**SMALL**	**MEDIUM**	**LARGE**	**GIANT**
WEIGHT	10 lb (4.5 kg)	20 lb (9 kg)	40 lb (18 kg)	70 lb (32 kg)	150 lb (68 kg)
CALORIES REQUIRED	200	600	900	1,700	2,500
DRY FOOD REQUIRED	2 oz (60 g)	6 oz (170 g)	10 oz (280 g)	17 oz (480 g)	25 oz (700 g)

ASK THE VET
DOGS EAT MEAT, RIGHT?

Most dogs certainly like to eat meat, but dogs living with humans have evolved over time to be omnivores, and are not strictly speaking carnivores. In other words, dogs can also digest plant foods, and in fact virtually every major pet food sold today is a mix of meat and vegetables. Many dogs can also be healthy on a carefully crafted vegetarian diet, but few commercial vegetarian dog foods are available. Remember that just like people, dogs need a healthy balance of nutrients, so simply feeding your dog cuts of meat (which is just muscle, and all the parts of the prey that a wolf in the wild would consume) does not provide your dog with the nutrition he needs.

191
UNDERSTAND THE IMPORTANCE OF PLAY

Dogs are highly intelligent animals that thrive on social interaction. They simply can't be happy without sufficient physical exercise and mental stimulation. For most domestic dogs, who no longer need to hunt beyond the kitchen floor for their breakfast, mental stimulation comes in the form of play, both with their human pack and their canine companions at the local dog park. If your dog has a canine companion at home, or a feline one who doesn't totally ignore him, you'll notice that the two friends spend a lot of time entertaining each other, which can save you a lot of effort (though it's still important to get your dogs out and about to meet and greet at the dog park). But if you are a single-dog family, it's even more important to spend quality playtime with your pooch, and to provide him with a range of toys that stimulate him physically and mentally. What's more, playing with dogs is great fun, provides exercise for you and your family, and is a fantastic opportunity for bonding. Playing with your dog also helps to cement your authority as pack leader, because it is you who provides the precious toy, and it is you who offers, throws, or tugs the toy to get the action underway.

GAME OF THROWS Throwing games, with a ball or Frisbee, provide maximum exercise for your dog with minimal effort on your part. Chasing games stimulate instinctive canine behavior. It's even more fun when two or more dogs can race for the ball (as long as play doesn't get too competitive!).

POWER PLAY Most dogs love to play tug-of-war, and any toy, rope, or stick will do as far as they're concerned. Tugging games stimulate a dog's natural prey instinct, and may not be appropriate for dominant or aggressive dogs, except as part of power play with an experienced trainer or handler. Dogs should instantly release the tug toy (or any toy) on command.

RACE AND CHASE When two or more dogs get together, they often don't need a toy to get the fun started and they can race and chase each other around the field to exercise and entertain themselves for as long as you allow them. This is the main reason why dog parks are so great!

WRESTLING AND ROUGHHOUSING Just like many human children, dogs love to spend a little time tumbling with each other. Well-socialized dogs will playfight without getting overly competitive or aggressive, but it's up to you to ensure the play stays friendly.

CHEWING FUN Even when home alone, a dog can entertain himself for hours with the right kind of chew toys. Some toys have a center in which a tasty treat can be hidden, so that your dog finds the toy even more tempting and is mentally challenged and rewarded for his chewing efforts.

192 STOCK UP THE TOY CHEST

Working dogs, herding dogs, hunting dogs? Some would argue that all dogs are "toy" dogs! Certainly, the majority of dogs love to chase, chew, or catch, and there are toys to suit every kind of dog—from high-flying Frisbee fans to stay-home-and-chew champs. Here are a few ideas from the seemingly endless range of possibilities out there. With all toys, be sure to select the right type and size for your particular dog.

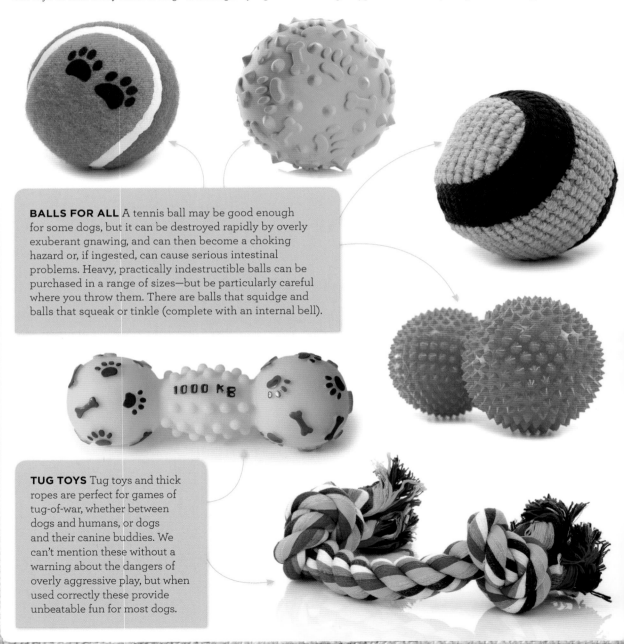

BALLS FOR ALL A tennis ball may be good enough for some dogs, but it can be destroyed rapidly by overly exuberant gnawing, and can then become a choking hazard or, if ingested, can cause serious intestinal problems. Heavy, practically indestructible balls can be purchased in a range of sizes—but be particularly careful where you throw them. There are balls that squidge and balls that squeak or tinkle (complete with an internal bell).

1000 KG

TUG TOYS Tug toys and thick ropes are perfect for games of tug-of-war, whether between dogs and humans, or dogs and their canine buddies. We can't mention these without a warning about the dangers of overly aggressive play, but when used correctly these provide unbeatable fun for most dogs.

FRISBEES There are a wide range of Frisbees designed especially for dogs. They are made of special plastics that are extra durable to contend with strong teeth, and yet gentle on your dog's mouth. If you intend to play at the beach, you might want to check that your Frisbee floats as well as it flies.

CHEW TOYS Of all the toys out there, chew toys are a must for practically all dogs. A suitable ball can double as a chew toy, but there are a huge range of toys in a variety of materials (plastic, rubber, rawhide, etc.) specifically designed to keep dogs entertained even when left alone at home.

BALL THROWING AIDS Nowadays, even the feeblest human can hurl a ball huge distances with the aid of special ball throwers now available from most pet stores. They let you pick up a ball without touching it, and hurl it across an entire field. Alternatively, choose a ball or Kong with a rope attached, which can be slung for a considerable distance (although not always in the intended direction, as a glance into the trees around your local dog park will testify).

193
CHECK OUT THE ULTRASONIC OPTION

There are chew toys that squeak and, better still (if you like a bit of peace at home), there are toys that don't. Best of all, there are chew toys that are designed to squeak at a pitch above the 20 kHz frequency at which sounds become inaudible to humans—but not to your pooch. That makes the toy super exciting for your dog, but satisfyingly silent for you!

194
LEARN THE ADVANTAGES OF BALL THROWERS

Forget the tennis racket. Now, with a ball thrower, you don't have to bend down to pick up the ball, you don't have to hold a ball drenched in drool, and you can throw it as far as you like. That means more fun for you and more exercise for your dog. The ball throwers are available with a short handle for convenient storage, or a longer handle for extra leverage. And if you're tossing a ball a distance in dim light, some balls even flash so that they can be seen in the dark (but it's probably not a good idea to hurl a ball in the dark unless you're 100 percent certain there's no one else around to be struck).

195 LET LEAPING DOGS FLY

Some dogs love to run, some love to swim, and some just love to leap. Jack Russells and collies are especially renowned for their jumping-jack habits, but almost any dog can be bitten by the bouncing bug. If your dog is a natural-born bouncer, then Frisbee is definitely the game for her. This may be something you reserve for the dog park or the beach, but if your dog shows real talent, then consider entering her into your local "disc dog" event. This event took off (quite literally) in the 1970s, and is a competition that judges your dog's skill in events such as "distance catching" and the often spectacular "freestyle catching." This sport is hugely enjoyable for the dog, the handler, and the spectators alike.

196 AVOID DANGEROUS TOYS

If your dog loves to play fetch it can be tempting to throw a stick, but this can be dangerous if the stick splinters, causing a choking hazard or mouth injuries. If you own a very fast dog, such as a Whippet, or you are not able to throw the stick very far, your dog may arrive before the stick and get hit on the head. Every year, dogs are injured in this way, sometimes impaling themselves as a sharp stick bounces awkwardly. Other impromptu toys, such as ropes and stones that your dog drops at your feet as an invitation for frolics, can be similarly hazardous. Even toys from the pet store can be dangerous if they are too small for your dog or are poorly constructed. Don't let playtime turn into a horror story. Choose your toys carefully, when in doubt consult with your local pet-store staff or your vet.

197 KNOW WHEN ENOUGH IS ENOUGH

Different dogs have different exercise requirements. All puppies should have their playtime limited, so they can put their energy into growing and avoid injuring delicate bones and muscles. Some dogs seem to have boundless energy and require lots of exercise to keep content. Other dogs need only short bursts of exercise and can become exhausted if encouraged to play for too long. Of course, as a dog gets older his exercise requirement decreases; short walks once or twice a day may be ample for an old timer. If in doubt, check with your vet to find out how much daily exercise your particular dog requires, and make sure you know when to call "time-out" on play. Remember, even older dogs will continue to play when their joints are starting to hurt, and you don't want your dog to pay a price when you get home.

198 PICK UP YOUR DOG PROPERLY

It is important for you to know how to pick up your dog in a way that does not injure her or you. Practice this technique regularly so that your dog is comfortable being picked up before you actually need to pick her up to bathe her or place her on a vet's table. Never pick up your dog by her tail or ears. And always place your dog down gently, releasing your hold only when she is safely on her feet.

STEP 1 Stand beside your dog before picking her up. Talk to her gently to reassure her.

STEP 2 Bend down (bending your knees, not your back), place one hand under her chest, and reach your other hand over her back and around her belly (A).

STEP 3 Lift your dog slowly to ensure you don't drop her. Use your legs and not your back to lift to avoid injury if your dog is heavy (B).

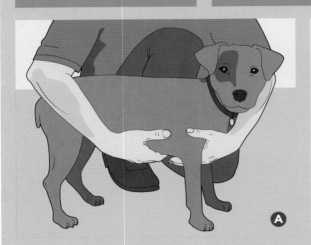

A

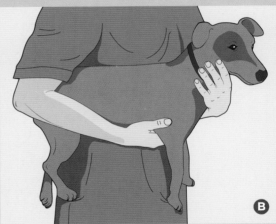

B

199 LEARN SOME BATH TIME DOS AND DON'TS

DO	DON'T
• Introduce your dog to the bath by degrees.	• Don't call your dog to come to you in the bath; go to him and calmly lead him or carry him to his watery ordeal.
• Have all the necessary bathing tools within arm's reach.	• Don't remove your dog's collar at bath time.
• Close the bathroom door.	• Don't leave the bathroom door open.
• Check with your vet how often your dog should be bathed.	• Don't let shampoo get into your dog's eyes.
• Follow the shampoo manufacturer's instructions.	• Don't use water that is too hot.
• Give him plenty of praise and treats during and immediately after bath time.	• Don't use soaps designed for humans; they may irritate your dog's skin.

200 PREP YOUR DOG FOR BATH TIME

Even water-loving dogs such as retrievers can find bath time daunting at first, and for some dogs that love nothing more than getting down and dirty in the nearest convenient mud pit, bath time is a positive nightmare. But practically any dog can learn to tolerate or even love bath time if it involves a generous splash of the three Ps: patience, praise, and petting.

Patience is particularly important the first time you bathe your dog. Don't wait until your dog rolls in something hideous before giving him his first bath. Then

the stakes for success are high and the pressure is on to have a great bath when your dog is not yet used to the experience. Instead, plan to make bathing a regular event that becomes part of his routine. Prep your dog for bath time in the four stages outlined below. And no matter how successfully you think you've prepared your dog for his first introduction to soapy water, when it comes to the big day when you're actually going to take the plunge, do a quick check of the house to ensure all the doors are closed (if he's ever going to make a break for it, this is the time).

STAGE 1 Introduce your dog to where he will be bathed. If you intend to hose him down in the yard, this is not as much of an issue, but if you intend to work with him indoors in the actual bathtub (in which case it's best to have a shower with a flexible hand-held sprayer), take him into your bathroom a few days before you plan to give him his first bath. Give him time to explore the room without running a tap; let him get used to the feel of the tiles and the strange, soapy odors.

STAGE 2 On the next visit (or after a few visits if you feel he needs a little time), pick him up and gently place him in the tub on a rubber mat. Give him lots of praise for tolerating the strange new environment, stroke him and scratch him behind his ear, and give him a tasty treat to seal the deal. If you plan to plug your dog's ears with cotton balls while you bathe him, now's a good time to practice putting the plugs in and taking them out.

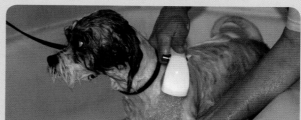

STAGE 3 Repeat the process for a couple of days, and then, without putting him into the tub, turn on the tap to get him used to the sound of running water. Make sure the bathroom door is locked so that he isn't tempted to bolt, and pet and praise him when he stays calm—or at least stays put! Again, give him a tasty treat and take him out of the room. If he seems calm, you can perhaps demonstrate the shower hose at this stage—again, without spraying him.

STAGE 4 On the big day, do not remove his collar, as you will almost certainly need to hold him at first. Place a mat in the tub for traction; run a shallow, lukewarm bath; and lift him gently into the tub. Have everything you need close at hand so that you don't need to let go of him. If you have to stand up to fetch the dog shampoo from the bathroom cabinet, he will almost certainly leap out of the bath and skid around on the wet tiles in a frantic effort to escape, and all your patient prep work will disappear down the drain.

201 GEAR UP FOR BATH TIME

The only required equipment for bath time is dog shampoo and conditioner, a plastic cup or jug, a couple of towels (and perhaps a hair dryer), and some cotton balls to use for earplugs. There are a wide variety of canine shampoos available, but a mild, odorless, puppy shampoo is probably the best bet to begin with. There are other specialty shampoos to treat a variety of skin conditions, which your vet might recommend from time to time, and there are flea-treatment shampoos should the need arise. A rubber mat for the bottom of the bath can reassure your dog by making it less likely that she will slip and slide. Finally, a highly recommended piece of bath-time equipment for you: a long, waterproof apron.

202 ASSOCIATE BATHING WITH GOOD THINGS

Just as your dog links his leash to walks and the car with trips to the dog park, you can make bath time a whole lot easier by encouraging your dog to associate bath time with things he especially enjoys. Save a special treat, such as a piece of cooked chicken, for bath time only. Bring out a favorite toy or play a boisterous game of tug-of-war once bath time is over. Better still, follow bath time with a walk in the park to show off your pristine pooch to the admiring neighbors. Be careful, though, because some dogs will run right to the mud and roll in it to get the smell of shampoo off their fur. Whatever fun experience you decide to share, the trick is to be consistent so that your dog learns to associate the fun thing he loves with the not-so-fun thing he tolerates.

203 BATHE YOUR DOG

As well as keeping those doggie odors in check, regular bathing can help keep certain pesky parasites at bay. It can also help treat a range of skin conditions, with special treatment shampoos for oily and dry skin and everything in between (just like with humans). If your dog has a long coat, start the bathing ritual by brushing out any tangles that will be difficult to comb out when wet. Brushing also has the practical benefit of removing any loose hairs that could accumulate and block your drain.

STEP 1 Place a rubber bath mat in the tub and run a shallow, lukewarm bath. Lift your dog carefully and place him onto the mat. Plug his ears with dry cotton.

STEP 2 Hold your dog firmly by his collar and pour warm water over his back to thoroughly wet his coat. Avoid the head at this point. Give him a treat and reassure him with soothing praise.

STEP 3 Shampoo your dog all over his body and legs, working up a good lather and massaging the soap into his coat to loosen grime and dead skin (A). Tell him what a "good boy" he is.

STEP 4 Carefully wet your dog's head, being sure not to splash soap in his eyes or mouth. Lather the back of his head gently and use a damp sponge to wipe any grime from his face.

STEP 5 Rinse your dog thoroughly with lukewarm water. If you have familiarized your dog with the shower hose, this is ideal (B). But, again, make sure that the temperature is just right!

STEP 6 After rinsing, you may want to use a conditioner to moisturize your dog's skin and minimize matting if he has long fur. Be sure to read the instructions carefully to see if the conditioner requires rinsing.

STEP 7 Now's the time to thoroughly dry your dog, so start by draining the bath, or if you're washing your dog in a free-standing tub, lift him out and wrap him in a large towel. Finally, use a blow dryer to dry his fur (C).

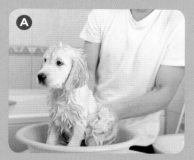

ASK THE VET
MY DOG HAS A LUMP ON HIS SKIN. WHAT DOES THIS MEAN?

If during your regular grooming session you come across a lump on your dog's skin, it is important to have it checked out by your vet as soon as possible. Lumps are common in dogs, and include abscesses, cysts, and warts. An abscess might be treated simply by bathing the area regularly in salt water. If the lump feels hard, it could be a cyst. If the lump is crusty around the base, it is probably a wart. The worst-case scenario is melanoma, which is a common type of cancer in dogs. Selective breeding has led to certain breeds being particularly prone to melanoma, including the hugely popular Golden Retrievers, as well as Boxers, Chihuahuas, Doberman Pinschers, Chow Chows, Springer Spaniels, Boston Terriers, and Cocker Spaniels. Tumors are most prevalent in older dogs of any breed, and they are often slow-growing and benign. Malignant tumors tend to grow more rapidly, are often painful, and can be fatal if left for too long without treatment. The crucial thing with any lump is to get an early and accurate diagnosis from your vet. Warts, cysts, and tumors all need to be removed by a professional, and malignant tumors require prompt and aggressive medical attention.

204

PREPARE FOR POST-BATH PANDEMONIUM

The relief of finishing her bath can send a dog wild with excitement. Left to her own devices, she will immediately shake any excess water on her coat all over you and her immediate surroundings. Released from the confines of the bathroom, she is liable to tear off at full speed around the house, rolling over on the carpet and rubbing herself against the furniture. If you've been unwise enough to leave a door to the yard open (or if one of your kids has left the door open), your dog may race into the yard and head straight for the nearest patch of dust or convenient flower bed and bring you right back to square one. It's far better to lock your dog in safe area like the kitchen while she decompresses for the first few minutes after bath time.

205 MAKE BATH TIME THE BEST TIME

If you don't want to risk wreaking havoc in your pristine bathroom, here are a few alternatives.

KITCHEN SINK For a very small dog, the kitchen or bathroom sink can be the perfect place for bath time, especially if the sink has a hose attachment. Just be doubly sure that your dog won't try to leap out from his high-rise hot tub.

PLAY POOL A plastic play pool placed on the lawn can be a great option during the warm summer months. The low sides provide excellent access (but also present your pooch with a tempting leap to freedom).

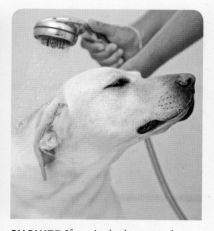

GARDEN HOSE If your dog enjoys playing with water streams, and some dogs really do, you can incorporate an impromptu bath time into these summertime frolics. After a few minutes of play, unleash the shampoo!

DOG BATH Consider investing in a specially designed plastic dog tub, which usually comes complete with a handy leash clip so Rover can't roam. High-end models have hoses, drains, shampoo caddies, and all manner of accessories. At the lower end, there's the plain old washtub.

SHOWER If you're lucky enough to have a separate shower area in your home, this can be the perfect place to launder a large dog. Again, a hose attachment is ideal for thorough rinsing.

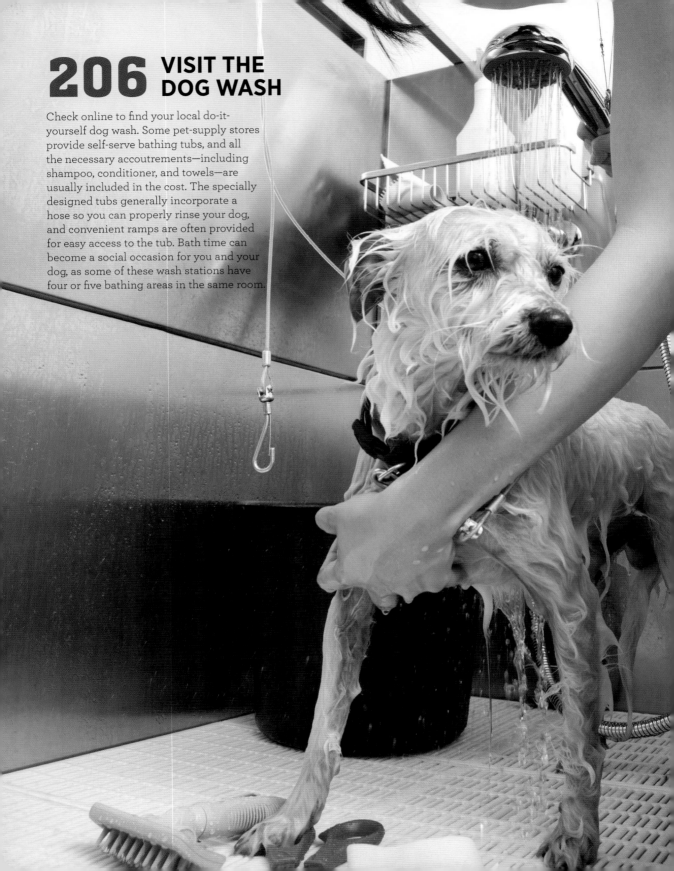

206 VISIT THE DOG WASH

Check online to find your local do-it-yourself dog wash. Some pet-supply stores provide self-serve bathing tubs, and all the necessary accoutrements—including shampoo, conditioner, and towels—are usually included in the cost. The specially designed tubs generally incorporate a hose so you can properly rinse your dog, and convenient ramps are often provided for easy access to the tub. Bath time can become a social occasion for you and your dog, as some of these wash stations have four or five bathing areas in the same room.

207 CALL IN THE PROFESSIONALS

If your dog is too heavy to lift into the tub, has special grooming needs due to her breed, is generally too much of a handful to bathe at home, or you simply don't have the time to dedicate to regular grooming routines, consider calling in the professionals. Ask your vet, check online ratings, or put the word out among your local dog-park network for recommendations for the best professional groomers in your area. Such grooming facilities can provide a one-stop shop for all your coat-grooming needs, including bathing, brushing, combing, clipping, and shaping. Some will come to you and work from a specially prepared van. Most will also trim your dog's nails, which can be a nerve-wracking experience to carry out at home even for those who do have the time and the tools. However, professional grooming can be a scary event for your dog the first couple of times, so make sure you find the right professional for your dog.

208 TURN SCARY INTO FUN

There may occasionally be tasks you need to perform (or equipment you need to use) that scare your dog. This could include brushing your dog, clipping his nails, or even bathing him. While it is always important to try to do these tasks in a way that causes the least stress possible for your dog (keeping the activity short, for example), you can also help calm him by associating the activity with something positive like food. This can be as easy as holding the brush or clippers when you give your dog a treat, or giving him a treat when he's near the tub or hose. This positive association won't make your dog love the activity all by itself, but it can help normalize the activity and remove at least some of the stress around it.

209 RECOGNIZE CANINE COAT TYPES

Selective breeding by humans has led to an enormous range of coat types in domestic dogs. These were often developed for a specific purpose, such as the poodle's woolly coat and cut that aid swimming; the Wire-haired Terrier's tough coat for protection against thorny undergrowth; or the characteristic thick, fluffy coat of spitz-type dogs, designed to protect them from extreme cold. In recent years, dogs' coats have been selected purely for aesthetic purposes, but the different coat types still require different kinds of routine maintenance.

SMOOTH COAT
Smooth coats have very short and relatively sparse hair, which appears almost like bare skin rather than fur. These require little more than a weekly brushing to clear shed hairs and keep the coat looking glossy.

SHORT COAT
Short coats are relatively dense and may comprise an outer coat of thick, straight hair with a downy undercoat close to the skin. Short-coated dogs should be groomed at least once a week.

LONG COAT
Long-coated breeds often have a straight outer coat combined with a dense undercoat. They require daily grooming and, depending upon the breed, may require regular trimming.

SILKY COAT

Silky coats are straight or slightly wavy with a natural sheen. Dogs with these coats are often single coated, and shed seasonally twice a year. Popular breeds with silky coats include the Cocker Spaniel and the Australian Silky Terrier.

WIRY COAT

Wirehaired types are often recommended for allergy sufferers since they do not shed; however, they still need to be brushed at least once a week to prevent matting and require regular hand-stripping or clipping.

CURLY COAT

Poodles, Portuguese Water Dogs, and other curly-coated types have distinctive, non-shedding, waterproof coats. However, the coats need to be clipped at least every two months.

210 CHOOSE THE IDEAL GROOMING KIT

A professional grooming table is a luxury for most dog owners, but can be a real advantage if your dog requires much daily grooming. Getting your dog used to being groomed on a table has certain benefits, including easier access, and it can help to focus your dog's mind on the task at hand—she knows that the grooming process is going to commence when she's lifted onto the table, and she knows that it's over once her paws are back on terra firma. Whether or not you use a table, it is vital that the rest of your equipment is designed for your dog's specific coat type. Your vet will be able to advise you if you are uncertain as to the type of equipment you need.

TABLES AND RESTRAINTS

Hydraulically adjustable tables are available for professional groomers or dog owners with a number of dogs that require extensive coat care. Such tables are very expensive, however, and for most dog owners, a folding table is more than adequate. Even if you use a regular kitchen table, you may want to invest in a grooming arm—a metal bar with strategically placed "eyes" to attach chains, loops, and other restraints that help to keep your dog still and prevent her from falling off the table. Such bars are equipped with strong clamps to secure them to the table. Of course, the cheapest option is a pair of knee pads and a dog that's trained to stand still on command.

TOOTHBRUSH

A toothbrush and toothpaste are essential for keeping your dog's teeth and gums in good shape. Special wipes containing methanol are also available to help keep your dog's teeth clean and fresh.

CLOTHS AND COTTON BALLS

A microfiber cloth is useful for bringing out the shine in a smooth coat, and cotton balls are a must for cleaning around sensitive areas, such as the eyes and ears, as well as for cleaning underneath facial skin folds in certain dog types.

BRUSHES AND COMBS

Brushes and combs help keep your dog's hair from becoming matted and tangled. Wire brushes are best for woolly coats and for grooming dense undercoats, while combs compete with stubborn tangles. A stripping knife can be useful for wire-haired dogs. Rubber brushes help to get rid of dead hair and massage your dog's skin.

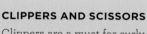

CLIPPERS AND SCISSORS

Clippers are a must for curly-coated dogs, and can be useful for dealing with a heavily matted coat. Use scissors to remove stubborn knots or for fine styling of longer hair. Nail clippers are a must if you intend to trim your dog's nails yourself. It is not a good idea to cut your dog's nails with regular scissors, as it's easy to accidentally cut him if he resists.

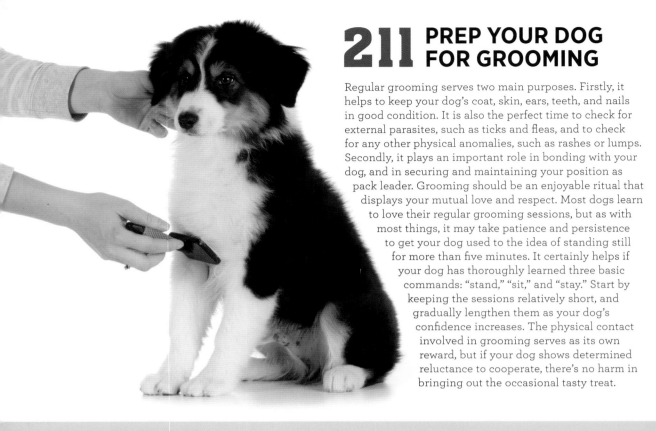

211 PREP YOUR DOG FOR GROOMING

Regular grooming serves two main purposes. Firstly, it helps to keep your dog's coat, skin, ears, teeth, and nails in good condition. It is also the perfect time to check for external parasites, such as ticks and fleas, and to check for any other physical anomalies, such as rashes or lumps. Secondly, it plays an important role in bonding with your dog, and in securing and maintaining your position as pack leader. Grooming should be an enjoyable ritual that displays your mutual love and respect. Most dogs learn to love their regular grooming sessions, but as with most things, it may take patience and persistence to get your dog used to the idea of standing still for more than five minutes. It certainly helps if your dog has thoroughly learned three basic commands: "stand," "sit," and "stay." Start by keeping the sessions relatively short, and gradually lengthen them as your dog's confidence increases. The physical contact involved in grooming serves as its own reward, but if your dog shows determined reluctance to cooperate, there's no harm in bringing out the occasional tasty treat.

212 CLEAN FIDO'S FACE

Your dog's monthly bath time isn't the only time you should be cleaning her face—you should do it every time you groom her. The process takes a matter of minutes—just follow these three simple steps.

STEP 1 Use a damp cotton ball to gently bathe the skin around one of your dog's eyes, then use a fresh ball for the other eye to avoid transferring any infection. Carefully, check for discharge or inflammation.

STEP 2 Clean inside your dog's ears with a moist cotton ball. Again, use a separate ball of cotton for each ear. Don't probe into the ear canal, and never attempt to use a cotton swab unless directed by your vet.

STEP 3 Wipe your dog's forehead and muzzle gently with a damp cotton ball, taking care to clean inside folds and under creases to clear dead skin and prevent the accumulation of bacteria.

213 PREP FOR DENTAL CLEANING

Do you really need to clean your dog's teeth? Absolutely! Allowing bacteria to build up can lead to tartar and gingivitis, which in turn can lead to gum disease (what your vet may call "periodontal disease") or painful dental abscesses. These conditions are bad enough in themselves and can result in tooth loss, but they can even become life threatening if left untreated, as they can spread systemically to other areas of the body, including the liver, kidneys, and heart.

214 TAKE IT SLOW

If your dog isn't used to having his teeth cleaned, the last thing you want to do is frighten him by rushing into the process. Approach him calmly and reassure him in soothing tones. Choose a toothpaste flavor that you think your dog might enjoy, and offer him a sample taste to make sure. Canine toothpaste is available in a variety of flavors, including, mint, malt, beef, chicken, and even cheese. Finding a flavor that your dog enjoys can make the brushing experience more pleasant for your dog and a whole lot easier for you. Once again, the trick is to associate an unfamiliar process with positive rewards.

STEP 1 Start by gently lifting his lip to inspect his teeth. Even this simple act may startle a nervous dog, in which case stop there, praise him, and reward him with a tasty treat. Repeat the process the next day, and for as long as necessary until your dog is comfortable with you messing with his mouth.

STEP 2 Put a little toothpaste on your finger and rub it onto your dog's teeth. Don't use a brush at this stage, since the unfamiliar object may frighten him. Save that for the next step, and just let him enjoy the tasty paste as a reward in itself.

STEP 3 Now introduce the brush, flavored with a little of his favorite toothpaste. Brush one or two teeth, but don't be tempted to rush the process—you're almost there. Stick with it for a few more days, cleaning two teeth each day if necessary, and soon your dog will accept brushing as a part of his regular daily routine.

ASK THE VET
MY DOG KEEPS SHAKING HIS HEAD— WHAT'S UP?

Head shaking, along with ear scratching, can be a sign of an ear disorder. If the behavior persists, it's a good idea to make an appointment to visit your local vet. Some foreign body, such as a seedhead, may have become lodged in your dog's ear, and the vet should be able to dislodge the offending item using special tweezers designed to negotiate the L-shaped tunnel of your dog's ear canal. Ear mites could also be the reason for your pup's agitation and discomfort. These miniscule beasties irritate the ear canal and can stimulate excessive wax production. Your vet will prescribe insecticidal eardrops to clear the mites. Because these mites can also survive outside the ear, you vet will also prescribe an insecticidal shampoo to eliminate ear mites from your dog's coat.

215 CLEAN YOUR DOG'S TEETH

Ideally, you should clean your dog's teeth every day, or at least once a week, to ensure her mouth remains healthy. The key is to familiarize yourself with how her mouth looks when it's in good shape so that you will recognize any changes that may signal a problem. If you notice anything unusual, bring it to the attention of your vet, who will be able to reassure you that everything's okay, or will advise you to make an appointment to take prompt remedial action if something's amiss. When brushing your dog's teeth, make sure you select a soft brush that is the right size for your dog.

STEP 1 Gently lift your dog's upper lip to carefully inspect her teeth and gums. Check for the buildup of tartar on the teeth and watch out for chipped or broken teeth. Also, check for reddening of the gums, which can signal gingivitis, and look out for lumps in the gums, which may indicate the growth of an abscess. Finally, check your dog's breath for any unusual odors that may be a sign of ill health.

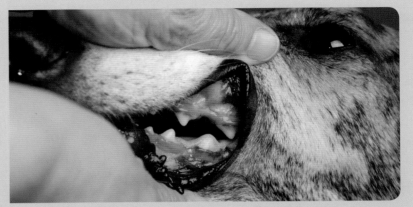

STEP 2 If you're trying a toothpaste flavor for the first time, dip your finger into the paste and rub a little onto your dog's teeth to check that she approves. Then squeeze a pea-sized amount of toothpaste onto your dog's special toothbrush. Lift her lip and gently scrub the outside of the teeth using a circular brushing motion. Over ninety percent of tartar occurs on the outside of the teeth, so you don't have to worry about brushing the back of the teeth. Pet and praise your dog for her cooperation!

DENTAL DOS AND DON'TS

DO	DON'T
• Check your dog's teeth every day.	• Don't use toothpaste designed for humans.
• Use a pet-approved toothpaste.	• Don't use toothbrushes designed for humans
• Feed your dog a healthy diet that promotes dental hygiene.	• Don't give your dog sweet treats—these can upset her stomach and damage her teeth.
• Try a range of toothpaste flavors.	• Don't persist with a toothpaste flavor that your dog clearly doesn't enjoy.
• Give your dog vet-approved chew toys.	

MY DOG'S BREATH SMELLS AWFUL. WHAT SHOULD I DO?

Bad breath is usually caused by a buildup of bacteria in your dog's mouth and stomach. The most common culprit is poor dental hygiene, which allows the accumulation of plaque and tartar to escalate to dangerous levels. Diet can also be a factor, especially if you regularly feed your dog canned food. If you improve your dog's dental regime and change his diet but his breath still smells foul, it could be a sign of a more serious issue, such as diabetes or kidney disease. Be sure to check out the problem with your vet.

216 CLEAN YOUR DOG'S EARS

As part of your grooming routine, regularly check your dog's ears to make sure that they are clean and healthy. Apart from the obvious dangers—bits of debris that might have found their way into your dog's ear during his adventures in the dense undergrowth of the local park—signs of potential trouble can include a buildup of wax, inflammation, or an unpleasant odor. Familiarize yourself with the appearance of your dog's inner ear when he's healthy, and consult your vet if you see anything out of the ordinary. For cleaning the ears, there are plenty of decent over-the-counter cleaning fluids. Always follow the instructions on the bottle. Again, when in doubt, check with your vet. Also, some dogs are very sensitive about their ears being manhandled, so take things slow.

STEP 1 Dampen a cotton ball with ear-cleaning fluid, and carefully lift the earflap. As always, reassure your dog with calming words. Clean the top part of your dog's ear. Don't try cleaning the ear canal until you have been given the okay and clear instruction by your vet (and certainly don't use cotton swabs in the way you would to clean your own ears) without first consulting your vet (see item 217).

STEP 2 Use a fresh cotton ball for the other ear and follow the same procedure. Again, focus on the upper ear and use reassuring words as you gently clean the earflap. Give your patient pet plenty of praise and a tasty treat when the procedure is finished.

ARE BONES GOOD FOR MY DOG?

Wolves and wild dogs eat bones, so they must be safe for domestic dogs too, right? Not necessarily! Cooked bones are more brittle than raw bones and they are likely to splinter, potentially causing injury to the mouth or stomach. They also present a serious choking hazard. Recreational raw bones, on the other hand, can help to break down tartar and reduce the risk of gum disease. Even with raw bones, however, it's best to supervise your dog closely while he's gnawing the bone. When the bone has been reduced to a size that your dog could potentially swallow, throw it away. When in doubt consult your vet or pet store about the safest options.

217 DEEP CLEAN THOSE EARS

With your vet's permission, you may have to treat chronic ear wax with a deep clean by pouring a little cleaning fluid directly into the ear canal and massaging the base of the ear to break up the wax. Never use soap and water, which will not evaporate in the way that cleaning fluids do, and can lead to ear infections. Your vet may show you how to carefully use a cotton swab to remove most of the broken-down wax from your dog's ear canal. However, your dog should instinctively shake his head to clear most of the debris himself (which is a good reason to perform this exercise outdoors if possible). If he doesn't shake his head, try blowing gently on his ear—that usually does the trick! As ever, when in doubt, leave this job to your vet or professional groomer.

218 PREP FOR NAIL TRIMMING

If you hear your dog's nails clicking on the floor, or if you notice them getting snagged on the carpet or in grass at the dog park, it's time to bring out the nail clippers. Although this job is fairly straightforward, many of us are nervous about trying it for the first time, and rightly so. If you accidentally trim your dog's nails back too far, you can cut into the quick, or nail bed. The quick contains the blood supply (so, yes, it will bleed) and nerves (so, yes, it will be painful for your pup!). So, if you have any doubts the first time around, do this under the supervision of your vet or professional groomer. You'll quickly become an expert, and you (and more importantly your pooch) will be far more comfortable with the whole procedure. As far as prepping your dog for trimming, you should make it a part of your daily grooming routine to check your dog's paws for dirt or debris between his toes, or splinters or cuts on his paw pads. Introduce him to the clippers even when you're not ready to use them. Start by clipping a very thin slice off a nail tip so that there's no way you could cut into the quick, and reward him for his tolerance with a tasty treat. Go through this process over a couple of days, trimming a thin slice of each claw on each foot (including dew claws), and then you'll both be more relaxed and ready for the real deal.

219 TRIM YOUR DOG'S NAILS

Whatever you do, don't just ignore your dog's nails because you're worried about hurting her with clippers. Letting them grow could lead to a far more painful experience for your dog as she rips out a claw on the carpet or develops an uncomfortable gait that eventually leads to muscle and joint problems. Follow these two simple steps to trim her nails. All you need is clippers, a nail file, and some styptic pads just in case you do cut into the quick. Again, if you really can't face it, call in the professionals!

STEP 1 Ask your dog to lie down on her side so that you can access each of her paws. Spread each of your dog's toes and remove any dirt or debris with a damp cloth or cotton swab. Clip a thin slice off each nail at a 45-degree angle. By cutting very thin slices rather than making one single cut, you are less likely to cut deeply into the quick, which would be extremely painful.

STEP 2 Repeat the process patiently until you see a gray or pink oval starting to appear, which tells you that you are near the quick and it's time to stop clipping. If you do accidentally cut the quick, apply a styptic pad with a gentle pressure to stop the bleeding.

STEP 3 Finally, file each of the nails to smooth any splintering. Use a gentle pressure, working from the back of the nail toward the tip. Give your dog a high-value treat for her patience and to let her know that nail trimming comes with serious advantages.

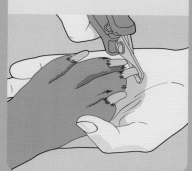

220 GROOM A SMOOTH COAT

Smooth coats are the easiest to maintain. A weekly grooming session can be sufficient to keep your dog looking sleek and shiny. Use the session to check your dog's skin condition and watch out for ticks, fleas, and other external parasites. Follow these three simple steps using a rubber brush, a bristle brush, and a microfiber cloth.

STEP 1 Begin by brushing against the direction of the fur using a rubber brush to loosen surface grime and dead hair. Keep talking to your dog while you work from head to tail.

STEP 2 Now brush the coat again, using a bristle brush to remove dead hair. This time brush briskly with the direction of the coat and, once again, make sure you cover the whole body.

STEP 3 Finally, polish the coat to a lustrous sheen using a cloth. Keep telling him what a good boy he is, and when the job is done reward him with a tasty treat or a favorite toy.

ASK THE VET
MY DOG HAS DRY SKIN. HOW CAN I HELP?

If your dog is continually scratching at his skin, he likely has fleas, or some other skin irritation perhaps caused by an infection or allergy, and you should contact your vet. Left untreated, your dog can create sores known as "hot spots" that are not only painful, but also can lead to infection and other complications. However, if your dog's skin is simply a little dry, or he has what looks like dandruff, this can be normal. Try these techniques to clear up the problem.

1 If you never bathe your dog, try giving him a bath with a medicated shampoo, or a shampoo designed to replenish your dog's natural skin oil.

2 If you give frequent baths to your dog, this may be causing the problem as baths stop your dog's natural skin oil from lubricating his fur. Try bathing less frequently.

3 Ask your vet about what types of foods might support your dog's skin and coat.

4 If you live in a dry climate, try using a humidifier in the room where your dog spends most of his time or sleeps.

221 GROOM A SHORT COAT

Short-coated dogs often have a double coat and need to be groomed more frequently than smooth-coated types—otherwise matting can occur in their relatively dense fur. They also shed more heavily, and this is a problem all year round if your dog spends a lot of time indoors shedding on your furniture. Nevertheless, twice-weekly grooming should be sufficient to keep them looking their best.

STEP 1 Begin by using a slicker brush to free up matted areas and release dead hair from the undercoat. Follow the lie of the coat with the slicker brush and pull dead hair out of the brush to keep it working effectively.

STEP 2 Switch to a bristle brush and briskly groom the coat from head to tail. This step will remove dead hair and any remaining grime from the surface of the coat.

STEP 2 Finally, ask your dog to stand if she isn't already, and use a metal comb to remove tangles from any longer fur, such as feathering on the tail or the back of the legs.

222 GROOM A LONG COAT

Long coats can look spectacular when kept in good condition, but they can quickly become untidy and uncomfortable for your dog if they are allowed to get dirty and matted. Daily grooming is a must for long-haired dogs, especially those dogs with dense undercoats as well as a long top coat.

STEP 1 Use a slicker brush to untangle any matted hair. Brush gently at first to establish where any knots are lurking. Use a wide-toothed comb to break down knots where you can, and be prepared to resort to scissors if a knot proves too stubborn to untangle.

STEP 2 Repeat the process using a pin brush. This time you should meet no resistance from knots or tangles. The brush will quickly fill with dead hair, which must be discarded after every few brushstrokes to keep the brush working efficiently.

STEP 3 Now tidy the feathering on the chest, legs, ears, and tail with a wide-toothed comb. Be particularly careful combing around the ears, as dogs are very sensitive in this area.

STEP 4 Now use the scissors to carefully trim any excessively long hair around your dog's feet, where dirt and debris can accumulate and cause discomfort. You may also wish to trim untidy hairs from the feathering behind the hocks and beneath the dog's tail.

223 GROOM A SILKY COAT

Some dogs have long, luxurious, silky coats but no dense undercoat. They can be groomed in much the same way as other longhaired dogs, but extra care must be taken to avoid scratching the skin. A final flourish with the bristle brush can really bring out the shine in a silky coat. Some purebred dogs, such as Yorkshire Terriers, have been selectively bred over centuries specifically to develop an extravagant silky coat. These dogs need regular attention from a professional groomer to keep their coat in good condition, as well as daily grooming from their owners simply to maintain their coat.

224 CLIP A COAT

The majority of dogs molt all year round, and require little more than a weekly brush to remove dead hair in a controlled way to prevent it from covering the couch. However, some dogs have distinctive curly coats that keep growing and need to be maintained through regular clipping, normally every six to eight weeks depending on the season. This is a complex procedure, which many owners believe is best left to the professionals. Even if you do not want to completely clip a coat, though you must be prepared to clip it occasionally to prevent it from becoming tangled. If you have a thick-coated dog and you live in a hot climate, you may want to give him a full-body clipping to help him stay cool. But leave enough hair length to make sure no skin is exposed to direct sunlight.

225 HANDSTRIP A WIREHAIRED DOG

Wirehaired dogs have to be hand-stripped every three to four months. This process involves pulling out dead hair and/or raking the coat in the direction of growth with a stripping tool (A). Hand-stripping should not cause your dog any discomfort. Specialty stripping knives are also available to aid the process—you can pull the dead hair out between your thumb and the serrated blade, which has no cutting edge (B). Clippers can be used to tidy long hair on the chest area (C).

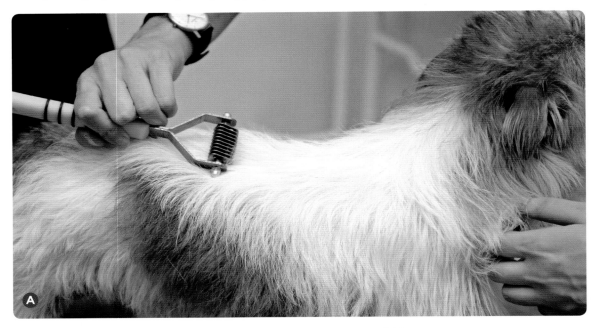

A

B

C

STRIPPING TOOL

226 DRESS TO IMPRESS

One of the benefits of training your dog to sit placidly while you pamper and fuss over her is that she's then more likely to be comfortable with a bit of fun dressing up from time to time. It's not for everyone; some dogs simply hate having things like clothes placed on their body, but many more are pretty neutral and seem willing to have some fun—especially if treats are in store! Small dogs, particularly, can look irresistibly cute with the simple addition of a bow in their hair (and with certain dogs, such Yorkshire Terrier mixes, this can also have the highly practical purpose of enabling your dog to see out from beneath very long fur).

227 CONSIDER CANINE COUTURE

Canine couture is big business today, with a plethora of pet fashions appearing on the market. Harrods of London even has an annual fashion show for pets called Pet-a-Porter, and acclaimed fashion designers, including Vivienne Westwood, often create designer clothes for dogs. Some believe dressing up a dog is cruel and even humiliating. You can decide if your dog is having fun, getting irritated, or just feeling too hot or uncomfortable.

In these days of instant imaging and frenzied social-media file sharing, it's hard to resist dressing up our pets once in a while for laughs, and that's great—as long as your dog's having fun too! Use your common sense and ask yourself a few simple questions before splurging on your dog's designer wardrobe.

IS SHE TOO HOT? An obvious concern is that most dogs already have a warm coat, and making your dog wear clothing on a hot day because you think she looks cute could lead to hyperthermia. Experts generally agree that clothing may be necessary for small, short-coated dogs on very cold days, but otherwise nature generally has it covered.

IS SHE TOO RESTRICTED? Some clothing is restrictive and prevents your dog from going about her normal doggie business. This could be okay for a quick photo, but is undoubtedly cruel if left for too long.

IS SHE COMFORTABLE? Any clothing that is going to be worn for anything other than a brief photo session should be fitted properly for maximum comfort. Clothing that is too tight or too loose can cause discomfort and can potentially be dangerous if your dog becomes entangled.

IS SHE HAVING FUN? Never force your dog to do something she doesn't want to. If you're powers of persuasion are not working when it comes to your dressing-up plans, drop them. Keep it fun.

BONE OF CONTENTION
DOG HAIR TO DYE FOR?

A worrying trend in doggie fashions is the use of hair dyes. Currently, there are no hair dyes made specifically for dogs and their skin can be sensitive to some of the chemicals used in the production of hair dyes, such as ammonia and hydrogen peroxide.

It's easy to see why many of us find these images amusing, but until someone comes up with a safe wash-in, wash-out hair dye specifically for dogs, stick with photo manipulating tools to color your dog's hair—the end result is the same.

228 DRESS UP FOR HALLOWEEN

Dogs especially love the "treat" part of the trick-or-treat season, which can be a reward for wearing a costume. Just remember, the treat must be a doggie treat, and not an actual candy treat for kids!

Picking the right costume for your pet and getting him comfortable wearing it for the full duration of your trick-or-treat rounds or Halloween gathering can take some planning and training. If your pet has never worn a costume, you should start out slowly. Let your dog smell the costume, and give him treats so he associates the costume with good things. Ask him to sit and stay, and reward him as you put the costume on. Don't be too ambitious to begin with—start with a velcro shark fin before working your way up to the full Elvis jumpsuit with wig and sunglasses. If you have an active dog, playing with a toy or taking him for a walk after you put the costume on can distract him from wanting to get the costume off, and get him used to the feeling of having it on, so he ignores it like he does his collar. Here are some more tips to keep the horrible howls out of your Halloween pet-costume fun.

THINK SAFETY FIRST

We all know what to expect at Halloween and half the fun is being a little scared, but recognize that your dog may be freaked out by some of the strangely costumed creatures leaping around him—he may prefer to stay at home.

AVOID FLAMES

Fireworks are increasingly popular at Halloween, but the noise can be terrifying for dogs and sparks can cause accidents. Candles, of course, are everywhere on Halloween and the naked flames and often highly flammable costumes can be a real danger for dogs and children alike. Keep your dog on a leash and away from fire.

CHOOSE QUICK-RELEASE CLOTHES

Go for a costume that can be taken off quickly, like those with velcro straps (shark fin, angel wings, etc.).

SUPERVISE DRESSING UP

Never leave your pet unsupervised wearing a costume for any length of time. He may try to escape from his clothes and this could result in a serious injury.

KEEP IT FUN!

Again, if your pet continues to struggle or seems unhappy or scared after one or more short sessions, wearing a costume is not fun for him, and you should never force your pet to dress up. Costumes are meant to be fun!

PILE ON THE PRAISE!

Most dogs love to be admired and told how cute they look, so don't forget to lavish your dog with compliments about how adorable he looks in his costume.

229 TAKE PICS OF YOUR POOCH

Halloween is a great time to have your pup join in the dress-up fun, and it's never been easier to share your spooky snaps with the rest of the dog-loving community by posting your pics on social media. The online options are growing every day, but Facebook is still the top social networking service and the obvious first port of call for sharing photos with friends and family. Flickr, too, is highly recommended as a great way to store, sort, and share your photos online. Meanwhile, Instagram allows you to share your snaps in a snap using your mobile phone, and links to the big guns at Facebook and Twitter. YouTube is still the best place to visit for sharing video footage with the world, especially if you think your pet has the potential to reach real superstar status.

However, it's only worth posting a photo if it's a great shot, and we all know how tough it can be to get our pets to say "cheese." But fear not: internationally renowned animal photographer Tracy Morgan is here to help by sharing her top ten tips to get professional results next time your dog's on the catwalk.

TOP TEN TIPS FOR PET PORTRAITURE

1 CLEAR AWAY CLUTTER Yes, you can crop it later and get rid of the bargain bucket in the background, but only at the expense of image quality. Clearing away any distracting objects from the background—or as much as is possible—is the simplest way to heighten the impact of your portrait.

2 FOCUS ON THE NOSE You generally focus on the eyes when taking portraits of people and flat-faced, pug-like pooches. However, with the majority of dogs, focusing on the eyes puts the nose out of focus. Focus, instead, on that big, shiny, black nose.

3 GET THE ANGLE RIGHT The temptation is to photograph from above, since your eye level is, we're guessing, higher than your pet's. Shake things up and get down to photograph your pet at her eye level, or even below, for a more striking and original image.

4 FILL THE FRAME If you don't have time to clear away clutter—your dog might not still be playing the banjo by the time you've finished spring cleaning— move in close to avoid background noise and maximize dramatic effect.

5 TAKE CANDID SHOTS Where possible, use the zoom function rather than trying to physically sneak up on your dog. The most interesting shots are often taken when our loved ones are unaware. Dogs aren't especially self-conscious, but they will be curious about what you're up to and will switch their attention to their beloved pack leader before you can say, "Darn it, that would've made a great photo!"

6 RELAX AND ENJOY Once again, your greatest friends when dealing with pets are patience and persistence. If you're determined to take a great shot and you get too worked up about it, your supersensitive pal will pick up on the vibe and start to look nervous. Take your time, don't bark commands, and don't get tense. If you enjoy the experience, chances are she will too.

7 GET THE LIGHT RIGHT Even though the cameras on most mobile phones these days will deal remarkably well with low light levels, it is still better to shoot in a brighter area when possible. Direct sunlight, however, can cast distracting shadows, so choose diffused light. You can reflect some light back into shadows using a white blanket or, better still, a piece of cardboard wrapped with aluminum foil. This, of course, only works if your dog is super well-behaved and happy to sit still in that tutu while you buzz around with bed sheets and baking foil.

8 AVOID USING DIRECT FLASH Flash can be great for freezing an action shot, such as a dog leaping for a ball, which might come out as a big blur leaping for a smaller blur in low-light conditions. But in portraits, direct flash can produce a boring flat image. Worse still, your cuddly pooch could turn into a devil dog with ghostly, glowing eyes due to the tapeta-lucida effect. Perfect for Halloween, though!

9 PAY YOUR SUPERMODEL We've mentioned patience and persistence, but don't forget positive reinforcement. A favorite toy will help to keep her mind focused on the task at hand. If she isn't watching her waistline, food treats may help, too—unless she's hungry and particularly prone to drooling!

10 TELL A STORY We all know our own pooch is the most beautiful in the world, but do others get the same emotional jolt just by looking at her cute little face? Maybe, if she really is that cute, but usually it's safer to have some kind of story going on that people can get excited about. Halloween is perfect, but coming up with a good story is possible at any time of year.

230 GET THE FACTS ON FLEAS

Have you ever had an itch that just wouldn't stop itching? You've probably got one now from just thinking about it! Imagine if you had that all the time and in many places on your body. That is what it's like for a dog who has fleas that go untreated. And not only is it a constant painful annoyance, but it can also lead to other diseases and infections as well, including tapeworms, anemia, and even plague!

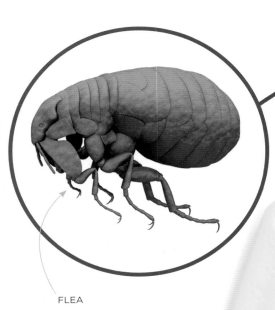

FLEA

FLEA COMB

231 CHECK YOUR DOG FOR FLEAS

You can check your dog for evidence of fleas right now with this quick, three-step test. All the equipment you'll need is a plain paper towel or tissue and a flea comb from your vet's office or local specialty pet store.

STEP 1 Have your pet lie in the "belly-rub" or "roll-over" position. This will help you to get a good, clear look at his or her skin where the hair is less dense. Do you see any fleas or little black specks (possible flea poop)?

STEP 2 If you didn't see anything alarming in step 1, gently run the comb through the fur on your dog's chest just to make sure. When you pull your comb away, do you see little black specks?

STEP 3 If you do find black specks, you need to know if it's just plain dirt or dastardly flea poop. Using a clean and damp white paper towel, wipe the black specks. If they turn red when they come in contact with the towel, you may have a flea infestation. It's time to see your vet.

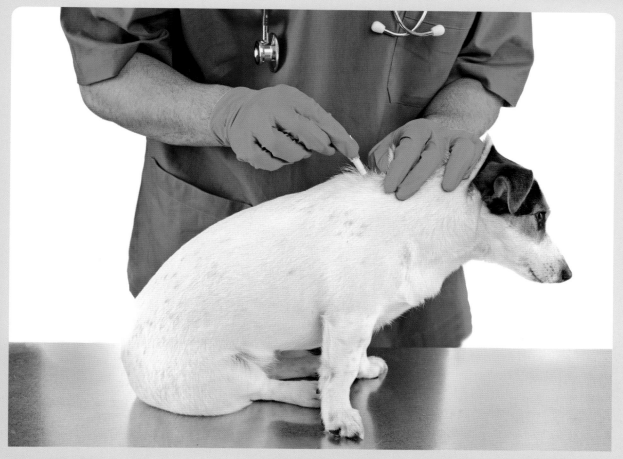

232
FREE YOUR HOME FROM FLEAS

Fleas are a very common problem for dogs. Fleas are just as happy inside or outside your house, and they jump onto your dog and bite her to feed. In the home, they spend most of their time in your carpet and upholstery. If they are in your house, they may be biting you but you might not notice. Or, you might notice small red bug bites around your feet and ankles.

The trick to controlling fleas is to deal with both your dog and your home environment. There are several ways to keep fleas at bay, and most veterinarians will recommend starting a regular routine to keep your pet safe.

FOR YOUR DOG

You can treat your dog to remove fleas in a number of ways. Most vets now recommend topical treatments that are applied to your dog's skin about once per month, and which then spread through the skin to kill the fleas. Also, flea-repellent powders can be sprinkled on your pet's coat every few weeks, and your dog can wear special flea-collars. The occasional bath with a shampoo designed to kill or repel fleas and ticks is a good idea, too.

FOR YOUR HOME

Fleas live in carpets, under furniture, or anywhere that they can safely hide. Vacuuming frequently helps, but is often not enough. There are products that use borate powder, which is a natural pesticide that's safe for your pets. Brushing these powders into your carpet makes it impossible for fleas to survive there. Finally, be sure to spray your dog's bedding with suitable biological spray to stop flea eggs from hatching and rebooting the parasitic cycle.

233 RECOGNIZE COMMON EXTERNAL PARASITES

PARASITE	DESCRIPTION AND SYMPTOMS	REMEDY
BLOWFLY MAGGOTS	Fly larvae are small white grubs that feed on dead flesh and fecal matter, performing a fabulous, free waste-disposal service in nature. However, they are also the cause of the dreaded "fly strike" in dogs and other pets. This problem is most prevalent in older dogs that are kept outdoors and have trouble cleaning themselves, in any dogs that are neglected with dirty and matted fur, or in dogs that are suffering from diarrhea. Blowflies most commonly lay their eggs around the anal region, and the resulting maggots infest the area and damage the skin.	This extremely unpleasant condition needs to be treated immediately. The maggots are removed using hydrogen peroxide, and the infected area is treated with an antiseptic. Prevention is simple: Keep your dog clean and apply a fly repellent in the summer months. If your dog has long fur, it helps to trim the hair around your dog's anus as part of his regular grooming routine to help keep the area clean and less likely to attract flies.
CHEYLETIELLA MITES	Often mistaken for dandruff, these highly contagious white mites are barely visible to the naked eye. Infestations result in actual dandruff forming on your dog's back and can cause a rash to form on the skin—on humans as well as dogs.	Your vet will prescribe an insecticidal shampoo to destroy the mites. Be sure to use the shampoo on all your dogs, even if only one appears to be infected. Also, clean all your dogs' bedding to ensure the pesky beasts don't make a comeback.
DEMODEX CANIS	Invisible to the naked eye, these cigar-shaped mange mites can result in very nasty rashes and/or pustules if left untreated. They live in or close to canine hair follicles and are most commonly a problem in elderly dogs (although they can infect younger dogs, too). The most common sites for early appearance of this form of mange are the face and forelegs.	Your vet will prescribe an insecticidal treatment to be applied on a weekly basis until the infection clears up. Pustules indicate a secondary bacterial infection that can be treated with antibiotics.

PARASITE	DESCRIPTION AND SYMPTOMS	REMEDY
HARVEST MITE, TROMBICULA AUTUMNALIS	Also known as a "chigger," this tiny red mite appears in the fall and lays eggs in damp soil. It is the barely visible larval stage of the mite that emerges and climbs up the nearest blade of grass to hitch a ride on the next passing mammal, which may be your dog. This mite tends to irritate paws specifically, and you may notice your dog licking his feet obsessively to alleviate the discomfort.	The larvae abandon their host after a few days and develop into adults in the soil, ready to begin the next cycle. Your vet can deal with the mite using insecticidal shampoos and anti-inflammatory drugs.
LICE, TRICHODECTES CANIS	Clearly visible to the naked eye, these flat-bodied lice slowly crawl around on a dog's skin to feed and glue their tiny, white eggs, known as "nits," to the fur. Female lice lay up to a hundred nits at a time, so infestations can occur rapidly. These lice are known to transmit tapeworms to dogs. Heavy infestations of lice are intensely irritating, but are rare in domestic dogs unless they are neglected.	Treatment involves a combination of combing with a special nit comb, and bathing the dog with a medicated shampoo.
SARCOPTIC MANGE MITE, SARCOPTES SCABIEI CANIS	This microscopic parasite burrows into a dog's skin to and causes canine scabies, or sarcoptic mange, which is agonizingly irritating. Symptoms include frantic scratching, rashes, and hair loss. Humans, too, can be briefly infected, although the symptoms are far less severe. Early infestation in dogs usually appears around the ears and elbows, which become scaly and scabby.	Your vet will prescribe a month-long course of insecticidal-shampoo treatments to destroy the mites. However, mites are able to survive for several days off the dog, so all bedding should be destroyed to avoid a recurrence of the infection.
TICKS, IXODES SP., DERMACENTOR SP.	Although often difficult to spot at first, ticks quickly engorge themselves on their host's blood and swell to become clearly visible unless concealed on the dog's skin—for example, beneath an ear flap or between the toes. Some *Dermacentor* ticks in the United States can cause paralysis, and the deer tick *Ixodes scapularis* can transmit Lyme disease, which can spread to humans.	Regular and thorough grooming will expose ticks attached to your dog's skin. Any ticks should be removed as quickly as possible using tweezers and rubbing alcohol.

234 TERMINATE THAT TICK

As a dog owner you have to learn not to be squeamish when it comes to dealing promptly with these bloated little devils. If left untreated they can lead to a range of serious secondary ailments. However, make sure you don some rubber gloves so that you don't inadvertently make direct contact with the tick or the bite area. Once you've removed the tick, it is advisable to keep it stored in a sealed container to show to your vet should your dog subsequently fall ill with a secondary infection. Throwing ticks in the garbage or even down the toilet will not necessarily destroy them. The best option is to put it in a small, screw-top jar containing some rubbing alcohol.

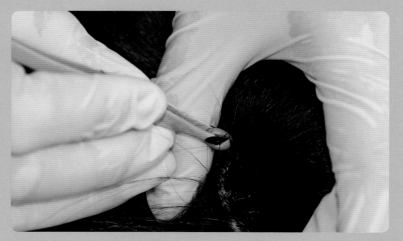

STEP 1 Swab the tick and the skin on which it is feeding using a cotton ball or a tissue soaked in rubbing alcohol.

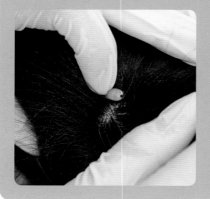

STEP 2 Using a pair of tweezers, grasp the tick as close to your dog's skin as possible. Take care to avoid pinching his skin. Pull straight upward with an even pressure to remove the tick, and take care to remove the head and mouthparts as well as the body.

STEP 3 Clean the bite area thoroughly with a suitable disinfectant. If any mouthparts remain, do not try to dig them out with tweezers. Instead, apply a warm compress and allow the dog's body to expel them naturally.

STEP 4 Dispose of the tick by placing it in a jar of rubbing alcohol. Do not crush the tick, as its gut content may contain infectious fluids. Remember to sterilize your tweezers by cleaning them in alcohol, or if they're made of metal briefly—and carefully—holding them over a naked flame.

STEP 5 Ask your vet about topical tick preventative treatments to avoid further bites. Tick bites are dangerous for your dog and must be prevented.

235 USE A TICK LASSO

Tweezers are not the only option for removing ticks, and they are not always the best tool for the job. If you live in an area where ticks are rampant, it's worth investing in a specialty tool such as a tick "lasso," which is a pen-shaped device with a thin wire at the end that loops over the tick and tightens to reliably remove the parasite, mouthparts and all. Because the lasso adapts to the size of the tick, a firm grip can be maintained on even the tiniest of these troublesome parasites.

ASK THE VET

MY DOG RUBS HIS REAR ALONG THE GROUND. WHAT'S UP?

If your dog adopts a sitting position and drags his rear along the ground with his back paws raised, it is commonly a sign of impacted anal glands. This semi-comical action is usually accompanied by excessive grooming in the anal region.

However, bottom-dragging can also be a sign of worm infestation. Check for signs of rice-like eggs attached to the hair around the anal region, which could be a sign of tapeworm infestation. When in doubt, consult your vet for a check up.

236 DEAL WITH INTERNAL PARASITES

Parasitic worms, such as roundworms and whipworms, can cause your dog considerable discomfort and can sometimes result in vomiting or diarrhea. All puppies should be routinely dewormed from two weeks of age.

Puppies may become infected with roundworm before birth, which causes them to gain weight poorly and have a distinct potbelly and a dull coat. Some worms can be passed on to humans.

INTERNAL PARASITES			
ROUNDWORM *Toxocara canis*	**TAPEWORM** *Dipylidium caninum*	**WHIPWORM** *Trichuris vulpis*	**HOOKWORM** *Uncinaria stenocephala*
SYMPTOMS Growing up to 6 inches (15 cm) long, roundworms are spaghetti-like parasites that can lead to vomiting and diarrhea containing the pale worms.	Growing up to 18 inches (46 cm) long, tapeworms have a segmented, flat body. They lead to increased appetite, but rarely cause clinical symptoms.	Growing up to 2 ½ inches (7 cm) long, whipworms live in the intestines and have a short, fat body with a longer, thinner tail. They can cause diarrhea and anemia.	Invisible to the naked eye, these microscopic parasites feed on blood in the small intestine and can cause severe anemia and diarrhea.
REMEDY Deworming medicines that destroy all stages of the life cycle are readily available from pet stores or your veterinarian clinic. All dogs should be dewormed every three months to prevent the worm from reappearing.	Deworm your dog regularly with a medication approved by your local vet. Also, control fleas, as your dog can become infected with a tapeworm by swallowing an infected flea while grooming herself.	You will need to consult your vet, who will perform special tests to confirm the infestations and will provide the appropriate treatment. Improve hygiene, as whipworms usually occur in young dogs kept in unhygienic conditions.	You will need to consult your vet, who will provide the appropriate treatment. Improve hygiene; hookworms infest damp, unhygienic bedding and the larvae can cause skin irritation.
PARASITE			

237 GIVE YEAR-ROUND CARE

Although a dog's basic needs don't change from one day to the next—he'll always need food and water, a good daily walk in all but the most extreme weather conditions, and year-round love and affection—be aware of the changing conditions, hazards, and responsibilities that come with the changing seasons. Seasonal festivities and celebrations can also pose specific problems for our canine companions.

SPRING

Spring arrives and we love to see the sunshine returning and flowers starting to bloom. But did you know that a lot of spring plants are actually toxic to pets? Tulips, hyacinths, and daffodils are especially dangerous, particularly if you have a pup who likes to dig and can't resist chewing those tasty-looking bulbs.

SUMMER

As temperatures rise, dogs left outside, in cars, or in non-air-conditioned rooms are endangered by heat-related problems such as heatstroke—not to mention scorching sidewalks. This is peak season for fleas and other parasites. Barbecues also present a host of dangers for dogs, and Fourth of July explosions cause many dogs stress and even make them jump fences.

FALL

With extra rain and mud, extra grooming may be required, and colder days mean older dogs' arthritis might start to act up. Fall is the major mushroom season, so be particularly vigilant on woodland walks. And snakes can get grumpy at this time of year. Also, Halloween and Thanksgiving bring a host of hazards for dogs.

WINTER

Snow and ice bring their accompanying delights and dangers, including salt and antifreeze. People are less inclined to take long walks, so dogs may need more indoor playtime. Frostbite and hypothermia are the real dangers when temperatures plummet. Like us, dogs gravitate to hot spots indoors, so pet-proof your fireplace.

238 WATCH OUT FOR WINTER HAZARDS

The holiday season brings many pleasures to our four-legged friends: family gatherings, special trips, and in many areas some chilly white fluffy stuff to frolic in.

However, many pet owners don't realize that when the temperatures drop, the unexpected risks for pets rise. Here are the main things to watch out for.

ROCK SALT If you live in a cold climate where winter brings snow and ice, then you're familiar with rock salt. Rock salt, also called road salt, is sodium chloride mixed with other chemicals, and is used to keep sidewalks and roadways free from ice. While the mixture works well, it is very tough on our pets' paws and can be extremely dangerous if ingested. Other de-icing agents should also be avoided in areas where pets congregate. If you must walk your dogs on surfaces with rock salt, purchase non-slip dog booties to protect their paws.

HEATING SOURCES Dogs may enjoy cozying up near the fireplace to bask in the warmth, but this activity (or inactivity) is dangerous because of the exposure to flames and high temperatures that can potentially burn their skin. In addition, pet parents need to be extra cautious when exposing their furry friends to electric blankets and space heaters because these electrical items can also create too much heat for your pet.

ANTIFREEZE Dogs may be drawn to engine coolant because it has a sweet taste, and this exceedingly toxic substance that contains ethylene glycol can be found anywhere vehicles drive or park, including streets, roadways, parking lots, or even your own driveway. If ingested, this fluorescent green fluid can cause kidney failure or even death in pets. Since it's used to control the freezing and boiling point of liquids, antifreeze is not exclusively a winter hazard, but is also quite dangerous during the warmer months.

FESTIVE FOODS
Meats and sweets are treats that dogs beg for, but they can be serious no-nos when it comes to her health. Turkey and other holiday meats are very high in protein, but if meats in their natural form are not a regular part of your dog's diet, they can be hard to digest, which can lead to

vomiting, diarrhea, or inflammation of the pancreas. Chocolate may be the best-known food danger for dogs because it contains caffeine. Dogs do not metabolize this stimulant in their liver, and elevations in heart rate and blood pressure, or even seizures, coma, or death can occur. Of course, all candy is high in sugar, which can cause digestive issues and dental problems for pets.

WINTER PLANTS Although they look pretty, many holiday plants can be poisonous to pets. Mistletoe, poinsettias, holly, and Christmas cactus are all extremely toxic and can cause severe gastrointestinal, cardiovascular, and neurological effects if ingested. Christmas trees are also hazardous, not only because the pine needles are poisonous, but also because of the bacteria and fertilizer harbored in the water stands (which dogs are known to drink from). Additionally, decorations such as tinsel can be very noxious if consumed. So if you have these decorations, keep them elevated and away from your dog.

239 EXPLORE THE SNOW

You only have to watch your dog frolic around to appreciate that deep snow can be just as much fun for your dog as it is for you and your kids. Many dogs are equipped to cope, sporting thick double coats that can withstand biting cold. However, dogs with smooth coats don't do well in the cold, and most types are vulnerable to frostbite and hypothermia when conditions are freezing, especially when there's a strong wind. Examine your pet's feet and ears, which will be the first to show signs of frostbite by turning cold, pale, and insensitive.

240 GIVE AN ADOPTION OPTION FOR THE HOLIDAYS

You should never give a pet as a surprise gift to anyone. Having a pet is a lifelong commitment and requires a lot of forethought and preparation. If, however, you already intend to adopt a pet, have done all your preparation, and are just waiting for the right time, then adopting a pet during the holiday period can be a wonderful family event. It can be a life-changing reward for a well-behaved child who has been asking for a dog, and a life-saving opportunity for a dog who has been looking for a new family to adopt her.

PICK THE PERFECT PET Take your child or loved one to your local shelter and let them help you pick out their new pet. Remember, however, that your child may find that Lab-mix puppy adorable, but you may see a huge commitment and a serious shoe-destruction risk. You might prefer to adopt a calmer, likely-past-the-worst-chewing-stage adult dog . . . or a cat!

GIVE A DONATION AS A GIFT Certain loved ones might prefer that you spend your money in their honor to help a pet in need, rather than spending it on a gift that may not hold as much meaning. Consider what you would have spent on a gift, and, instead, make a donation in honor of your loved one to your local animal shelter or rescue organization.

BE RESPONSIBLE Parents should know that children may promise they will be fully responsible for a pet's care, and be passionate and persuasive and absolutely mean it at the time, but they don't always fully appreciate the time and effort involved. Ensure there is a resident adult who is willing to take full responsibility for exercise, training, feeding, and vet care for the pet's entire life.

GIVE YOUR PUP A PRESENT When it comes to gift giving, don't forget to give your pup a gift as well. This could be a new toy, a special outing to the dog park, or some new, tasty dog treat. Be wary, however, of leaving an edible treat beneath a Christmas tree—your impatient pup may be tempted to open it early. Holidays are our time to show we care, so show you care about your pup, too!

241 DRESS FOR WINTER

Dogs that don't have a double coat, or older and/or smaller dogs that feel the cold despite their extra layer, may need a little help to get through the chilliest winter months. Naturally, there are high-quality designer products out there for those with the budget, and you can make your own clothes as long as they don't restrict your dog's natural movement and behavior. Boots are a must for many dogs when temperatures plummet.

DESIGNER This specially designed waterproof jacket with its fake-fur-lined hood is both trendy and practical for a dog who's clearly meant for warmer climes. Chihuahua mixes need extra layers in winter.

MADE TO ORDER If someone in your family has the necessary skills, it can be nice to make clothes for your best friend. Here, a child's sweater has been adapted to provide sleeves for this terrier.

SUITED AND BOOTED Despite her thick double coat, this miniature mutt benefits from added protection. Fit boots at the pet store to guarantee that they're the correct size and won't fall off.

ASK THE VET
MY DOG HAS HYPOTHERMIA! WHAT CAN I DO?

Hypothermia is most common in dogs that have fallen into freezing water. Initial signs are shivering and weakness, with breathing difficulties developing in more severe cases. If you suspect your dog is suffering from hypothermia, wrap him in a blanket or a thick, dry towel to keep him warm, and take him immediately to a veterinarian.

242 KEEP YOUR DOG SAFE IN SUMMER

The sun is out and it's fun, fun, fun for dog owners and their pets, with more quality time together on summer vacations and more day trips to the beach and countryside. However, summertime also presents its own specific risks to your dog's health and safety. Here are some summertime hazards to watch out for.

BLOCK SUNBURN Believe it or not, dogs can get sunburned, too, either on their nose or on exposed skin. Your dog should always have access to shade and shelter, especially during the summer months, but on really hot days, it may make sense to use a sunscreen specifically designed for dogs.

STOP HEATSTROKE Never leave your dog in the car for any length of time on a hot day. Even with the window left open, the interior can get hot and your dog could suffer from heatstroke, signalled by drooling and rapid, heavy panting, which can very rapidly prove fatal.

TEST THE TARMAC Surfaces can get baking hot in summer, and we shoe-donning humans don't always notice that our dog's foot pads are in danger of serious burns. Hold your hand to the floor for a few seconds. If it's too hot for you, it's too hot for your dog. Those booties aren't just useful in winter!

AVOID DEHYDRATION During the hot summer days, dogs need water more than ever. Keep an extra-keen eye on the water bowl and replenish it regularly. If you keep your dog outdoors, never leave his water bowl in direct sunlight, where the water can quickly become hot and evaporate.

BEWARE OF PICNIC PERILS For many of us, summertime means barbecues, cookouts, and other outdoor fun. But many of the parties and activities that are fun for humans can present real dangers to pets. Keep your pets safe indoors, or at least away from the food and flames.

BEAT THE BUGS Remember, ticks, fleas, and other pesky parasites are most prevalent during the summer months. Keep a special lookout for signs of parasitic infestation when grooming, and ask your vet for advice on topical flea and tick preventatives, and other ways to keep your pet safe.

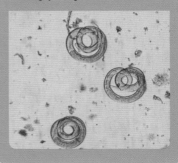

243

BEAT THE BBQ BLUES

Before your next big backyard bash, beware of the dangers listed below. Once you've read up on these picnic perils, you may decide that it's best to keep your dog indoors during the party, or at least keep him in an enclosed area or on a leash so that he is kept safely away from the fires, food, and lighter fluid.

HARMFUL FOOD Picnics and barbecues mean foods that can be harmful to your dog. Most prepared human food isn't good for pets, including potato salad and other rich dishes they might be able to get at during a picnic or barbecue. Pancreatitis can be brought on by eating overly greasy or fatty foods, many of which are found at barbecues.

GOOEY-EYED GUESTS Remember that you might not feed your pets from the table, but can you guarantee that your guests will be able to resist those doe eyes? Even if you warn your guests not to feed the dog (and they stay determined and sober enough to follow your rules), your dog might just take the opportunity to jump up and sneak a bite where he shouldn't, or provide a quick cleanup of someone's spilled food.

LETHAL LEFTOVERS After parties, there are often food scraps on the ground, and certainly in the garbage. These scraps may include cooked bones, which are very harmful to dogs because they create sharp splinters when chewed. Trash can also contain all kinds of other foods and plastics, which are all very harmful to your dog if ingested. So be sure to keep your dog's environment clear and separated from this kind of trash.

LIGHTER FLUID AND FLAMES It's not just the food at the barbecue that can harm your dog. Lighter fluid is also dangerous, because it is highly flammable if spilled and highly toxic if ingested. The fire itself, of course, can be very dangerous for your dog, especially as he may jump up, or wildly wag his tail close to the flames. Fire that is "baited" with tasty food is doubly dangerous for your dog.

BUG SPRAYS Bug repellents meant for people can be harmful to your pet if ingested. Be sure to keep them locked away and out of your dog's reach. Never spray an insect repellent designed for humans onto your dog's coat. Your dog will almost certainly try to clean his coat with his tongue, which can lead to serious risks of illness and poisoning.

CALLIE—MORE THAN JUST A PRETTY FACE

Getting abandoned animals and new families together isn't easy at the best of times. In Houston, Texas, where temperatures soar to more than 90ºF (32ºC) from June to October, adoption work can become impossible in summer, as many adoption venues are forced to shut down. The heat is just too hard on the animals, the volunteers, and the potential adopters alike. SAVE Rescue, based in Santa Fe, Texas, decided to meet the problem head-on and built a completely self-contained, air-conditioned adoption trailer to provide a storefront for rescue groups in the Texas area.

One particularly lucky pet who has been helped by SAVE is Callie, a small Maltese mix, who was abandoned with what are believed to be her two daughters in a trailer park in a small town outside of Houston. The three dogs were left cold and tired, but were glad to be in the shelter when they arrived. However, the small shelter that took in the pups filled up quickly and their time was soon up, which was when a volunteer contacted SAVE to ask if they could take them. SAVE took in all three, and the two younger dogs were adopted shortly afterward (together) by a wonderful family.

The custom-designed, 30-foot (9-m) vehicle houses up to 20 dogs (or cats) in its upper and lower kennels, and SAVE hopes that having the trailer as a comfortable, professional venue to showcase their abandoned pets at special events in high-traffic areas will increase summertime adoptions dramatically. The signs are positive, as the trailer's first two events resulted in three new adoptions. Of course, the trailer—with its portable generator, refrigerator, and amenities for volunteers—serves the group just as well in the winter months. With the help of sponsorship and donations from the public, SAVE intends to keep the "Maxmobile" on the road year-round so that more animals can be saved each year.

For little Callie, however, the adoption journey was far from over. Callie had a bad skin condition, which she battled for three months. She had transformed from a mangy, ragged pup into a budding beauty, but her troubles continued: She was taken on a sleepover by a couple and returned when it was discovered that her skin issue had still not completely resolved. No one could figure out why Callie's otherwise pretty face just would not heal. Finally, one of SAVE's wonderful vets looked closely at Callie's teeth and discovered she had a very bad abscess that was continually breaking through to the skin on her face. The mystery was finally solved. The tooth came out and Callie was really on the mend this time.

Throughout this experience Callie was a little trouper, never grumpy and always loving to her foster mom and family. The hair on her face was still growing in, but SAVE decided that it was time for her to go out and meet the public again. SAVE had their new trailer out for the second time and Callie was at the event. She was getting ready to take a walk when a lovely couple walked in. They were actually there to see another dog, but their eyes fell on Callie, with her "slightly crooked smile," and it was love at first sight. After some questions, an application, and a meet and greet with her new brother Doxie, Callie went "home"

for the first time in months. She came back to visit a few days later, and although she was still very friendly, she was ready to go back to her new "mom" right away. She knew she was where she was meant to be. Her adoring foster mom missed her very much, but she was so glad that Callie "had finally found her forever home."

SAVE received a grant from Adopt-a-Pet.com to enable them to complete the graphics for the outside of the trailer, so that it could also act as a rolling billboard for adoption events and for adopting a pet in general. The pictures here show the adoption trailer at one of its first events— before it was spruced up with its wonderful new graphics.

The photos also show the brave little trouper Callie—at the shelter during her recovery, and with her new loving family.

244 COPE WITH FEAR OF THUNDER

Does your dog start trembling the moment he hears the low rumbling of thunder in the distance? Does he dive under the bed or even into the bathtub (yes, it does happen!) trying to escape from the "attack" of thunder and lightning? Some pets will go into a total panic attack trying to run away from the terrifying noise, even to the point of hurting themselves. Some will become incontinent with fear, so be prepared, and be understanding. It is thought that dogs can sense a storm's approach by the rapidly falling barometric pressure, and so can begin to show signs of anxiety even before the storm can be heard. But there's good news: While thunderstorms can instill fear in dogs, they can learn to manage their reactions and feel calmer through all the noise and bright flashes. Here are five tips to help your dog get safely through any passing thunderstorms.

1 No surprises here, but it's worth repeating: Be sure that your dog's identification tag is securely fastened to his collar in case he makes his own lightning-fast bolt out of the front door. Haven't gotten a microchip yet? Now is a great time. If your dog already has a microchip, make sure it's registered with your current information.

2 If your dog spends a lot of time outside, bring him indoors until the storm blows over. Dogs that are outdoors are more likely to be lost or even injured if they flee from their yards during a storm. Once your dog is safely inside, close all the windows and draw the curtains to dampen the noise and hide the flashes.

3 Create a peaceful den where your dog can feel safe. This is another time when having an indoor kennel or crate where your dog feels secure can be a real boon. It can also protect your property, as some dogs react to fear by chewing furniture or engaging in other unintentionally destructive behaviors.

4 Keep calm and carry on! Dogs can sense fear in their human family, so if you panic, it's more likely that he will too. Play a game with your dog or enjoy an impromptu grooming session. Music, played at normal volume, can also help to soothe your dog. Although it's tempting to try to calm him with soothing words, experts believe that this will sound like praise and may actually heighten his agitation.

5 Keep your dog away from doors that lead outside, as he may bolt if another family member opens the door unexpectedly. As well as the risk of your dog being lost or injured, there is also a danger that the person returning home may be knocked over and injured.

245

PLAN YOUR VACATION CAREFULLY

When planning a vacation, decide right away whether your dog will be coming with you or staying home. If your dog is going to stay at home, you'll need to find a trusted friend or professional pet sitter to care for him while you are away. Remember to leave that person with more than enough food, very clear written instructions about your dog's feeding and walking habits, emergency numbers for other friends and family and your vet, and any other info you want the person to know. Tape a copy of all instructions to a kitchen cupboard. Call each day to check on your dog—if your dog sitter became incapacitated, how else would you know?

246

TRAVEL SAFELY WITH YOUR DOG

If you are bringing your dog with you on a trip, be sure to check with all the places you intend to stay to make sure they allow dogs. If it is a car trip, plan on frequent stops to let your dog out for a drink and to do his business. Be sure to always pull off the main road or highway, onto a smaller street, and always keep your dog securely leashed or harnessed. Having your dog run away on a crowded or unknown street would be a nightmare—and very dangerous for your dog. If you are traveling by plane, be sure that the airline allows dogs, that you have alerted them your dog is coming and paid any fees, and that you are abiding by all of their regulations regarding safely transporting a dog on a plane.

247 HIRE A DOG WALKER OR SITTER

Ideally, you will have a good friend or family member who knows and loves your dog and who is delighted to look after her while you are away. If not, however, there are some excellent professionals out there who can do just as good a job of caring for your dog. In fact, it can be better to leave your dog in the hands of caring professionals—rather than with well-meaning friends or neighbors who don't have the time or experience to look after your pet properly. But don't leave it to the last minute to decide, because good professionals are in high demand, especially in the peak holiday season.

1 Do they have liability insurance and bonding, and how much coverage? Accidents can happen, so you want to make sure they are professionals and have proper insurance in place.

2 Are their pet sitters actual employees or independent contractors? This is important for liability reasons. If a company hires actual employees, then you know they're more likely to be around for a while. In addition, you'll know they are a legitimate company and that they value their sitters.

Also, you need to run a very careful check on the company to make sure your dog (not to mention your house) is in safe hands. Whether you're considering an independent pet sitter or a company, make sure a background check has been run on anyone who will be working with you. Even if they tick all the boxes on your checklist (see below), you should still leave your dog with them for a day or a weekend before leaving her in their charge for a week or more. Here are the top ten questions to ask—and you can probably think of plenty more that are specific to your particular dog.

3 Is there a background check on all sitters? Some pet sitters/dog walkers may seem great when you meet them and say all the right things, but you are trusting them with your pets and access to your home, so it makes sense to be extra cautious.

4 Are they members of any professional pet sitting organizations? For example, Pet Sitters International is a good association to be aligned with.

5 How do dog walkers/sitters keep track of their schedules? You want to make sure that their time is well organized for your pets.

6 Will they give you the same walker/sitter each day, or each time you call? If not, how does the interview process work with each sitter that will come into your home?

7 What methods of payment do they accept? This can help you gauge if they are a full-service company.

8 For dog walking, how many dogs do they walk at once? In addition, are there certain types of collars, harnesses, or leashes that they use or do not like to use? Many pet sitters/dog walkers will not use certain types of collars and leashes for safety reasons, and they limit the number of dogs they will walk at one time. This ensures the safety and well-being of the animals they are responsible for.

9 What are the company's mission, values, and ethics? Check the company's website and marketing literature. What is their reputation in the community? You can ask around at vets, groomers, pet stores, pet rescues, etc., to see if they know anything about that company. It's also important to note if they work with or donate to local shelters and animal rescues. A dog walking/sitting company that is also compassionate and involved in helping animals is a good sign.

10 Last but not least, ask for at least two references from current clients that use their services. It is very important to know if they have happy clients, so don't be shy about asking for references.

248 CHECK OUT KENNELS IN ADVANCE

If you decide to board your dog at a kennel, ask your friends, your vet, or the local animal shelter if they know a kennel they would recommend personally. You can check online or in the local phone books to find a kennel, but be sure to investigate the facilities in advance, and if possible, bring your dog by a few times to get him used to the kennel and the people there. Remember, most kennels will require you to show proof of current vaccinations, so you must obtain this before you leave. This requirement should not in any way discourage you from choosing a kennel; in fact, it should be a major factor on your quality checklist, because it protects your dog and other animals.

BOARDING KENNELS CHECKLIST

❏ **CHECK CERTIFICATION** Ensure the kennel you are considering displays a current license or certificate showing that it meets the state's mandated standards for boarding kennels.

❏ **INSPECT HYGIENE** Ask to see all the places that your pet will be taken and check that they look and smell clean. Also, does the kennel provide additional services, such as bathing and grooming?

❏ **ENSURE COMFORT** Is a comfortable temperature maintained at all times, and is there adequate ventilation and light? Also, is the bedding clean and comfortable?

❏ **CONSIDER EXERCISE** Is the exercise schedule adequate for your dog's needs? Also, are the outdoor run and exercise areas adequately protected from the elements?

❏ **TALK TO STAFF** Does the staff seem knowledgeable and caring? Does your dog respond positively to them when you introduce him? Inform them of any special issues your dog may have, such as a fear of thunder.

❏ **CHECK VACCINATION REQUIREMENTS** Are all pets required to be up-to-date with vaccinations, including the vaccine for kennel cough? Also, what veterinary services are available to the kennel?

❏ **ASK ABOUT FEEDING** Check how often the dogs are fed, and make sure you're permitted to leave your own usual food for your pet.

❏ **PROVIDE CONTACT DETAILS** Make sure you give the kennel your pet's medications and special foods as appropriate, the number of your own vet, and contact details for yourself and another trusted friend or family member.

❏ **LOOK ONLINE** You can learn more by searching online to see if you can find any reviews. Be wary of a company that doesn't have an online presence.

249
CALM YOUR PET ON THE FOURTH OF JULY

Many animal shelters experience their highest single-day intake rates of stray dogs on the evening of July 4th. Pre-Fourth preparations can save a lot of heartache. So check that collar and ID tag and, if necessary, update your dog's microchip registration details. That done, consider the following tips to help your dog stay safe and calm on Independence Day.

BRING YOUR DOG INDOORS Even if they are usually fine outdoors and have been fine in previous years, there is a reason so many pets end up in the shelters on July 4th. You never know when someone is going to set off a firework close enough to frighten your pet into bolting, even over or through a fence that contained her before.

DON'T BRING YOUR PET TO THE PARTY Your pet is safest inside your own home, so don't bring her to celebrations. If you are having people over, even just a few, lock your dog in a bedroom or in a crate, and ask each guest not to let her out, no matter what.

KEEP WINDOWS AND DOORS CLOSED Startled pets have been known to push or jump through screens or even cracked windows. Keep doors to the outside closed on July 4th to prevent pets from bolting and slipping past you as people exit or enter. Pets can stay stressed for hours after the fireworks stop—don't discount the possibility that they may bolt even after the fireworks have died down. If possible, keep pets locked out of rooms where a door to the outside might be opened.

TURN ON THE TV Use the TV or music system to muffle any fireworks noises—it doesn't have to be blasting. Sound therapy CDs and digital downloads specially designed to help your dog stay calm during fireworks can be a genuine help on July 4th.

IGNORE FEAR Let your pet hide if she wants, but don't coax or pay attention to a pet exhibiting fearful behavior. You don't want to unintentionally reward (and therefore reinforce) scared behavior. Ignore your own fear, too: If you are calm and relaxed, this can help your pet stay relaxed, too.

ENGAGE WITH A SPECIAL TOY Give your pet a super-yummy food-stuffed toy or long-lasting chew treat. Some pets are too scared to eat, but for food-motivated ones, this can at least distract them and help them to stay calm.

GET SOME EXERCISE Exercise helps relieve stress, so your dog's daily release is a huge help. On July 4th, schedule your dog walk for early morning when fireworks are least likely to go off, and give him an extra-long walk to tire him out.

CONSULT YOUR VET If you know your pet gets dangerously distressed during fireworks, talk to your vet about possible short-term medication.

250 FIND YOUR LOST DOG

No caring pet owner plans on their pet getting out and getting lost, but it happens. The crucial thing is to act quickly and, as horrible as it feels, don't panic—you won't be able to help yourself or your beloved pet if you panic. So stay calm, but act quickly: Every minute your dog is out there, he is in danger of being injured on the road. Never assume that your dog will turn up on his own.

RALLY TROOPS If your dog has been lost in your local area, get out and call him. Recruit willing friends and neighbors to help in the search, and be sure to ask anyone you pass if they have seen your pet. It is best to head out on foot or on a bicycle initially, so that you can keep calling for your pet and talk to as many people as possible. If you draw a blank, stop by your neighbors' houses and let them know your dog is missing. Someone may have taken your dog in, planning to look after him while trying to find the owner through the local police or animal rescue service.

TELEPHONE FOR HELP Inform your microchip company that your dog is missing and double check that your contact details are up to date. Call all your local vets and rescue centers to give them a description of your dog in case somebody contacts them with news about your pet, or an injured dog is brought in that fits your pet's description. Call your local animal control agency or animal shelter; these are the institutions that people are likely to contact if your dog is involved in an accident or reported as a stray.

POST A FLYER Prepare a flyer with a picture of your pet. Include your pet's name and a brief description of when and where he was lost. Also include your own name, your home and cell number, and your e-mail address. Offer a reward; it doesn't need to be much, but the word "reward" may attract more eyes to your flyer. Post the flyers around the place where your dog was lost, in local pet stores, newsagents, veterinary clinics, and in any local community buildings where people are most likely to look. When posting outdoors, on trees and lampposts, be sure to protect the flyer from the elements by covering it in clear plastic.

USE LOCAL MEDIA Post an ad in the lost-and-found section of your local newspapers. Be sure to check the newspaper listings for any found dogs. Check online for local and national resources set up to reunite lost pets with their families.

REMEMBER—PREVENTION IS POWER!

MICROCHIP Haven't gotten a microchip for your pet yet? Now is a great time. If your pet has one already, call the microchip company to make sure the chip is registered with your current information.

COLLAR AND ID TAG Check to make sure pet collars are secure and tags are up-to-date and readable.

PHOTOS OF YOUR PET If she gets out, you'll want photos to make lost pet flyers. Have a clear body shot and face shot somewhere you can access quickly.

PET GPS Several companies now sell a GPS transmitter designed to attach to your pet's collar. The units are suitable for dogs who weigh at least 10 pounds (4.5 kg).

251
DEAL WITH A DOG BITE

If your dog is attacked by another dog or becomes involved in a serious fight, you will need to check your dog carefully for bite wounds. Punctures and lacerations will often be clearly visible, but damage to the soft tissue below the skin may not be immediately apparent. Use scissors to carefully clip away hair from around a puncture wound and bathe the region with warm water containing a mild skin disinfectant. Gently apply a little petroleum jelly to soothe irritation. Even with an apparently minor injury, it is worth making an appointment with your vet, who may recommend a course of antibiotics to prevent infection. If your dog has more severe cuts, your vet will be able to advise you whether or not he requires stitches.

252
TREAT AN INSECT STING

It isn't only cats that get into trouble because of curiosity—dogs are also naturally curious creatures and they love to chase things, including insects. Insect stings usually result in relatively short-term irritation and mild swelling in the affected area. But if your dog has an allergic reaction, if he is stung multiple times, or if he is stung inside the mouth or throat, stings can be life threatening and an urgent trip to the vet is required. Dogs are most commonly stung by bees and wasps.

BEE STINGS A bee's stinger is barbed and becomes embedded in your dog's skin. If possible, use a magnifying glass to locate the sting and remove it carefully with a pair of tweezers. Apply an antiseptic cream or use an ice pack to reduce swelling.

WASP STINGS A wasp sting isn't barbed, but it is more painful than a bee sting. And a single wasp can sting repeatedly if it's really riled up. Apply a weak mixture of water and baking soda to the sting site to help reduce the pain. Then keep a careful eye on your dog for signs of an allergic reaction.

SIGNS OF A REACTION A life-threatening reaction can occur if your dog is stung multiple times or if he is allergic to the poison in the insect sting. Signs will include a large swelling at the site of the sting, lethargy, and breathing difficulties.

253 HANDLE A TOAD ENCOUNTER

Toads are generally easygoing critters that just like to be left alone. If they feel threatened, however, toads can excrete toxins onto their skin and some can even squirt the poison up to 7 feet (2 m) if needed. Contact with, and ingestion of, these secretions can cause serious problems for your pooch. Symptoms include salivation and possibly vomiting. In the worst-case scenario, absorption of toxic toad secretions can also lead to seizures, convulsions, and cardiac arrest.

ACT QUICKLY You can keep things under control if you act quickly and clear the substance from your dog's mouth and wipe it away from his lips, eyes, paws, and other points of contact as soon as possible. A jet of water from a water sprayer or hose is ideal for flushing out his mouth. But don't allow your dog to drink the water. If possible, use your cell phone to snap a picture of the toad in case you need to take your pet to the vet, which you will need to do if your dog shows continuing signs of discomfort or irritation.

254 KEEP A CANINE FIRST-AID KIT

Keep a first-aid kit at home and another in your car in case you are out and about when an accident occurs. You only need to stock a few basic items, such as scissors, tweezers, a thermometer, antiseptic cream, cotton wool, and a selection of dressings. However, it is important to remember that overly zealous first aid can actually do more harm than good, especially when time is of the essence. Your veterinarian's office will want you to contact them immediately if you have any doubts about the seriousness of a condition or injury.

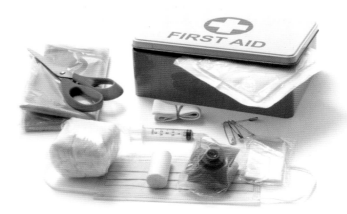

RATTLESNAKES
MAY BE FOUND IN THIS AREA

GIVE THEM DISTANCE
AND RESPECT

255 MANAGE A SNAKE SIGHTING

The United States has around 20 species of venomous snakes, including 16 species of rattlesnakes. Every state has at least one species of venomous snake. If you see or hear a snake, calmly and slowly back away from the snake until you are no longer within striking distance (about the snake's length). Then carefully leave the area, because if there is one snake, there are likely to be more in that same area.

256 AVOID RATTLESNAKES

Rattlesnakes can be common in the parks and trails that many dog-lovers use for hikes and walks with their dogs, and more and more homes are being built in areas that were previously rural, making encounters with wildlife even more common. Rattlesnakes can be a life-threatening danger to dogs of all sizes (especially small dogs). But with just a few preventive steps, you can reduce the chances your dog will get bitten and die from a rattlesnake bite.

WALK YOUR DOG ON A SHORT LEASH Vets say the vast majority of rattlesnake bites occur when a dog is off-leash or on a retractable leash. Having your dog on a short, 6-foot (2-m) leash when in areas that could have rattlesnakes keeps her from moving quickly enough to startle a snake, and lets you pull the leash back if you hear the telltale rattle of the snake's tail.

AVOID ROCKY OR DENSE BRUSH OR GRASSY AREAS On your walks with your dog, stay on the trail, and choose wide trails or roads over narrow brush-bordered trails if possible. That way you are more likely to see a snake sunning itself across your path, and be able to stop and avoid it in time. Also, keep the grass in your yard cut short and eliminate brush and piles of cut wood and rocks—snakes like to sun themselves in these spots, as well as hide and hunt for rodents.

257 RECOGNIZE RATTLESNAKE-BITE SYMPTOMS

If your dog is bitten, there is a treatment at the vet's office, but time is of the essence. The actual moment a dog is bitten is rarely seen, so it is important to be aware of the symptoms. Depending on how much venom the bite injected into your dog, and the size of your dog, symptoms may become more severe very quickly or within a few hours of the bite.

IMMEDIATE SYMPTOMS

- puncture wounds (can be bleeding)
- severe pain
- swelling
- restlessness, panting, or drooling

LATER SYMPTOMS

- lethargy, weakness, sometimes collapse
- muscle tremors
- diarrhea
- seizures
- neurological signs including depressed respiration

RESPONSE Limiting the dog's activity as you rush to the vet will limit the venom moving around in his body, which is better. Dogs are most frequently bitten on the head or legs. Do not apply a tourniquet if your dog is bitten on his leg. And do not cut into the wound and attempt to suck out the venom, as this only increases the blood flow and speeds up the spread of the poison. If ice is readily available, apply an ice pack to the wound to slow down the blood flow. If you can, carry your dog to your car. If you can't carry your dog, walk him to your car. And if you have someone with you, ask them to call the vet while you drive. It will save time, and possibly save your dog's life, if you alert the vet so she can have the treatment ready as soon as you arrive.

258 SPOT THE SIGNS OF ILL HEALTH

One of the most difficult things about having a dog is their inability to tell us directly when something is wrong. Your human child can specify if she has a headache or a stomachache, but a dog often suffers in silence. However, there are signs that you can watch out for when your dog is ill or injured—clearly visible signs such as limping or vomiting, and more subtle signals such as uncharacteristic lethargy or loss of appetite. Here are some tips on how to spot when your dog is not feeling well, and the appropriate response.

SYMPTOM	RESPONSE
LOSS OF APPETITE Your dog is not eating his normal amount, or not eating at all. Just like people, dogs can catch viruses, or otherwise feel under the weather. Unlike people, they don't complain about it. But if your dog suddenly loses his interest in food, this is something you should pay attention to.	If the food is wet food and will dry up or go bad, remove it. His discomfort may pass and he may eat more in a few hours. It is also possible the batch of food you provided was somehow spoiled, so open a different can of food just to be sure. If your dog still isn't eating on the following day, make an appointment with your vet.
VOMITING Although not uncommon in dogs, vomiting should not occur frequently or repeatedly. Sometimes a dog just eats too quickly or too much, or gets into something in your yard that upsets her stomach.	Verify that your dog has not had access to anything poisonous such as herbicides, insecticides, or household chemicals. If your dog is otherwise energetic after vomiting, simply offer food again in a few hours. If your dog vomits more than once, or is showing other signs of low energy or any form of distress, call your vet immediately.
EXCESSIVE THIRST Your dog's water bowl should always be full and accessible, but what if you notice that you are refilling the bowl more frequently than normal? If your dog is drinking an unusual amount of water—other than on an unusually hot day or after a lot of exercise—it could indicate a problem.	Drinking large amounts of water, while not an emergency, can be a sign of a kidney or liver malfunction, or an adrenal or pituitary gland disorder. Schedule an appointment with your vet, who can run a series of tests to find out if there is a problem.
TIREDNESS AND LETHARGY Dogs, like people, can feel under the weather. And, just like us, they slow down with age. However, if your normally active dog is lacking energy and seems unusually lethargic. it could signal a blood disorder or heart trouble.	If the low energy does not pass within 24 hours, make an appointment to see your veterinarian, who can check for signs of anaemia, worm infestations, heart valve malfunctions, or other symptoms that might lead to lethargy. Your vet may recommend a simple change in diet or a more drastic course of treatment depending on the diagnosis.
LIMPING If you notice that your dog is limping, or walking in an unusual way, it may be that he has a minor external injury such as a splinter in his paw, or it could be an internal problem affecting the muscles, bones, or tendons. Young dogs are especially prone to leg injuries, and arthritis is a common problem in some types of dog as they age.	Examine the relevant paw to see if something has lodged itself in the foot pad or between his toes. If you are unable to see or remove the object yourself, visit the vet. Your vet will look for signs of injury, such as swelling or tenderness. If there is no visible reason, it is likely an injured joint or tendon, or it may be a chronic problem, such as arthritis.
WHINING OR CRYING Although, sadly, dogs are unable to specify where they have a problem, they can let us know that they are in distress when they whimper or cry. They do this when they are sad if they know you are about to leave, or if they are outside and want to come in— but what if there is no apparent reason for their distress?	If there is no obvious reason your dog is whining, it may be that she is suffering acute pain. Treat this as an emergency and drive your dog to the vet immediately. Dogs do not easily display pain, so if your dog is letting you know something is wrong, something is likely very wrong and may need immediate medical intervention.

MY DOG EATS GRASS. IS THIS OKAY?

Puppies will chew anything, grass included. And some adult dogs seem to simply enjoy eating grass and will munch on blades of grass at any opportunity. However, if your dog only rarely eats grass, it could be a sign of abdominal discomfort, which your dog is attempting to self-medicate. If your dog seems subdued and perhaps has lost his appetite for his normal food, consult your vet.

259
NURSE YOUR POOCH

Dogs tend to recover more quickly when they are cared for at home in familiar surroundings among the people they love. However, be sure to follow your vet's advice to the letter when your dog is recovering from an illness or injury at home. Give your convalescent canine his medicine at the appointed times and feed him only on recommended foods if his diet is to be restricted. As ever, make sure that plenty of fresh, clean water is available, and if your dog is unwilling or unable to drink properly, use a syringe to feed water into the side of his mouth. Your pet's body temperature can drop when he is sick, so make sure he has clean, comfortable bedding. Your vet may even recommend you use a lukewarm hot-water bottle to warm your dog's bed. Make sure your pet has access to a toilet area, and be prepared to carry him there if necessary. Make sure that your dog is not disturbed by young children, who may not understand your pet's predicament. If, for whatever reason, you are unable to carry out your vet's instructions or find the necessary procedures too upsetting, it is best to ask that your dog be hospitalized until he is more fully recovered.

260
GIVE YOUR DOG A PILL

If your dog is prescribed a course of tablets, make sure you give them regularly at the appointed times. Ask your vet to demonstrate how to give your dog a pill so you can see how well your dog does with a professional, and you can witness the procedure firsthand. The idea is to get your dog to swallow the pill without trying to chew it or reject it.

OPEN WIDE Place your left thumb and index finger over the top of your dog's snout, at the very back of his lips, and pinch softly but firmly with your fingers to open his mouth.

POP IN THE PILL With your right hand, place the pill as far back as possible on your dog's tongue. Be sure the pill is centered on the tongue or he might start to chew it.

SWALLOW THE PILL Use your left hand to gently hold his mouth closed, and with your right hand, firmly stroke his throat downward to encourage him to relax and swallow the pill. Your dog will lick his lips, which is a sure sign that he has swallowed the tablet. Remember to praise your dog when he takes his medicine.

261 SEE THE SIGNS OF OLD AGE

Dogs don't live as long as people, so it is very likely your dog will die before you do. It is important to recognize this, and to understand how to help your dog to remain comfortable and as healthy as possible in his old age. Like people, dogs have a range of life expectancies—some will die younger and some older. Generally speaking, small dogs under 20 pounds (9 kg) have an average lifespan of 15 years, medium-size dogs have an average lifespan of 11 years, and big dogs over 90 pounds (40 kg) live on average about 8 years. It's important to be sensitive to when your dog is showing signs of aging. Since we can't always see changes that are happening slowly every day, sometimes it takes a comment from someone who only sees your dog occasionally, like an old friend or a pet sitter, to make us realize that our dog is showing signs of age.

SLOWING DOWN

As much as we hate to admit it, everyone gets older, and just like people, dogs slow down and need special care as they age. They can develop health issues that might include cancer, and even a very healthy senior dog is still likely to develop arthritis that will require you to modify many aspects of her daily routine. Dogs, like people, can start showing gray hair around their face as they age. They may continue to eat well, but eat a little less. They may not jump or run as much as they used to, and they may spend more time sleeping than they used to. All of these are normal changes, and you should modify your dog's routine to cater to her changing needs.

HEARING DETERIORATES

EYESIGHT DETERIORATES

GRAY HAIR ON MUZZLE

COAT IS THIN AND DRY

JOINTS STIFFEN

MUSCLES WEAKEN

262 CHANGE YOUR ELDERLY DOG'S ROUTINE

Any dog, just like any person, will begin to develop some joint pain and lose some muscle mass as they get older. Be sensitive to this, especially if you have an active dog. Perhaps your dog always went with you on your runs and now is not showing as much enthusiasm. Perhaps he is starting to lag behind on runs, and is no longer able to play for hours on end. It is important to see these changes and modify your daily routine based upon what your dog is able to do—and what he wants to do.

FEEDING Elderly dogs don't need as much protein in their food, and changes in their digestive system demand changes in their diet. Consult with your veterinarian on when it might be time to switch to a food specifically designed for senior dogs.

GROOMING You might need to invest in a softer brush—your dog's coat and skin are thinner than they once were, so you need to be especially gentle when brushing an elderly dog. Grooming is more important than ever, because an old dog cannot groom himself as well as a younger dog. Plus, you need to be especially vigilant when it comes to lumps that may indicate cancer and other age-related illnesses.

HYGIENE Keep checking your dog's gums for signs of infection, which can be more prevalent in old age. Regularly clear mucus from around your dog's eyes using damp cotton balls, and check inside the ears for any buildup of ear wax, which can lead to painful ear infections. Keep the fur clean and trimmed beneath your dog's tail, where he may no longer be able to clean himself properly.

DOG TALES

JASPER, ABANDONED BUT NOT FORGOTTEN

Forget Me Not is the only animal shelter in Ferry County, a relatively low-income rural district in Washington State. Ferry County has an area approximately the size of Delaware, including large swaths of state and national forest. Kim Gillen, the Volunteer Executive Director for the shelter, laments, "We seem to be a magnetic dumping ground for unwanted pets by people who just can't afford to care for their pet. Many of these otherwise great animals are lucky to be found by hikers, often several miles from the nearest home. The number of abandoned cats and dogs in our county far exceeds the number of available adoptive homes; as a result, we have built a thriving (though costly) distance adoption program. Our distance adoption program relies heavily on the advertising provided by Adopt-a-Pet.com."

The adoption process at Forget Me Not is thorough, but that's standard practice for most pet rescue groups. Adopters fill out an online application, and the Forget Me Not team then checks the adopters' property records, landlord permissions and requirements (if applicable), vet references, and personal references. Forget Me Not also requires photos of the home and an interview with the potential adopter, all to be sure the pet and family will be a great match. About 80 percent of the group's placements are outside Ferry County.

Once a month, Forget Me Not drives those fortunate dogs to meet their potential adopters at a rendezvous point in Seattle and Spokane, where they and their new families are introduced. They then begin a 30-day trial adoption. Forget Me Not has a money-back guarantee on every pet they place, and work with their distance adopters throughout the trial period and beyond to help them succeed with their new family members. If a placement does not work out for any reason, the group will pick the pet up on the next delivery run. The work they put in prior to placement has thankfully kept their return rate extremely low; only a handful of pets each year end up coming back into the adoption program, with the most common reason being undiscovered allergies.

Jasper arrived at Forget Me Not as an old boy reaching the end of his natural life. He was an 11-year-old Labrador/Boxer mix, who was impounded by the county after his owners moved away and left him at their former rental home. They had told the landlord they would be back for their dogs (Jasper came in with a five-year-old Boxer and an elderly Chihuahua), but after a month had gone by, the landlord had no choice but to ask the sheriff to come get the abandoned dogs he had been caring for.

I would highly recommend that anyone adopt a senior dog.

"From the first day, Jasper decided I was his main person and he has never wavered in his devotion. He has learned who his people are and does his 'happy dance' when they show up at the door. Thankfully, his health is exemplary except for the expected arthritis in his hind legs. We have about the same level of energy and stamina so we urge each other on for our daily exercise. He loves riding in the car with his head hanging out the window. I hear people talking to him when I am at stoplights and have even had people take his picture. The blissful look on his face is pretty wonderful.

"Again, my thanks for trusting me with this beautiful animal."

The owners were located and came to Forget Me Not, where they paid the impound fee for the Chihuahua and took him away. They told Forget Me Not, "You can have the other two," leaving Jasper and his Boxer friend homeless.

Jasper seemed to really enjoy his time at the shelter. The team at Forget Me Not believe it is most likely that Jasper was left outside all the time with his former family, so the one-on-one indoor attention and play time he received from the wonderful volunteers must have seemed like a great improvement to Jasper.

Forget Me Not did worry about Jasper, however. Life in any animal shelter, however well run, is not the same as living in a comfortable home with a loving family—and it is often difficult to find a home for a dog nearing the end of his life. Nevertheless, they optimistically listed him and hoped for the best, while continuing to make him happy and comfortable for what could be the rest of his life at the shelter.

Thankfully, Forget Me Not's distance adoption program did the trick for Jasper, and he was matched to a wonderful, loving woman named Jane in the Seattle area. The picture of Jasper resting his head on Jane's lap while she reads speaks for itself—while no one can say how many years Jasper has left, it is all but certain that he will spend his last years happy and loved.

Jane says, "Jasper is doing better than ever and I am forever grateful for having him in my life.

263 JUST SAY NO TO JOINT PAIN

A common ailment for elderly dogs is arthritis that causes joint pain. They do not run as much, and are less able to jump on and off a bed or go up or down stairs, and they generally slow down. You may notice that they walk with their head held lower, or seem to have stiff back legs or hips.

CHANGE HIS DIET Ask your veterinarian to examine your elderly pup. There may be a drug that can help with your dog's joints. There are also supplements you can get from the pet-supply store that can be added to your dog's food to help his joints. Simple changes to your dog's diet can sometimes give him a new lease on life.

TRY MASSAGE THERAPY Gentle massage of the muscles and joints is great for older dogs. When they are resting, gently press and glide your fingers down the joints and limbs. You can also gently manipulate their limbs to help them stretch and maintain flexibility.

264 GIVE YOUR DOG A HAND TO STAND

As dogs age and lose strength and flexibility in their legs, they may struggle to stand up or sit down, and they may have trouble getting traction on slippery surfaces. Here are some tips to help your elderly pup.

STEPS If your dog loves to be on your bed but is having trouble jumping up or down, a small set of steps will make it easier for him to get on or off. Be sure to gently train your elderly pup on the use of the steps, and place something soft on either side in case he stumbles.

RAMPS If your dog is too big for you to easily lift in and out of your car, you can build or buy a simple ramp that slides in and out of your car. Your dog can use the ramp to walk up into the backseat or the rear area of the car. Make sure the ramp has a suitable non-slip, textured surface so that your dog doesn't fall and injure himself.

HARNESSES If your dog's hind legs are becoming weak, you can buy a special handheld harness that takes some of the weight off his rear legs, making it easier for him to walk. Also, there are wheeled apparatuses you can purchase that are custom-made to your dog's size and allow him to walk using his front legs.

265

TALK ABOUT YOUR DOG'S LAST DAYS

Unless an emergency comes up or your dog suddenly passes away, chances are you will have some time and a tough decision to make as your dog reaches the end of his days. We have the power and the responsibility to decide to end our pets' lives and save them from suffering when we know they will not recover. This is likely the hardest decision you will ever make regarding your pet, but you do not need to make it alone. Talk to your vet and make the decision together.

CONSIDER THESE QUESTIONS:

1 What is the quality of life for your dog today? When your dog is gone, will you remember today as a day you are glad he had, or will you wish he hadn't had to struggle through this day? If on balance, your dog has some joy and not too much suffering, then today is not the day to say goodbye.

2 Is there less suffering in sight if you can just make it through the day, or is each day likely to get worse for your dog? Remember, you can't change the inevitable. The best you can do is to speed the end along to prevent your dog from suffering for no reason.

3 Are you keeping your dog here for you, or because it is the right thing to do for him? People in this harrowing situation generally feel they make a decision to say goodbye too soon or too late. It's hard to feel like you got it right, and here is where a veterinarian can be very helpful. They have a clearer understanding of what your dog is likely to go through, so trust their opinion on whether it makes sense to keep fighting, or peacefully say goodbye.

266

REMEMBER YOUR DOG

Once a beloved pet dies, your vet is still there to help you and discuss the options available to you. Many people have their pet's body cremated. Your vet can arrange that for you, and you can have the ashes returned to you if you pay for a private cremation—though it is fine to simply say goodbye, and perhaps keep your dog's collar or favorite toy as a reminder.

Other people opt to bury their dog, either in a pet cemetery or on their own property. If you do bury your pet on your own property, be sure the grave is at least 3 feet (1 m) deep to safeguard against scavengers. Perhaps plant a flower or a tree on the spot as a lasting reminder of your old friend.

267
SHARE YOUR GRIEF

Once your dog is gone, she is free. Take comfort in knowing that there is no more pain or struggle. The pain is now yours, as you miss your beloved friend and family member, and you should be very kind to yourself and rely on those who love you to help you through your loss—especially other family members who are also grieving. But consider, too, that people you don't expect might have had similar experiences and could really understand what you are going through. If you don't find all the help you need from your family and friends, you can look online for pet-loss support groups—sometimes it helps to talk to others who are going through similar experiences.

UNDERSTAND YOUR GRIEF Don't think "it's just a dog." A dog is part of your family—a part of your life every day over many years. For many people, their relationship with their dog is as meaningful as any human relationship they have. You have a right to be sad and to be comforted. You may not expect people to understand, but they will; so be willing to tell people about your loss.

LET IT OUT The devastation in your heart will pass, but it is helpful to truly recognize the loss of this significant relationship, and to allow yourself to feel deeply so that you can move through the grieving process. Embrace your sadness—cry, scream, run, punch a pillow, do whatever you need to do to get through the initial, often overwhelming, wave of sorrow.

CREATE A TRIBUTE Creating a tribute is a wonderful way to reminisce about the good times and share them, as well as to honor what your pet meant to you. Whether you write a story or poem, pour your heart out to your lost friend in the form of a letter, make a photo album, or put together a video, paying homage can help you heal.

268
FIND A
NEW FRIEND

Some people react to the loss of a pet by
immediately wanting another one. Others
take months or years to recover before
deciding the time is right. There is no
right or wrong here—only what feels right
for you. But do remember that once your
dog is gone, he is okay, free from pain,
and would want you to be happy. And
somewhere within your reach is another
living dog—one who does not have a
home today—who you can save. So when
you are ready, whether that is today or in a
year, consider visiting Adopt-a-Pet.com or
Petfinder.com, opening your heart again,
and saving another life. There is a special
someone waiting for you right now.

INDEX

Numbers refer to the item number. Unnumbered items are indexed by the numbered item that they follow. For example, "following 54" means that you can find this information in the box that appears after the text numbered 54.

A

adjustment period, 11, 22, 28, 94
adopt-a-pet.com, *introductory pages*, 18, 20–21, *following 243*, *following 262*, 268,
adopting dogs
    adopting friends for your dog, 59
    benefits of owning dogs, 1, *following 1*
    choosing to fit lifestyle, 5
    after the death of previous pet, 268
    giving adoption options as gifts, 240
    lifetime commitment, 2
    searching for dogs to adopt, 20–26
adult dogs, 6, 9, 16, 35, 236, *following 258*
Afghan Hounds, 73
aggression
    Alpha Roll, *following 35*
    bark signals, 36
    dog parks and, 173
    ear signals, 38
    eye contact, 39–41
    guard dogs, *following 77*
    lip curling, 47
    play and, 191
    reasons to spay and neuter, 52
    tail signals, 45
    teaching children how to behave around dogs, 37
    types of, 51
    working dogs category, 80
agility training, 84
allergies, 9
Alpha Roll, *following 35*
American Cocker Spaniels, 76
American Hairless Terriers, 9
American Pit Bull Terriers, 10, 69, 90
animal shelters, 22
ankle biting, 82
antifreeze, 238
apartments, 7
Australian Cattle Dogs, 10, 85
Australian Shepherds, 10
Australian Silky Terriers, 209

B

bags, carrying dogs in, *following 91*
balls, *following 57*, 75, 113, 125, 144, 191–192, 194
barking
    boredom, 79

    excessive, *following 78*
    identifying signals, 36
    training to bark, 151
    training to stop, 79, 152
Basset Hounds, 73
bathing
    associating with good things, 202
    decompressing after, 204
    do-it-yourself dog washes, 206
    dos and don'ts of, 199
    equipment for, 201
    hiring professionals, 207
    locations for, 205
    preparation for, 200
    steps for, 203
Beagles, 10, 31, 59, 66, 72, 73
beanbags, 13
Bearded Collies, 85
Bedlington Terriers, 9, 90
beds, 13, 129–130
begging, 41, 143, 238
behavior. *See names of specific behaviors*
Belgian Shepherds, 10, 85
Bergamascos, 85
biking, 168–170
biscuits, 96
bites, treating, 251
Black & Tan Coonhounds, 73
blinking, 42
Bloodhounds, 72, 73
blowfly maggots, 233
bones, 187, *following 216*
Border Collies, 10, 43, 66, 81, 85
boredom barking, 79
Borzois, 73
Boston Terriers, *following 203*
bowls, 13
Boxers, 77, 80, *following 203*
breeding dogs, *following 54*
breeds, 70–71. *See also names of specific breeds*
Briards, 85
brushes, 210, 220–223

C

canine couture, 227
canned food, 189
cat food, *following 186*, 187
catapults, 192, 194

cats, 19, 67, 114, 181
chamois cloths, 210, 220
chasing
    games and play involving, 191
    runners, 68
    tail, *following 47*
    teaching children not to chase dogs, 123
chew toys, 13, *following 57*, 117, 191–193, 215
chewing, 117, 127, 191
chews, 96
Cheyletiella mites, 233
chiggers (harvest mites; *Trombicula autumnalis*), 233
Chihuahuas, 46, *following 203*
children
    benefits of having dogs, 1
    building relationship between puppy and, 125
    choosing dogs for households with, 6
    coping with puppies and small children, 124
    dog parks and, 173
    giving dogs as gifts, 240
    introducing puppies to, 116
    teaching how to behave around dogs, 6, 37, 123
    training puppies to stop nipping, 126
Chinese Crested Hairless, 9
chipping, 15, *following 250*
choke chains, 155, *following 159*
Chow Chows, 77, 80, *following 203*
clickers, 113, 148–150
clippers, 210, 224
coat types, 209
Cockapoos, 9
Cocker Spaniels, *following 203*, 209
collars, 13, 154–155, *following 250*
combs, 210, 221–222
"come" command, 83, 102, 136, 139–141
coonhounds, 72
cotton balls, 200, 210, 212
crates
    choosing right time for, 117
    closing door of, 122
    for crying, 60
    for destructive chewing, 117
    getting puppies used to, 121
    how long to leave dogs in, 118
    selecting, 13, 113, 119
    for separation anxiety, 58, 117
    for toilet training, 117

where to put, 120
cropping ears, *following* 38
crying, 60, 258
curly-coated breeds, 209. *See also* names of
specific breeds

D

Dachshunds, 73
Dalmatians, 10
Dandie Dinmont Terriers, 90
day care, 58
dehydration, 242
Demodex canis, 233
dental cleaning, 213–215, *following* 215
DHLPP vaccines, 175
digging, 87–89
Doberman Pinschers, 77, 80, *following* 203
docking tails, *following* 44
dog sitters, 247
dog walkers, 247
doghouses, 182, 184
Dogo Argentinos, 80
Dogue de Bordeauxs, 80
dominance and submission
    Alpha Roll, *following* 35
    bark signals, 36
    blinking, 42
    ear signals, 38
    eye contact, 39–41
    identifying dominance, 46
    identifying submission, 53
    pack behavior, 51
    submissive urination, 55
    tail signals, 43–45
dressing dogs, 92, 227–228, 241
dried food, 189
dry skin, *following* 220

E

ears
    cleaning, 216–217
    cropping, *following* 38
    scratching, *following* 38
    sense of hearing, 31
    signals, 38
elderly dogs
    assistance to stand or move around, 264
    changing routine for, 262
    joint pain, 263
    signs of old age, 261
end of life issues, 265–267
English Cocker Spaniels, 76
English Mastiffs, 80
English Springer Spaniels, 76
exercise

agility training, 84
apartment-dwelling dogs, 7
benefits of dog ownership, 1, *following* 1
building relationship between puppy
    and children through, 125
dogs as biking partners, 168–170
dogs as running partners, 10, 167
playing to release energy, 75
proper limits, 197
providing, 12
to stop crying, 60
eyes
    contact, 37, 39–40, *following* 40, 41
    sense of sight, 31
    signals, 39–40

F

face, cleaning, 212
fear
    of fireworks, 249
    identifying signs of, 54, 123
    of thunder, 244
    turning scary tasks into fun, 208
fences, 153
fetching, 144–145, 196
fighting
    breaking up dogfights, 50
    ear signals, 251
    play-fighting, 35, 191
    spaying and neutering to prevent, 52
    treating dog bites, 251
financial issues
    benefits of spaying and neutering, 52
    determining costs of dog ownership, 14
    large dogs and, 8
    veterinary expenses, 177, 179
first-aid kits, 254
fleas, 230–232
food
    barbecues, 243
    biscuits, 96
    calorie counting, 190
    cat food, *following* 186, 187
    chews, 96
    disturbing eating dogs, 37, 123
    dog parks and, 173
    eating grass, *following* 258
    elderly dogs, 262
    holiday, 238
    loss of appetite, 258
    meat, 191
    prepared, 189
    proper nutrition, 185
    separate food bowls, 188
    storing safely, 181
    table manners, 128

ten commandments of feeding, 187
    treats, 113
    types of, 189
fostering, 30
Fox Terriers, 90
freeze (statue) game, 172
Frisbees, 192, 195
fundraising, 179

G

German Shepherds, 43, 81, 85
gifts, giving dogs as, 2, 240
Golden Retrievers, 10, 76, *following* 203
GPS transmitters, *following* 250
Great Danes, 7, 8, *following* 8, 80
greeting rituals, 33, 162
Greyhounds, 7, 23, 66, 72, 73
grooming
    clipping coat, 224
    elderly dogs, 262
    equipment for, 210
    hair dye, *following* 227
    handstripping wirehaired breeds, 225
    long-coated breeds, 222
    preparation for, 211
    short-coated breeds, 221
    silky-coated breeds, 223
    smooth-coated breeds, 220
grooming kits, 13
grooming tables, 210
growling, 36–37, 47–48, 54
guard dogs, *following* 77

H

hair dye, following 227
hairless dogs, 9
hand signals, 136, *following* 136
handstripping wirehaired breeds, 225
harnesses, 158, 264
harvest mites (chiggers; *Trombicula
autumnalis*), 233
head halters, 160, 161
head shaking, *following* 214
health and safety
    assistance to stand or move around, 264
    backyard safety, 182
    creating safe environment, 4
    dehydration, 242
    diarrhea, *following* 186
    dog parks and, 173
    dogs as biking partners, 168
    dogs as running partners, 167
    dressing dogs, 227–228
    ear scratching, *following* 38
    first-aid kits, 254

fleas, 230–232
giving pills, 260
health insurance, 178
hiding toxins, 181
hypothermia, *following* 241
identifying signs of ill health, 258
importance of play, 191
joint pain, 263
leaving dogs in cars, 165, 242
"lifesaver" commands, 102
nursing sick dogs, 259
parasites, 176, 233–236, 242
pool hazards, 183
purebred dogs, *following* 69
seasonal issues, 237, 238–239, 242–243
skin issues, *following* 203, *following* 220
snake encounters, 255–257
spaying and neutering, 52
starting training slowly and safely, 103
storing food, 181
swimming, 146–147
toad encounters, 253
toys, 13, 196
travel, 164–165
treating dog bites, 251
treating insect stings, 252
vaccinations, 175–176
veterinarians, 176, 177, 179
wet versus dry nose, *following* 72
health insurance, 178
hearing, sense of, 31
heartworm, 176
heatstroke, 242
herding dogs category, 71, 81–85. *See also
names of specific breeds*
hide-and-seek, 125, 171
home
    apartments, 7
    backyard safety, 182
    creating safe environment at, 4
    eliminating fleas from, 232
    hiding toxins, 181
    pool hazards, 183
    puppy-proofing, 174
    residential rules regarding pets, 3, 7
    setting house rules, 174
    storing food, 181
    toilet training, 131–133
    training to stay off furniture, 129–130
hookworm (*Uncinaria stenocephala*), 236
hounds category, 71–73. *See also names of
specific breeds*
housetraining. *See* toilet training
humane societies, 24
humping, 52
Huskies, 43, 59, 77, 80

I
identity tags, 13, 15, *following* 250
insect stings, treating, 252
Irish Setters, 66, 76

J
Jack Russell Terriers, 7, *following* 8, 10, 46,
66, 71, 90, 195, 197
Jackapoos, 9
Jacobson's organ, 31
joint pain, 263
jumping, 61–63, *following* 63, 108, 195

K
kennels, 248
Komondors, 85

L
Labradoodles, 9, 224
Labrador Retrievers, 10, 74, 76
leash aggression, 161–162
leashes, 13, 113, 156–157, 159–160
lethargy, 258
lice (*Trichodectes canis*), 233
licking, 64
"lie down" command, 135–136
"lifesaver" commands, 102
limping, 258
lip curling, 47
long-coated breeds, 209, 222. *See also
names of specific breeds*
lost dogs, 250, *following* 250
low-dander dogs, 9

M
Manchester Terriers, 90
martingale (no-slip) collars, 155
microchips, 15, *following* 250
Miniature Poodles, 76
mixed-breed dogs, 9–10, 17. *See also names
of specific breeds*
Morgan, Tracy, 229
mouthing, 65
multiple-dog households
    adopting bonded pairs, 29
    adopting friends for your dog, 59
    benefits of, following 28
    introducing new dogs into, 28
    separate food bowls, 188
    training to respond to team names, 110
muzzles, 113

N
nail trimming, 218–219
names, 27, 109, 110
neutering, 52, *following* 52
nipping, 126
"no" command, 112
nose
    sense of smell, 31
    sniffing, 32–33
    wet versus dry, *following* 72
no-slip (martingale) collars, 155
Nova Scotia Duck-Tolling Retrievers, 76

O
obedience classes, 95
Old English Sheepdog, 85
oxytocin, *following* 40

P
pack behavior, 51
parasites, 176, 233–236, 242
parks, 173
Pekingeses, 91
petting, patting versus, 57, 123
photography, 229, *following* 250
picking dogs up, 198
pills, 260
Pit Bulls, 10, 69, 90
play bow, 34
play-fighting, 35, 191
Pointers, 76
Pomeranians, 71
Poodles, 9, 10, 74, 76, 209
Poogles, 9
Portuguese Water Dogs, 209
positive reinforcement, 100, 104, 108,
148–150
possessive aggression, 51
prey drive, 67
puppies
    building relationship with children
    through play, 125
    coping with puppies and small
    children, 124
    getting used to crates, 121
    introducing to children, 116
    play-fighting with adult dogs, 35
    puppy-proofing home, 174
    socializing, 115
    training, 111
    training to stop nipping, 126
puppy mills, 26
purebred dogs, 18, *following* 69

R

racing dogs, 23
ramps, 264
rattlesnakes, 255–257
rescue organizations, 23, 25
resource guarding, 78
retractable leashes, 159
Rhodesian Ridgebacks, 10
rock salt (road salt), 238
rolling over, 33, *following* 35, 39, 53, 142
Rottweilers, 77, 80
Rough Collies, 10, 81, 85
roundworm (*Toxocara canis*), 236
routines, establishing, 180
rubbing rear on ground, *following* 235

S

Saint Bernards, 77, 80
Salukis, 73
sarcoptic mange mites (*Sarcoptes scabiei canis*), 233
Schnauzers, 9
scissors, 210
Scottish Terriers, 90
semi-moist food, 189
separation anxiety, 58, 117
short-coated breeds, 209, 221. *See also names of specific breeds*
shyness, 56
Siberian Huskies, 10
sight, sense of, 31
silky-coated breeds, 209, 223. *See also names of specific breeds*
"sit" command, 51, 62, 128, 134, 136, 162, 172
"6-6" rule, 124
size of dogs, 7–8, *following* 8
sleep, 37, 118
slings, 192, 194
smell, sense of, 31
smooth-coated breeds, 209, 220. *See also names of specific breeds*
snakes, 255–257
sniffing, 32–33
snug shirts, 60
Societies for the Prevention of Cruelty to Animals (SPCAs), 24
spaying and neutering, 52, *following* 52
sporting dogs category, 71, 74, 76. *See also names of specific breeds*
Springer Spaniels, *following* 203
Staffordshire Bull Terriers, 90
Standard Poodles, 76
statue (freeze) game, 172
"stay" command, 51, 102, 136, 137–138, 172
submission. *See* dominance and submission
submissive urination, 55

sun protection, 182, 242
swimming, 145–147, 183

T

tail
    chasing, *following* 47
    docking, *following* 44
    shapes of, 44
    signals, 43–44
    wagging, 45
tapeworm (*Dipylidium caninum*), 236
taste, sense of, 31
teething, 127
terriers category, 71, 86, 90. *See also names of specific breeds*
territorial aggression, 51
ticks (*Ixodes sp.* and *Dermacentor sp.*), 233–235
time-outs, 163
tiredness, 258
toads, 253
toilet training, 117, 131–133
toothbrushes, 210, 215
touch, sense of, 31
toy dogs category, 71, 91, *following* 91, 92. *See also names of specific breeds*
Toy Poodles, 76
toys, *following* 57, 60, 64, 113, 123, 173, 192, 193, 196. *See also names of specific toys*
training. *See also names of specific behaviors*
    consistency in, 94, 99, 136
    equipment for, 113
    introducing dogs to other pets, 114
    ten commandments of, 97–107
training pads, 113, 132
travel, 164–165, 242, 245–248
treat pouches, 113
treats, training using, 96, 101, 113. *See also food*
tug toys, 192
tug-of-war, 49, *following* 57, 191

V

veterinarians, 22, 176–177, 179
Vizslas, 10, 76
vomiting, 258

W

water
    accessibility, 186
    dehydration, 242
    excessive thirst, 258
    flotation devices, 147
    pool hazards, 183

safely, 146
    training to fetch from, 145
weight issues, 96, 167–168, 187, 190, 236
Weimaraners, 10, 76
Welsh Terriers, 90
West Highland White Terriers, 90
whining, 258
Whippets, 73, 196
whipworm (*Trichuris vulpis*), 236
whistles, 113, 141
Wire-Haired Terriers, 209
wiry-coated breeds, 209, 225. *See also names of specific breeds*
wolves, 66
working dogs category, 71, 77, 80. *See also names of specific breeds*

Y

Yorkshire Terriers, 8, 71, 223, 226

CREDITS

Photography courtesy of *Shutterstock Images*, with the following exceptions: Introduction *Adopt-a-Pet.com* (photo of David, photo of Abbie) *Megan Baggott* (photo of Pia) | About Adopt-a-Pet.com *Pia Salk* (dog in door), *Peter Neidell* (Pia on porch), *Steven Abbey* (David in New Orleans), others courtesy *Jennifer Warner Jacobsen and Adopt-a-Pet.com* | Arthur's tale of endurance and devotion *www.facebook.com/peakperformanceadventureracingteam* | Basic Training Hand Signals *Damien Moore and Eve Moore* | Sam and Bertie, "Mean and Wild" minis *Adopt-a-Pet.com* | 206 *www.luckydogsdiydogwash.com* | Callie—More than just a Pretty Face *Adopt-a-Pet.com* | Jasper, Abandoned but not Forgotten *Adopt-a-Pet.com*

Illustrations courtesy of *Philippa Baile* 43 | *Andy Crisp*: 36, 45, 55, 182, 198, 219, 233 | *Raymond Larrett*: 37, 60, | *Paula Rogers*: 57, 65

weldon**owen**

PRESIDENT & PUBLISHER Roger Shaw
ASSOCIATE PUBLISHER Mariah Bear
SVP, SALES & MARKETING Amy Kaneko
FINANCE MANAGER Philip Paulick
EDITOR Bridget Fitzgerald
CREATIVE DIRECTOR Kelly Booth
ART DIRECTOR William Mack
ILLUSTRATION COORINATOR Conor Buckley
PRODUCTION DIRECTOR Chris Hemesath
ASSOCIATE PRODUCTION DIRECTOR Michelle Duggan

1045 Sansome Street, San Francisco, CA 94111
weldonowen.com

© 2015 Weldon Owen Inc.

Weldon Owen is a division of **BONNIER**

Library of Congress Control Number
on file with the publisher.

ISBN 13: 978-1-61628-955-3
ISBN 10: 1-61628-955-4
10 9 8 7 6 5 4 3 2 1
2015 2016 2017 2018 2019
Printed in China by 1010 Printing International

MOSELEY ROAD INC

PRESIDENT Sean Moore
EDITORIAL DIRECTOR Damien Moore
PRODUCTION DIRECTOR Adam Moore
GENERAL MANAGER Karen Prince
DESIGN Philippa Baile, www.oiloften.co.uk

Special thanks tp Adam Moore for retouching various
images. Katharine Moore for editorial assistance, Kevin
Broccoli for index services, and Tracy Morgan for two
images used in the index and acknowledgments.

Special thanks to Jennifer Warner Jacobsen,
Katya Lidsky Friedman, and Dana Puglisi for
their contributions to this book.

ABOUT OUR SPONSORS:

For over 80 years,
Purina has used
its knowledge and
expertise to give pet owners the healthy pet food,
products, tools and advice they need to help enrich
their pets' lives. Purina offers programs that enrich
the lives of pets and the people who love them as
well, partnering with animal welfare organizations
throughout the year on various special programs.

Bayer HealthCare Animal
Health produces flea, tick
and heartworm products,
including Advantage Multi® for
Cats (imidacloprid+moxidectin),
Advantage Multi® for Dogs
(imidacloprid+moxidectin),
K9 Advantix® II for dogs,
Seresto® for dogs or cats and
Advantage® II for cats. Bayer's
Friends in Need program provides Bayer flea and
tick products at discounted rates to animal shelters
and welfare organizations.

The Petco Foundation
has raised more than
$125 million since it
was created in 1999 to
help promote and improve the welfare of companion
animals. In conjunction with Petco, the Petco
Foundation works with and supports thousands of
local animal welfare groups across the country and,
through in-store adoption events, helps find homes
for more than 350,000 animals every year.